METACOGNITION AND COGNITIVE NEUROPSYCHOLOGY

➤ ✻ ◄

MONITORING AND CONTROL PROCESSES

METACOGNITION AND COGNITIVE NEUROPSYCHOLOGY

➤ ❋ ◄

MONITORING AND CONTROL PROCESSES

Edited by

Giuliana Mazzoni
University of Florence, Italy
Thomas O. Nelson
University of Maryland

IEA LAWRENCE ERLBAUM ASSOCIATES, PUBLISHERS
1998   Mahwah, New Jersey   London

Lawrence Erlbaum Associates, Inc., Publishers
10 Industrial Avenue
Mahwah, NJ 07430

Cover design by Kathryn Houghtaling Lacey

Library of Congress Cataloging-in-Publication Data

Metacognitive and cognitive neuropsychology : monitoring and control processes / edited by Giuliana Mazzoni, Thomas O. Nelson.
    p. cm.
Includes bibliographical references and indexes.
ISBN 0–8058–2662–9 (Hardcover : alk. paper).
1. Metacognition.   2. Cognitive neuroscience.   I. Mazzoni, Giuliana.   II. Nelson, Thomas O.
BF311.M4485   1998
153—dc21   98–5819
                                                    CIP

Books published by Lawrence Erlbaum Associates are printed on acid-free paper, and their bindings are chosen for strength and durability.

Printed in the United States of America
10 9 8 7 6 5 4 3 2 1

To Tommaso, for his patience,
and to Tom Nelson's children,
Ashley Sinclair Nelson, and Jake Taylor Nelson

Contents

Preface

In the last two decades empirical efforts to understand cognitive monitoring and control processes have multiplied in the areas of metacognition and cognitive neuropsychology. However, researchers in these areas frequently used different conceptualizations of monitoring and of control, and even different labels for what might be the same cognitive activities. The combination of common interest with diverging approaches gave impetus to a conference during June 1994 at the University of Firenze, Italy, where scholars from both areas were brought together to discuss their research on cognitive monitoring and control processes. The goals were to facilitate synergistic activity and to determine some common starting points for future research.

Previous books on metacognition have contributed a set of core readings for researchers interested in metacognition (Nelson, 1992) and have described the state of the art of research on several aspects of metacognition (Metcalfe & Shimamura, 1994; Reder, 1996). But how should we conceptualize the cognitive monitoring of oneself, and the control of one's own cognitive processes? How are those activities reflected in brain functioning? The following chapters describe some current attempts to move toward answers to those questions.

In the first chapter, Schneider, taking off from the framework on metacognition proposed by Nelson and Narens (1990), focuses on developmental changes during childhood in the interaction between cognitive monitoring and control. This chapter is useful as a springboard for comparing what develops during childhood and what is seen to decline or disintegrate in patients with neuropsychological deficits.

The chapter by Hall and Bahrick illustrates the critical effect of training and the potential role of cognitive monitoring and control over long-term retention intervals.

The chapter by Umiltà and Stablum reviews several conceptualizations of cognitive control processes and proposes a new method to assess control deficits in closed-head-injury patients. These authors highlight the role of frontal lobe processing for cognitive and, potentially, metacognitive control processes.

The chapter by Darling, Della Sala, Gray, and Trivelli gives a historical overview of the functions attributed to the frontal lobes and describes the deficits that have been linked to damage in the frontal and prefrontal area (for a review of findings that implicated frontal lobe processing in traditional metacognitive research paradigms, see Shimamura, 1994). The chapter also offers an extended discussion of the methods used to assess frontal-lobes deficits.

The focus of the chapter by Koriat and Goldsmith is on the regulatory role of metacognition during the retrieval of information from memory. The authors stress the concept of accuracy in memory performance, showing that accuracy is under the participants' control. Emphasis is given to the two kinds of retrieval failure that can occur—omissions (i.e., failing to retrieve the answer) and commissions (retrieving the incorrect answer) that participants are able to eliminate under the appropriate circumstances.

The chapter by Schacter describes illusions of memory related to the aforementioned kinds of retrieval failures. The emphasis is on a cognitive neuroscience analysis that relates memory illusions (and therefore retrieval failures) to the functioning of various areas of the brain.

The aim of the chapter by Cornoldi is to elaborate on empirical findings that can show the influence of metacognitive knowledge on metacognitive control and hence on cognitive behavior.

The chapter by Nelson, Graf, Dunlosky, Marlatt, Walker, and Luce illustrates a psychopharmacological approach in which the temporary changes that occur in the brain during acute alcohol intoxication can affect cognitive and metacognitive performance, including the occurrence of omission and commission errors.

In the final chapter Metcalfe discusses the metacognitive aspects of a specific type of problem solving (i.e. insight) and includes some data from amnesic patients.

References

Metcalfe, J., & Shimamura, A. P. (Eds.). (1994). *Metacognition: Knowing about knowing*. MA: MIT Press.

Nelson, T. O. (1992). *Metacognition: Core readings*. Boston: Allyn & Bacon.

Nelson, T. O., & Narens, L. (1990). Metamemory: A theoretical framework and some new findings. In G. H. Bower (Ed.), *The psychology of learning and motivation* (Vol. 26). New York: Academic Press.

Reder, L. M. (1996). *Implicit memory and metacognition*. Mahwah, NJ.: Lawrence Erlbaum Associates.

Shimamura, A. P. (1994). Metacognition: Neuropsychological evidence. In J. Metcalfe & A. P. Shimamura (Eds.), *Metacognition: Knowing about knowing* (pp. 301–328). Cambridge, MA: MIT Press.

1

The Development of Procedural Metamemory in Childhood and Adolescence

Wolfgang Schneider
University of Wuerzburg, Germany

More than 25 years ago, Flavell (1971) coined the term metamemory to refer to knowledge about memory processes and contents. Although this concept has gained considerable attention in the literature and has proved important for describing and explaining developmental changes in the memory domain, it has also been criticized because of its obvious "fuzziness."

One major source of confusion concerning the widespread use of the construct is that it has been used to refer to two distinct areas of research, namely factual knowledge about memory and monitoring and regulation of memory processes. *Factual knowledge about memory* has also been labeled *declarative metamemory* and refers to the relatively stable, statable, often fallible, and late-developing information that children have about their own memory processes and those of others. In their taxonomy of declarative metamemory, Flavell and Wellman (1977) included categories such as knowledge about person characteristics (mnemonic self-concept), knowledge about task characteristics, and knowledge about potentially applicable memory strategies. Paris and colleagues (e.g., Paris & Lindauer, 1982; Paris & Oka, 1986) later introduced an additional component of declarative metamemory called conditional metacognitive knowledge that focused on children's ability to justify or explain their decisions concerning memory actions. Whereas declarative metamemory assessed by Flavell and colleagues focuses on "knowing that," the component added by Paris and coworkers deals with " knowing why" information.

The second area of metamemory research, *memory monitoring and self-regulation*, has also been labeled *procedural metamemory* in the literature (cf. Borkowski, Milstead, & Hale, 1988; Schneider & Bjorklund, 1998; Schneider & Pressley, 1997). Brown and her colleagues (cf. Baker & Brown, 1984; Brown, 1978; Brown, Bransford, Ferrara, & Campione, 1983) were the first to explore the procedural metamemory component, assessing children's ability to monitor and regulate their memory behavior during ongoing memory activities ("knowing how"). Here, the frame of reference was the competent information processor, one possessing an efficient executive that regulated cognitive behaviors. Brown and colleagues took the perspective that memory monitoring and regulation processes play a large role in executive actions, and that considerable developmental differences can be observed for these variables. In particular, it was assumed that monitoring and regulating behaviors are crucial in more complex cognitive tasks such as comprehending and memorizing text materials (e.g., Baker & Brown, 1984; Brown et al., 1983; Garner, 1987).

In this chapter, I want to summarize the state of the art regarding developmental trends in procedural metamemory. A more recent theoretical model relating memory monitoring and self-regulation is presented first, followed by an overview of developmental studies focusing on memory monitoring. Next, empirical research tapping the development of self-regulation skills and their interrelations with memory monitoring processes is discussed. Studies dealing with relations between both components of procedural metacognitive knowledge and memory performance as well as the developmental trends in these relations are summarized in the last section of the chapter.

NELSON AND NARENS' MODEL OF PROCEDURAL METAMEMORY

One possibility for exploring the role of procedural metamemory in actual behavior is to look at how children use their knowledge to monitor their own memory status and regulate their memory activities. According to Nelson and Narens (1990, 1994), self-monitoring and self-regulation correspond to two different levels of metacognitive processing. Self-monitoring refers to keeping track of where you are with regard to your goal of understanding and remembering (bottom-up process). On the other hand, self-regulation refers to central executive activities and includes planning, directing, and evaluating your behavior (top-down process).

Nelson and Narens (1990, 1994) referred to *servomechanisms* such as the thermostat in order to describe the interplay between components of procedural metamemory. In their model, a metalevel is distinguished from an object level of cognitive functioning (cf. Fig. 1.1.). Control processes are linked to the metalevel and are thought to directly influence the object level. It is assumed that the metalevel modifies the object level, but not vice versa. In particular, the information flowing from the metalevel to the object level either changes the state of the object level process or changes the object level process itself. Because control per se does not yield any information from the object level, monitoring processes are assumed to inform the metalevel about the current state of the object level. Nelson and Narens assume that this may change the metalevel's model of the situation and eventually lead to control activities. It seems important to note that whereas the metalevel has a model of the object level, the reverse is not true.

The various monitoring and self-regulation components assumed to be relevant for efficient information processing are shown in Fig. 1.1. They are depicted as a function of the stages of information acquisition, retention,

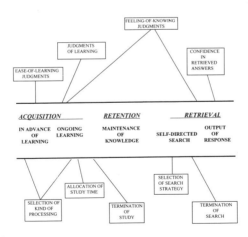

FIG. 1.1   The model of procedural metamemory developed by Nelson and Narens (1990).

and retrieval. So far, developmental research has focused on monitoring components such as ease-of-learning (EOL) judgments, judgments of learning (JOL), and feeling-of-knowing (FOK) judgments, and has also explored some aspects of control and self-regulation such as allocation of study time and termination of study. Empirical findings concerning developmental trends in these variables are summarized next.

DEVELOPMENTAL TRENDS CONCERNING PROCEDURAL METAMEMORY EOL

EOL judgments occur in advance of the learning process, are largely inferential, and refer to items that have not yet been learned. The corresponding memory paradigm is performance prediction in various retention tasks. Performance predictions, as the name implies, are made prior to study of the to-be-remembered material and involve estimation of how much will be learned. A form of performance prediction that has been used often in developmental research is prediction of one's own memory span (e.g., Flavell, Friedrichs, & Hoyt, 1970). Individuals are presented incrementally longer lists of materials to be learned (pictures, words, or figures) and are asked to indicate whether they could still recall a list that long. The child's memory span is then tapped using the same lists. Comparisons of the prediction value with actual memory span yields the metamemory indicator, which is usually interpreted as a by-product of memory monitoring (i.e., children who have monitored their memory proficiently in the past should be more aware of their memory span than children who have not monitored at all or not monitored well in the past). Performance prediction accuracy can be measured for a variety of memory tasks, with recent applications to text learning (e.g., Schneider, Körkel, & Weinert, 1990; Schneider & Uhl, 1990).

Most studies on EOL judgments using list-learning paradigms have found that preschool and kindergarten children overpredict their memory performance, whereas elementary school children are much more accurate (e.g., Flavell et al., 1970; Schneider, 1986; Schneider, Borkowski, Kurtz, & Kerwin, 1986; Worden & Sladewski-Awig, 1982; Yussen & Levy, 1975). Whether elementary school children over- or underestimate performance seems to vary with the memory task. For example, serial memory span is usually overestimated, whereas recall of categorizable lists is underestimated (cf. Flavell et al., 1970; Worden & Sladewski-Awig, 1982). The latter finding is probably not surprising given elementary-school children's lack of awareness of the effects of categorizing on memory. Recent studies also indicate that individual differences in aptitude do not have significant effects on estimation accuracy (cf. Alexander, Carr, & Schwanenflugel, 1995).

Several studies have tried to identify young children's difficulties in making accurate performance predictions. One likely possibility is that many memory tasks are completely unfamiliar to preschoolers. It was found that young children's predictions tended to be more accurate in familiar situations than in unfamiliar, laboratory-type situations. Thus preschool children make more realistic predictions when asked how far they can jump (Markman, 1973; Schneider, in press). Predictions are also more accurate when assessments of memory span are nonverbal rather than verbal (Cunningham & Weaver, 1989) or are conducted in a familiar context, such as a game (Wippich, 1981).

A particularly interesting question is whether predictions of overall performance improve in accuracy as experience with the memory task increases. There seems to be developmental improvement here. In the studies by Schneider and colleagues (Schneider, 1986; Schneider et al., 1986; Schneider & Uhl, 1990), participants made a prediction before attempting a list-learning task. Then, after completing the list-learning task and test of the material on the list, the participants were told that they would be doing another list-learning task and were asked to predict performance on this second list. Although first and second predictions did not differ in accuracy for Grade 2 and Grade 3 children, Grade 4 children's predictions became more accurate with practice. Pressley and Ghatala (1989) provided complementary data. In their study, Grade 1 and 2, Grade 4 and 5, and Grade 7 and 8 participants predicted performance on a vocabulary test, took the test, and then predicted performance on a future test of comparable difficulty. Although there was no evidence of prediction improvement from first to second prediction at the Grade 1 and 2 level, there was a strong trend toward improvement at the Grade 4 and 5 level and unambiguous improvement from first to second prediction at the Grade 7 and 8 level.

More negatively, prediction improvement may be limited to tasks involving fairly simple materials. When Schneider and Uhl's (1990) participants went through the prediction–learning–testing–prediction–learning–testing cycle with prose materials, there were no improvements in prediction with practice. Schneider and Uhl speculated that accurate awareness of the amount recalled on a test of prose content may be less certain than accurate awareness for list items, and thus, test monitoring during prose study and testing might not be sufficient to permit improvements in predictions about future prose learning.

One problem with the performance prediction paradigm is that it may not only tap metacognitive processes, particularly when it is carried out with young children. Researchers of achievement motivation (Stipek, 1984; Stipek & Mac Iver, 1989) using performance prediction in order to assess young children's level of aspiration in motor tasks found that children's performance predictions seem confounded by motivational factors such as wishful thinking. This means that young children are estimating what they would like to get rather than what they think they will get. In a subsequent study using both motor and memory tasks, Schneider (in press) confirmed this assumption. Like Stipek (1984), Schneider found that preschoolers and kindergartners can be rather accurate when asked to predict the perform-ance of other children, as compared to their own performance (cf. Fig. 1.2).

This finding is in line with the wishful thinking hypothesis: Given their egocentric stage, young children's desires are restricted to their own per-formance and do not necessarily generalize to achievements of their peers. However, this finding is not compatible with the metacognitive deficiency hypothesis because poor memory monitoring should yield similar outcomes in both conditions. Thus young children's poor EOL judgments seem not particularly due to deficiencies in memory monitoring, but may be strongly affected by motivational factors such as wishful thinking or beliefs in the power of effort (cf. Stipek, 1984; Wellman, 1985). However, because such motivational processes are not similarly influential in schoolchildren, there are subtle improvements over the elementary school years (Körkel, 1987, Pressley & Ghatala, 1990; Schneider et al., 1990; Schneider & Uhl, 1990).

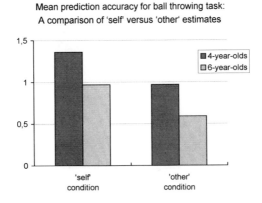

FIG. 1.2   Differences in estimating accuracy concerning one's performance versus another-child's performance (data from Schneider, in press).

JOL TASKS

Similar developmental trends were observed for performance on JOL tasks. In a few developmental studies, children's postdictions (i.e., their judgments of performance accuracy after the fact) were evaluated (Bisanz, Vesonder, & Voss, 1978; Pressley, Levin, Ghatala, & Ahmad, 1987). For instance, Pressley et al. (1987) compared 7- and 10-year-olds' postdictions for word lists and individual items. There were two major findings: (a) although rather accurate postdictions were found even for the younger age group, the older children were significantly better; and (b) those children who were most accurate with regard to estimating performance on individual items were not similarly accurate when asked to postdict performance on the entire list, and vice versa. It appears, then, that these two tasks tap different aspects of the estimation process.

In a more recent study, Schneider, Kettner, Schlagmüller, and Nelson (in preparation) used a different memory paradigm (i.e., paired-associate learning) to assess developmental trends in JOL judgments of Grade 2 and Grade 4 children. One of the major goals of this study was to explore whether children's delayed JOL judgments (given about 2 minutes after the learning process) would correspond more closely with actual learning outcomes than judgments provided immediately after learning the item pairs, a finding repeatedly reported for adults (cf. Mazzoni & Nelson, 1995; Nelson, 1996; Nelson & Dunlosky, 1991). Furthermore, judgments for individual item pairs were compared with aggregate judgments; that is, JOLs for the entire list of items. The major findings are summarized in Table 1.1.

TABLE 1.1

Means and Standard Deviations (in parenthesis) for Judgments of Learning (JOLs) in a Paired Association Task, as a Function of Age and Experimental Condition. (Data from Schneider, et al., in preparation)

	Age Group			
	Second Grade		Fourth Grade	
	Estimate	Hits	Estimate	Hits
Immediate	20.18	12.71	20.39	13.56
	(3.49)	(2.42)	(4.12)	(3.20)
Delayed	17.03	15.79	17.76	18.41
	(4.56)	(4.03)	(3.67)	(3.73)
Aggregate	14.00		14.79	
	(3.96)		(3.50)	

As can be seen from this table, delayed JOLs turned out to be more accurate than immediate JOLs in both age groups, thus replicating the findings obtained with adult samples. However, whereas adults' performance estimates based on individual items were always more optimistic and significantly higher than those based on the entire list, the difference in the mean level of aggregated versus individual items was not statistically significant for the children, regardless of age level. In accord with the findings reported by Pressley et al. (1987), however, only low to moderate correlations were found between the two estimation procedures. It appears, then, that they tap different aspects of the estimation process (see also Mazzoni & Nelson, 1995; Nelson & Narens, 1994).

In summary, the results of the JOL studies described here indicate that children's ability to judge their own memory performance after study of test materials seems to increase over the elementary school years. However, even young schoolchildren are able to monitor their performance quite accurately and to estimate future performance reasonably well when judgments are given not immediately after study but somewhat delayed. According to Nelson and Narens (1994), the difference in accuracy between immediate and delayed judgments could be due to the fact that immediate judgments are based on analyses tapping working memory, whereas delayed judgments are based on search processes addressing the contents of the long-term store. Regardless of whether this explanation holds or not, the processes causing the differences in immediate and delayed JOLs seem similar in children and adults.

FOK JUDGMENTS

A number of developmental studies have explored children's FOK accuracy (Brown & Lawton, 1977; Cultice, Somerville, & Wellman, 1983; DeLoache & Brown, 1984; Wellman, 1977). In a now classic study, Wellman (1977) studied the accuracy of children's feelings that they knew items, even when they could not recall them. Children were shown a series of items and then asked to name them. When children could not recall the name of an object given its picture, they were asked to indicate whether the name would be recognized if the experimenter provided it. Then, a recognition test was given in which the name of the object was provided with the child required to select the item from a group of pictures. When FOK ratings were related to performance on the recognition test, it was found that FOK accuracy increased from kindergarten (youngest children in the study) to Grade 3 (oldest children in the study). Wellman also noted that only the Grade 3 children registered the frustration that is typical of adults who have something on the tip of their tongue but cannot remember it (see the study by Brown & Lawton [1977] for similar developmental trends observed for children with learning difficulties).

In late elementary school, age effects in cognitive monitoring seem minimal. For example, Schneider and Körkel (1989) assessed FOK judgments on a multiple-choice completion task testing recognition of a previously heard story. 9-, 10-, and eleven-year-old children were equally able to accurately access their performance through these FOK judgments regardless of age, aptitude, and familiarity with the test materials (for similar findings, see Schneider et al., 1990).

Even young children seem to possess the skills relevant for FOK problems when task difficulty is adequate. Findings of a study by Cultice et al. (1983) revealed that preschoolers can be fairly accurate when the task is simply structured and involves highly meaningful test materials such as faces. In this study, participants were asked to name children who were depicted on photos presented to them. The pictures included very familiar faces (i.e., children from their own preschool group), somewhat less familiar faces (i.e., children from another group in the preschool), and completely unfamiliar faces. When the children could not name the person in the picture, they were quite capable of saying whether they would recognize the person when the name was provided. Thus, when FOK problems are simply structured and involve highly familiar materials such as faces, even preschoolers evidence the memory-monitoring competence tapped by the FOK task.

Taken together, the findings summarized here indicate that FOK accuracy can be already high in young children and seems to improve continuously during the early elementary school years. However, the pattern of developmental trends is not entirely clear. In particular, a study by Butterfield, Nelson, and Peck (1988) sheds doubts on the assumption of age-related improvement. This study avoided a methodological problem apparent in previous research on FOK judgments, that is, the confounding of the individual's threshold for "know" versus "do not know" responses with their knowledge about nonrecalled items. It also included an extensive practice period in order to ensure that children in the sample (first graders and fifth graders) clearly understood the task requirements. As a main result of their first experiment, Butterfield et al. (1988) showed that first-grade children's FOK judgments were actually more accurate than those of fifth graders and undergraduate students. Obviously, the results of this experiment do not square well with the findings of previous research. However, results of a second experiment conducted by Butterfield et al. (1988) yielded inconsistent findings for the sample of undergraduates, indicating that FOK judgments vary with method of assessment or materials. Thus more research is needed to explore developmental trends in FOK accuracy.

SELF-REGULATION AND CONTROL

As noted earlier, several studies investigated the development of children's control and self-regulation processes. In the following, I restrict the overview to two research paradigms, namely the knowledge of recall readiness and the allocation of effort and attention during study of task materials.

Knowledge of Recall Readiness

Recall readiness assessments are made after material has been studied at least one time. One variation involves asking participants to continue studying until their memory of the items to be learned is perfect. For instance, Flavell et al. (1970) asked their participants (kindergartners, Grade 1, Grade 2, and Grade 4 children) to study a word list long enough to be absolutely certain they would be able to recall the entire list perfectly. There was a clear developmental trend in estimation of recall readiness. Flavell et al. (1970) found that 5- to 6-year-olds were often too optimistic about their readiness for a test and had low levels of recall after they said they were ready for a test. In comparison, the Grade 2 and Grade 4 children were considerably more accurate. Flavell et al. concluded that older children's more accurate assessments were due to their greater use of self-testing during study.

One problem with this interpretation is that relatively short lists corresponding to each child's memory span were used in this study. Recall readiness assessment skills are typically overestimated when children learn materials that are not particularly difficult (Markman, 1973). In later studies that included memory tasks other than serial recall (e.g., free recall, memory for text), older elementary school children were not very good at determining when they had studied items long enough to master the material (e.g., Gettinger, 1985; Leal, Crays, & Moely, 1985). Self-testing strategies were rarely observed in these studies. Apparently, most grade-school children do not spontaneously use task-relevant regulation strategies in recall readiness tasks. Although there is no doubt that self testing occurs more frequently as a function of age, there is still room for improvement in this skill during adolescence and young adulthood.

Effort and Attention Allocation

Another nonverbal method of measuring online monitoring and control is to observe how learners deploy their attention and effort. The ability to attend selectively to relevant aspects of a memory task is a traditional index of learners' understanding of the task (cf. Brown et al., 1983).

Several studies examined whether schoolchildren and adults were more likely to spend more time on less well-learned material (allocation of study time). For instance, Masur, McIntyre, and Flavell (1973) asked first graders, third graders, and college students to learn a list of pictures for free recall. After the first study and first free recall trial, participants were instructed to select half the pictures for additional study. Although third graders and college students tended to select items not recalled correctly on the first trial, first graders did not seem to consider first-trial performance in selecting of items for additional processing. Similar findings were reported by Bisanz et al. (1978) for a paired-associate task. They found that fifth graders and college students were more likely than first or third graders to select items not learned on a first trial.

It is somewhat puzzling that young grade-school children do not choose to allocate more study to items that they have not yet mastered. It does not seem likely that it is because they are unaware which item materials are not known. For instance, Pressley et al. (1987) and Pressley and Ghatala (1989) both showed that even Grade 1 and Grade 2 children are aware of which test items they are almost certainly answering correctly and which are probably answered incorrectly, even though there is developmental improvement in these discriminations over the grade-school years. When processing differentially learnable text, even Grade 2 children know which parts of the text are easier than others (Danner, 1976). Apparently, knowing which information is known already or easier to learn and which information is unlikely to have been mastered is not sufficient to result in appropriate self-regulation (i.e., studying those items that have yet to be learned).

One problem with the studies by Masur et al. (1973) and Bisanz et al. (1978) is that children were forced to be selective. Thus we do not know how young children might behave in a more spontaneous study situation.

A study by Dufresne and Kobasigawa (1989) assessed spontaneous allocation of study time for children in Grades 1, 3, 5, and 7. Participants were
asked to study booklets containing either "easy" (highly related) or
"hard" (unrelated) paired-associate items until they were sure they could
remember all pairs perfectly. The results are given in Fig. 1.3.

Whereas Grade 1 and Grade 3 children spent about the same amount
of time on easy pairs as they spent on hard pairs, participants in the two
older age groups devoted considerably more time to studying the hard
items than the easy ones. These findings confirm the outcomes of
previous studies in that cognitive self-regulation can be observed in older
but not younger schoolchildren (e.g., Bisanz et al., 1978). Dufresne and
Kobasigawa (1989) noted that the younger children in their study were
well able to distinguish between hard and easy pairs. This suggests that
the major difference between younger and older schoolchildren is that
accurate monitoring leads to appropriate self–regulation in the older
participants but not in the younger participants. Although a more recent
study by Kobasigawa and Metcalfe-Haggert (1993) indicates that even
Grade 1 children can allocate study time differentially when differences
in item difficulty are particularly salient, this seems more an exception
than the rule. Using Nelson and Narens' (1990) terminology (cf. Fig. 1.1),
it appears that young children's self-regulation component is not developed well enough to respond appropriately to incoming information from
their monitoring component.

There is no doubt that performance on study time apportionment
tasks strongly depends on the difficulty and complexity of the memory

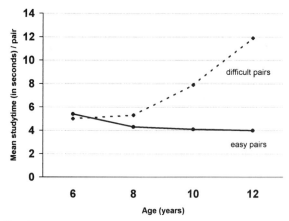

FIG. 1.3.   Developmental differences in study time apportionment (data from Dufresne &
Kobasigawa, 1989).

tasks involved. As illustrated by Brown and colleagues, judging one's mastery of the gist of texts is more difficult than judging verbatim recall of items (for a review, see Brown et al., 1983). Studies using the study time apportionment paradigm with texts revealed that sophisticated selection of text material for further study develops somewhat later than the grade-school years. One source of difficulty for schoolchildren is that they are not aware of the relative importance of different parts of complicated text (Brown, Smiley, & Lawton, 1978; Kurtz & Schneider, 1988), even though they can differentiate important from less important information in short texts and simple, conventionally-structured stories (e.g., Denhiere & LeNy, 1980; Yussen, Mathews, Buss, & Kane, 1980). Brown et al. (1978) demonstrated that between Grade 5 and college there is development in understanding of parts of texts not mastered during a first study–test cycle. Consistent with the hypothesis that elementary school children would not make effective use of additional study opportunity, Brown and colleagues showed that fifth graders' recall of text did not improve following 5 minutes of additional study. In comparison, Grade 7, Grade 8, and high school students did benefit from the additional study time, with the total pattern of data suggesting that knowledge of text parts that were not yet mastered may have directed restudy at those age levels.

All in all, the available evidence on the development of self-regulation skills shows that there are clear increases from middle childhood to adolescence. Effective self-regulation occurs only in highly constrained situations during the grade-school years and continues to develop well into adolescence. In contrast, the literature on the development of monitoring yields a less consistent pattern. Although most studies indicated a continuous increase with age, others showed just the opposite result. Developmental research using more sophisticated methodologies is needed to solve this puzzle and fill the gap.

Finally, it should be noted in this regard that although most grade-school children do show deficits in memory monitoring and do not spontaneously use task–relevant regulation strategies, there is no doubt that they can be successfully trained to do so. Several studies have shown that training in memory monitoring and self-regulation is responsible for the effectiveness and maintenance of strategy training (e.g., Ghatala, Levin, Pressley, & Goodwin, 1986; Paris, Newman, & McVey, 1982; Pressley & McCormick, 1995).

RELATIONS BETWEEN PROCEDURAL
METAMEMORY AND MEMORY PERFORMANCE

One of the main motivations for research on metamemory has been the theoretical conviction that there are important relations between knowing about memory and memory performance (cf. Flavell & Wellman, 1977; Schneider, 1985). However, it soon turned out that the links between knowledge and behavior are not very strong. A statistical meta-analysis of empirical studies on the metamemory–memory relation conducted by Schneider (1985) revealed an overall correlation (Pearson r) of .41, indicating a reliable but only moderate relation between knowledge about memory and memory performance. In the following, the developmental literature concerning possible links between various aspects of procedural metamemory and memory performance is briefly discussed.

Relations Between Prediction Accuracy and Memory Performance

Researchers exploring the link between prediction accuracy and recall assumed that people who are good information processors should have good memories, and presumably also monitor their performances better than poor information processors; thus they should know more about their memory capacities and limitations and be better able to predict their memory performances than other people.

The first explicit test of the relation between prediction accuracy and memory performance was conducted by Kelly, Scholnick, Travers, and Johnson (1976), who found no obvious relation between prediction accuracy and memory in their study. Ceiling effects may have played a part in this failure, however. because prediction accuracy was generally very high at all age levels, it does not come as a surprise that the correlations between prediction accuracy and recall were low (i.e., there was a restricted range in the metamemory measure).

Follow-up investigations were more successful in establishing accuracy–recall relations (Levin, Yussen, de Rose, & Pressley, 1977; cf. Levin, Wippich, 1981; Yussen & Berman, 1981;). There was clear evidence that prediction accuracy–performance relations were task specific (e.g., obtained with recall but not recognition, more likely in natural situations than in the laboratory). There were developmental trends, with increasing correlations between predictions and performance during the grade-school years. The correlations between predictions and performance were higher for noncategorizable than categorizable lists. This may be due to the fact that positive effects of list structure on recall were generally underestimated by younger children (cf. Schneider, 1985).

Relations Between Effort and Attention Allocation and Memory Performance

In the study by Masur et al. (1973) described earlier, children were asked to select items for additional study after an initial study-recall cycle. Participants were considered to be metamnemonically sophisticated when they selected items for further study that they had not recalled on the previous trial. Although both Grade 3 children and college students made appropriate item selections, only college students' memory performance was positively affected by selection of appropriate items. Thus it was only at the college level that adequate metamemory (i.e., knowing which items to select) corresponded with reliable memory improvement. Brown (1978) offered an interesting explanation of this pattern of results. She argued that in focusing attention on the items that were not learned previously, children failed to process additionally the items that were recalled previously. Possibly, these previously recalled items were not mastered so well that subsequent recall was certain without additional learning. Thus, even though memory of previously unrecalled items may have increased on subsequent recall trials, memory for previously recalled items would have declined, resulting in little advantage for the child participants who selected unrecalled items for further study. Brown (1978) suggested that effective restudy in this situation requires complex coordination (i.e., rehearsing previously recalled items in addition to relearning information not recalled) that has only been partially mastered by young grade-school children, if it has been mastered at all.

In addition to consideration of allocation of effort during encoding, there have also been studies of selective effort allocation during retrieval. Wellman (1979) reanalyzed his earlier (Wellman, 1977) data. He investigated whether there were correlations between children's FOK judgments and the effort deployed to try to retrieve the words. Although the relation between the strength of the FOK judgments and effort increased with age, it was already reliable for the youngest age group (i.e., kindergartners). This finding is consistent with the conclusion that even very young children can sometimes use their knowledge of information availability to guide strategic efforts.

Relationships Between Monitoring and Control and Text Processing

Consistent correlational relations were found between various types of metacognitive knowledge about text and various outcome measures that reflect text processing, such as comprehension and recall of what was read (e.g., Denhiere, 1988; Garner, 1987; Körkel, 1987; Körkel & Schneider, 1992; Schneider & Uhl, 1990). These correlations generally ranged from low to moderate (i.e., .10–.50).

One of the more completely researched correlational relations is between knowledge of the relative importance of information in text and recall of text. Even preschool children tend to remember more important information in text compared to less important information, even though they may not be aware of the differential importance of text units (cf. Brown & Smiley, 1978; Denhiere, 1988; Young & Schumacher, 1983). In fact, the evidence provided by Brown et al. (1983) suggests that monitoring and control of text processing based on knowledge of relative importance of text units occurs a number of years after correlations between recall and importance levels are present. Several studies using importance rating scales and short, meaningful stories found moderately high metamemory–memory links for children age 10 and older (cf. Denhiere, 1988; Yussen et al., 1980). Similar evidence was also reported by Brown and Smiley (1978), who used a study-time apportionment paradigm. Brown and Smiley inferred from recall patterns that Grade 7 and Grade 8 children directed their attention to the more important aspects of text when they were given additional study time. In contrast, fifth graders studied less selectively.

Other studies focused on the relation of various JOL variables and text comprehension and recall (Forrest-Pressley & Waller, 1984; Hasselhorn & Körkel, 1986; Schneider et al., 1990). For example, Hasselhorn and Körkel (1986) provided their participants with inferences drawn from a text that they had studied before. The children's task was (a) to judge the appropriateness of the text inferences and (b) to indicate how sure they were that their judgments were correct (confidence judgments). Hasselhorn and Körkel reported significant correlations between their sixth graders' confidence judgments and the correctness of inferences.

Schneider et al. (1990) explored the relative effects of domain-specific knowledge and metacognitive knowledge on text recall. Soccer experts and novices from Grades 3, 5, and 7 were presented with a narrative text dealing with a soccer game. Although the text was generally easy to understand even for novices, some important information was occasionally omitted and had to be inferred by the participants. Also, several contradictions were built into the text that could only be detected by careful reading. Regarding the importance of procedural metacognitive knowledge, it was assumed that it should be closely linked to the designated domain. That is, the hypothesis was that the quality of FOK judgments and importance ratings should depend on the familiarity of item materials. The data clearly confirmed this assumption. It was shown that both EOL judgments and FOK judgments not only correlated with expertise but also with text recall and comprehension.

Körkel and Schneider (1992) went one step further and explored the relative effects of domain-specific knowledge and metacognitive knowledge on text recall by using a more comprehensive statistical framework. That is, they used structural equation modeling procedures based on a latent variable approach (LISREL) to examine whether metacognitive knowledge significantly contributes to experts' memory performance. Several alternative causal models were estimated and tested. The model that fit the data best is depicted in Fig. 1.4.

It specified that both verbal and nonverbal intelligence should influence the three knowledge components considered (i.e., domain-specific knowledge and declarative and procedural metacognitive knowledge). As declarative and procedural metacognitive knowledge was conceived of as rather independent (cf. Brown et al., 1983), no relation between these two concepts was specified. It was further assumed that domain-specific knowledge should influence procedural metacognitive knowledge, which in turn should affect text recall.

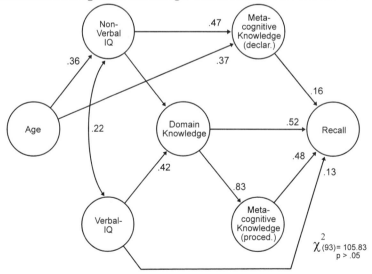

FIG. 1.4.   Structural equation model describing the impact of intelligence and various knowledge components on text recall (data from Körkel & Schneider, 1992).

The results of the causal modeling procedure basically confirmed these assumptions. As predicted, no link between declarative and procedural metacognitive knowledge was found. Whereas declarative metamemory only played a modest role in predicting text recall, procedural metamemory turned out to be a significant predictor of memory performance. It was strongly affected by domain-specific knowledge that showed substantial direct and indirect effects on text recall. Thus although the findings by Körkel and Schneider (1992) confirmed the crucial role of domain-specific knowledge on recall of information linked to the domain of expertise, they also indicate that domain-specific knowledge and procedural metacognitive knowledge are functionally related, and that procedural metacognitive knowledge has an independent, reliable direct effect on text recall. It appears, then, that procedural metacognitive knowledge does make a difference even in cases where domain-specific knowledge is particularly rich.

CONCLUDING REMARKS

Although the concept of metamemory has been studied for more than 25 years, the issue of definition and conceptualization of metacognitive knowledge is still controversial. In my view, however, the distinction between declarative and procedural metamemory has proven useful for empirical research. Similarly, distinction between monitoring and control processes within the procedural metamemory component suggested by Nelson and Narens (1990) makes a lot of sense.

From a developmental perspective, the research findings concerning the monitoring component reveal that basic competencies are already available from early ages on and that developmental trends are not similarly clear-cut as in many aspects of declarative metamemory. In comparison, we find substantial age differences in the competency to regulate and control one's own behavior. Obviously, young grade-school children have enormous problems responding appropriately to monitoring activities. As noted by Brown et al. (1983), the ability to monitor and regulate one's state of learning depends on the sensitivity one has to factors such as strategies, domain knowledge, material, and task demands. These all influence the degree to which a child will be able to engage in monitoring and coordinate his or her plans. There is no doubt that factors such as knowledge and strategies develop rather late and improve considerably over the elementary school years. This may explain the fact that flexibility in monitoring and self-regulation is rarely observed before sixth grade.

REFERENCES

Alexander, J. M., & Carr, M., Schwanenflugel, P. J. (1995). Development of metacognition in gifted children: Directions for future research. *Developmental Review, 15*, 1–37.

Baker, L., & Brown, A. L. (1984). Metacognitive skills and reading. In P. D. Pearson, M. Kamil, R. Barr, & P. Mosenthal (Eds.), *Handbook of reading research* (pp. 353–394). New York: Longman.

Bisanz, G. L., Vesonder, G. T., & Voss, J. F. (1978). Knowledge of one's own responding and the relation of such knowledge to learning. *Journal of Experimental Child Psychology, 25*, 116–128.

Borkowski, J. G., Milstead, M., & Hale, C. (1988). Components of children's metamemory: Implications for strategy generalization. In F. E. Weinert & M. Perlmutter (Eds.), *Memory development: Universal changes and individual differences* (pp. 73–100). Hillsdale, NJ: Lawrence Erlbaum Associates.

Brown, A. L. (1978). Knowing when, where, and how to remember: A problem of metacognition. In R. Glaser (Ed.), *Advances in instructional psychology* (pp. 77–165). Hillsdale, NJ: Lawrence Erlbaum Associates.

Brown, A. L., Bransford, J. D., Ferrara, R. A., & Campione, J. C. (1983). Learning, remembering, and understanding. In J. H. Flavell & E. M. Markman (Eds.), *Handbook of child psychology:* Vol. III. Cognitive development (pp. 77–166). New York: Wiley.

Brown, A. L., & Lawton, S. C. (1977). The feeling of knowing experience in educable retarded children. *Developmental Psychology, 13*, 364–370.

Brown, A. L., & Smiley, S. S. (1978). The development of strategies for studying texts. *Child Development, 49*, 1076–1088.

Brown, A. L., Smiley, S. S., & Lawton, S. C. (1978). The effects of experience on the selection of suitable retrieval cues for studying texts. *Child Development, 49*, 829–835.

Butterfield, E., Nelson, T., & Peck, G. (1988). Developmental aspects of the feeling of knowing. *Developmental Psychology, 24*, 654–663.

Cultice, J. C., Somerville, S. C., & Wellman, H. M. (1983). Preschooler's memory monitoring: Feeling-of-knowing judgments. *Child Development, 54*, 1480–1486.

Cunningham, J. G., & Weaver, S. L. (1989). Young children's knowledge of their memory span: Effects of task and experience. *Journal of Experimental Child Psychology, 48*, 32–44.

Danner, F. W. (1976). Children's understanding of intersentence organization in the recall of short descriptive passages. *Journal of Educational Psychology 68*, 174–183.

DeLoache, J. S., & Brown, A. L. (1984). Where do I go next? Intelligent searching by very young children. *Developmental Psychology, 20*, 37–44.

Denhiere, G. (1988). Story comprehension and memorization by children. In F. E. Weinert & M. Perlmutter (Eds.), *Memory development: Universal changes and individual differences.* Hillsdale, NJ: Lawrence Erlbaum Associates.

Denhiere, G., & Le Ny, J. F. (1980). Relative importance of meaningful units in comprehension and recall of narratives by children and adults. *Poetics, 9*, 147–161.

Dufresne, A., & Kobasigawa, A. (1989). Children's spontaneous allocation of study time: Differential and sufficient aspects. *Journal of Experimental Child Psychology, 47*, 274–296.

Flavell, J. H. (1971). First discussant's comments: What is memory development the development of? *Human Development, 14*, 272–278.

Flavell, J. H., Friedrichs, A. G., & Hoyt, J. D. (1970). Developmental changes in memorization processes. *Cognitive Psychology, 1*, 324–340.

Flavell, J. H., & Wellman, H. M. (1977). Metamemory. In R. V. Kail & J. W. Hagen (Eds.), *Perspectives on the development of memory and cognition* (pp. 3–33). Hillsdale, NJ: Lawrence Erlbaum Associates.

Forrest-Pressley, D. L., & Waller, T. (1984). *Cognition, metacognition, and reading.* New York: Springer-Verlag.

Garner, R. (1987). *Metacognition and reading comprehension.* Norwood, NJ: Ablex Publishing Corp.

Gettinger, M. (1985). Time allocated and time spent relative to time needed for learning as determinants of achievement. *Journal of Educational Psychology, 77*, 3–11.

Ghatala, L., Levin, J., Pressley, M., & Goodwin, D. (1986). A componential analysis of derived and supplied strategy-utility information on children's strategy selection. *Journal of Experimental Child Psychology, 41*, 76–92.

Hasselhorn, M., & Korkel, J. (1986). Metacognitive versus traditional reading instructions: The mediating role of domain-specific knowledge on children's text processing. *Human Learning, 5*, 75–90.

Kelly, M., Scholnick, E. K., Travers, S. H., & Johnson, J. W. (1976). Relations among memory, memory appraisal, and memory strategies. *Child Development, 47*, 648–649.

Kobasigawa, A., & Metcalfe-Haggert, A. (1993). Spontaneous allocation of study time by first- and third-grade children in a simple memory task. *Journal of Genetic Psychology, 154*, 223–235.

Körkel, J. (1987). Die Entwicklung von Gedächtnis- und Metagedächtnisleistungen in Abhängigkeit von bereichsspezifischen Vorkenntnissen [The development of memory and metamemory and its dependence on domain-specific knowledge]. Frankfurt: Lang.

Körkel, J., & Schneider, W. (1992). Domain-specific versus metacognitive knowledge effects on text recall and comprehension. In M. Carretero, M. Pope, R. J. Simons, & J. I. Pozo (Eds.), *Learning and instruction—European research in an international context* (Vol. 3, pp. 311–324). New York: Pergamon.

Kurtz, B. E., & Schneider, W. (1988). The effects of age, study time, and importance of text units on strategy use and memory for texts *European Journal of Psychology of Education, 3*, 191–199.

Leal, L., Crays, N., & Moely, B. E. (1985). Training children to use a self-monitoring study strategy in preparation for recall: Maintenance and generalization effects. *Child Development, 56*, 643–653.

Levin, J., Yussen, S., De Rose, T., & Pressley, M. (1977). Developmental changes in assessing recall and recognition memory capacity. *Developmental Psychology, 13*, 608–615.

Markman, E. M. (1973). *Factors affecting the young child's ability to monitor his memory.* Unpublished doctoral dissertation, University of Pennsylvania; Philadelphia, PA.

Masur, E. F., McIntyre, C. W., & Flavell, J. H. (1973). Developmental changes in apportionment of study time among items in a multitrial free recall task. *Journal of Experimental Child Psychology, 15*, 237–246.

Mazzoni, G., & Nelson, T. O. (1995). Judgments of learning are affected by the kind of encoding in ways that cannot be attributed to the level of recall. *Journal of Experimental Psychology: Learning, Memory and Cognition, 21*, 1263–1274.

Nelson, T. O. (1996). Consciousness and metacognition. *American Psychologist, 51*, 102–116.

Nelson, T. O., & Dunlosky, J. (1991). When people's judgment of learning (JOLs) are extremely accurate at predicting subsequent recall: the "delayed-JOL effect." *Psychological Science, 2*, 267–270.

Nelson, T. O., & Narens, L. (1990). Metamemory: A theoretical framework and new findings. In G. Bower (Ed.), *The psychology of learning and motivation* (Vol. 26, pp. 125–140). New York: Academic Press.

Nelson, T. O., & Narens, L. (1994). Why investigate metacognition? In J. Metcalfe & A. P. Shimamura (Eds.), *Metacognition: Knowing about knowing.* (pp. 1–25) Cambridge, MA: MIT Press.

Paris, S. G., & Lindauer, B. K. (1982). The development of cognitive skills during childhood. In B. Wolman (Ed.), *Handbook of developmental psychology* (pp. 35–60). Englewood Cliffs, NJ: Prentice-Hall.

Paris, S. G., Newman, R. S., & McVey, K. A. (1982). Learning the functional significance of mnemonic actions: A microgenetic study of strategy acquisition. *Journal of Experimental Child Psychology, 34*, 490–509.

Paris, S. G., & Oka, E. R. (1986). Children's reading strategies, metacognition, and motivation. *Developmental Review, 6*, 25–56.

Pressley, M., & Ghatala, E. S. (1989). Metacognitive benefits of taking a test for children and young adolescents. *Journal of Experimental Child Psychology, 47*, 430–450.

Pressley, M., & Ghatala, L. (1990). Self-regulated learning: Monitoring learning from text. *Educational Psychologist, 25*, 19–34.

Pressley, M., Levin, J. R., Ghatala, E. S., & Ahmad, M. (1987). Test monitoring in young grade school children. *Journal of Experimental Child Psychology, 43*, 96–111.

Pressley, M., & McCormick, C. (1995). *Advanced educational psychology for educators researchers and policy makers.* New York: HarperCollins.

Schneider, W. (1985). Developmental trends in the metamemory–memory behavior relationship: An integrative review. In D. L. Forrest-Pressley, G. E. MacKinnon, & T. G. Waller (Eds.), *Metacognition. cognition and human performance* (Vol. 1, pp. 57–109). Orlando, FL: Academic Press.

Schneider, W. (1986). The role of conceptual knowledge and metamemory in the development of organizational processes in memory. *Journal of Experimental Child Psychology, 42*, 218–236.

Schneider, W. (in press). Performance prediction in young children: Effects of skill, metacognition. and wishful thinking. *Developmental Science.*

Schneider, W., & Bjorklund, D. F. (1998). Memory. In W. Damon (Ed.-in Chief) & D. Kuhn & R. S. Siegler (Eds.), *Handbook of child psychology*: Vol. 2 Cognition, perception and language (5th ed.). New York: Wiley.

Schneider, W., Borkowski, J. G., Kurtz, B. E., & Kerwin, K. (1986). Metamemory and motivation: A comparison of strategy use and performance in German and American children. *Journal of Cross-Cultural Psychology, 17,* 315–336.

Schneider, W., Kettner, D., Schlagmuller, M., & Nelson, T. O. (in preparation). *Developmental differences in judgments of learning.* Unpublished manuscript, University of Wuerzburg, Wuerzburg, Germany.

Schneider, W., & Körkel, J. (1989). The knowledge base and text recall: Evidence from a short-term longitudinal study. *Contemporary Educational Psychology, 14,* 382–393.

Schneider, W., Körkel, J., & Weinert, F. E. (1990). Expert knowledge, general abilities, and text processing. In W. Schneider & F. E. Weinert (Eds.), *Interactions among aptitudes, strategies, and knowledge in cognitive performance* (pp. 235–251). New York: Springer-Verlag.

Schneider, W., & Pressley, M. (1997). *Memory development between 2 and 20* (2nd ed.). Mahwah, NJ: Lawrence Erlbaum Associates.

Schneider, W., & Uhl, C. (1990). Metagedachtnis, Strategienutzung und Gedachtnisleistung: Vergleichende Analysen bei Kindern, jungeren Erwachsenen und alten Menschen. [Metamemory, strategy use and memory performance in children, adults, and the elderly]. *Zeitschrift fur Entwicklungspsychologie und Padagogische Psychologie, 22,* 22–41.

Stipek, D. J. (1984). Young children's performance expectations: Logical analysis or wishful thinking? In J. G. Nicholls (Ed.), *The development of achievement motivation* (pp. 121–. Greenwich, CT: JAI.

Stipek, D., & Mac Iver, D. (1989). Developmental change in children's assessment of intellectual competence. *Child Development, 60,* 521–538.

Wellman, H. M. (1977). Tip of the tongue and feeling of knowing experiences: A developmental study of memory monitoring. *Child Development, 48,* 13–21.

Wellman, H. M. (1979). *The role of metamemory in memory behavior: A developmental demonstration.* Unpublished manuscript, University of Michigan, Ann Arbor, MI.

Wellman, H. M. (1985). A child's theory of mind: The development of conceptions of cognition. In S. R. Yussen (Ed.), *The growth of reflection in children* (pp. 169–206). New York: Academic Press.

Wippich, W. (1981). Verbessert eine Einkaufssituation die Vorhersage der eigenen Behaltensleistungen im Vorschulalter? [Does a shopping game ever improve predictions of memory performance in preschoolers? *Zeitschrift fur Entwicklunqspsychologie und Padagogische Psychologie, 8,* 280–290.

Worden, P. E., & Sladewski-Awig, L. J. (1982). Children's awareness of memorability. *Journal of Educational Psychology, 74,* 341–350.

Young, D. R., & Schumacher, G. M. (1983). Context effects in young children's sensitivity to the importance level of prose information. *Child Development, 54,* 1446–1456.

Yussen, S. R., & Berman, L. (1981). Memory predictions for recall and recognition in first-, third-, and fifth-grade children. *Developmental Psychology, 17,* 224–229.

Yussen, S. R., & Levy, V. M. (1975). Developmental changes in predicting one's own memory span of short-term memory. *Journal of Experimental Child Psychology, 19,* 502–508.

Yussen, S. R., Mathews. S. R., Buss, R. R., & Kane, P. T. (1980). Developmental change in judging important and critical elements of stories. *Developmental Psychology, 16,* 213–219.

2

The Validity of Metacognitive Predictions of Widespread Learning and Long-Term Retention

Lynda K. Hall
Harry P. Bahrick
Ohio Wesleyan University

Metacognition has become an important focus of cognitive research. As is often the case, the research began with the investigation of a specific phenomenon, in this case Hart's (1965) exploration of the feeling of knowing (FOK). It was soon recognized (Flavell, 1979; Hart, 1967) that FOK is part of a more general research domain that deals with understanding one's own cognitive processes. Nelson and Narens (1990) organized this research domain in their seminal paper that focused on the distinction between monitoring and control processes and described the available techniques of measurement.

Initial exploration of a phenomenon such as FOK may reflect the interests of a single investigator, but the rapid development of a research area requires a much wider recognition of the potential importance of the domain. Metacognitive research attracted the interest of the research community because it provided exactly the kind of information needed to support an ongoing transformation of learning and memory research. Prior to the 1960s, investigators of verbal learning and memory controlled their experiments by using tasks, materials, and directions that limited participants' strategy decisions and confined their role to relatively passive involvement (Nelson & Narens, 1994). With the onset of the cognitive revolution, investigators began to use a greater variety of naturalistic tasks in which participants made on-line decisions and selected strategies that had important consequences for their performance. The organization of encoding and retrieval processes became a focus of inquiry, and it was soon apparent that metacognitive research was needed to understand how cognitive strategies developed and were selected and implemented.

The past 20 years have produced an impressive array of techniques designed to find out how well and on what basis we monitor and control our cognitive processes. The literature now includes a book of readings edited by Nelson (1992) that focuses on basic theoretical and empirical issues as well as an edited volume (Metcalfe & Shimamura, 1994) of recent research programs on selected aspects of metacognition. This volume is evidence of continuing interest and progress in this rapidly developing domain. However, almost all of the empirical research on metacognition has been conducted in time-compressed laboratory investigations, and although the memory content is often acquired naturalistically at an earlier time, research on metacognitive accuracy and the consequences of interventions is subject to the usual temporal limitations of longitudinal and even single-session work. These constraints are not peculiar to metamemory research; rather, they are inherent in the experimental paradigm that has dominated all of memory research for the past century. Interventions and their consequences must be observed within the time limits available for longitudinal laboratory investigations. Most laboratory research has therefore used retention intervals of a few minutes or hours; only a few investigations extended observations several days or weeks. As a result, we have no knowledge of metamemory processes involved in monitoring and controlling acquisition or in maintaining complex knowledge systems, because such systems are acquired and maintained over much longer periods. Schmidt and Bjork (1992) reviewed evidence indicating that several conditions that enhance learning over short periods may actually have adverse effects on long-term memory. Based on this evidence, they challenged the assumption that short-term effects on acquisition will be identical to long-term effects on retention, and they advocated research exploring the long-term effects of independent variables. Our own research leads to the conclusion that laboratory memory investigations do not yield guidelines designed to support the long-term maintenance of knowledge (Bahrick, 1996), and Metcalfe (1994) and Bjork (1994) discussed these same issues in regard to metacognitive research.

The metamemory data we present here are based on three investigations in which extended retention intervals were used. We first discuss findings of two studies (Bahrick & Hall, 1991; Bahrick & Phelps, 1988) in which the spontaneous recovery of naturalistically acquired, marginal knowledge was observed 30 days after participants made metacognitive judgments regarding the likelihood of these changes in access. Next, we present the metacognitive findings of a longitudinal study of acquisition and maintenance of foreign language vocabulary (Bahrick, Bahrick, Bahrick, & Bahrick, 1993) extending over an acquisition period that ranged from 6 months to 4 years, with a retention interval of 1 to 5 years.

FEELING OF KNOWING AND THE RECOVERY OF ACCESS TO MARGINAL KNOWLEDGE

The purpose of the Bahrick and Phelps (1988) investigation was to explore interventions designed to restore recall access to marginal knowledge. A preliminary goal in this research was to identify marginal target items, that is, items likely to be failed on a cued recall test but correctly identified on a recognition test. Such items were obtained on the basis of pilot tests administered in three domains of knowledge: foreign language vocabulary, name recognition for portraits of famous individuals, and general information. Items were selected and participants were recruited in such a way to minimize extraexperimental exposure to the targets during the time of our investigation and during the year preceding our investigation. Original exposure to the information had generally occurred at an earlier time. The participants were presented with a series of 100 items in each domain. For each target they failed to recall, they gave an FOK rating on a 7-point scale. We used these ratings to assign items comparable in FOK to one of four treatment and intervention conditions. One intervention and treatment, administered 1 day after the recall test, consisted of a forced-choice recognition test for items previously failed on the recall test. We have now calculated Goodman–Kruskal gamma correlations (G) between the FOK ratings and performance on the recognition tests, and the mean correlation for each knowledge domain is presented in Table 2.1. These values are somewhat higher than those obtained for recently learned material (Leonesio & Nelson, 1990).

One fourth of the items failed on the original recall test were not subjected to any intervention, but were retested for recall 1 month after the original recall test. A high percentage of the previously failed targets

TABLE 2.1

Mean Gamma Correlations Between FOK Ratings and Performance on Subsequent
Memory Tests

| | Recognition Test | | Recall Test | |
Domain	Mean G	n	Mean G	n
GEN	.43** (.34)	27	.55** (.40)	23
PIC	.41** (.32)	23	.57** (.47)	21
VOC	.20* (.33)	12	.42 (.84)	7

Note: Standard deviations are in parentheses. GEN = general information. PIC = name recognition for portraits of famous individuals. VOC = foreign language vocabulary.
*$p < .06.$ **$p < .001.$

(between 18% and 24% for the three domains of knowledge) was successfully recalled on the second test, indicating a substantial reminiscence effect. Gamma correlations were calculated for each participant between recall on the second test and the FOK ratings the person had given a month earlier. The mean correlations are reported for each knowledge domain in Table 2.1. Note that we could only calculate gammas for seven participants on the foreign language vocabulary test.

These results show that FOK ratings predict not only performance on a recognition test, but also, with comparable validity, the likelihood of recovered recall access to previously inaccessible, marginal target items. Validity of the latter predictions is maintained over a 30-day interval between ratings and test, but note that the target items belong to knowledge systems acquired long before the ratings were obtained. Leonesio and Nelson (1990) also found that metacognitive ratings can predict performance for criteria other than those rated, but the gamma values they reported for predicting recognition on the basis of ease of learning ratings for recently acquired items were considerably lower.

Bahrick and Hall (1991) used items of general knowledge, foreign language vocabulary, and recall of names for portraits of famous individuals selected on the same basis as the items used by Bahrick and Phelps (1988). Participants were instructed not to guess and were asked to provide a metamemory rating for each question. When participants failed to recall a target, they immediately rated how likely they would be to recall the answer at a later time. These ratings were given on a 3-point scale of *very likely,* *likely, or not very likely.* Table 2.2 shows the percentage of upward and downward fluctuations for targets rated by participants as high, medium, or low in likelihood of fluctuation for tests readministered after intervals of 2

TABLE 2.2

Percentage of Fluctuating Items as a Function of Metacognitive Rating

Rating	Up-Fluctuations	Down-Fluctuations
2-hour interval		
High	41% (23 of 56)	20% (2 of 10)
Medium	19% (60 of 315)	9% (19 of 203)
Low	5% (60 of 1127)	2% (21 of 964)
Gamma correlation	.55	.28
1-month interval		
High	43% (9 of 21)	16% (3 of 19)
Medium	22% (61 of 274)	14% (46 of 340)
Low	8% (86 of 1072)	4% (32 of 885)
Gamma correlation	.46	.50

Note. From "Preventive and Corrective Maintenance of Access to Knowledge," by H. P. Bahrick & L. K. Hall, 1991, *Applied Cognitive Psychology, 5*, p. 9. Copyright © 1991 by John Wiley & Sons, Ltd. Reprinted with permission.

hours and 1 month, respectively. The gamma correlations are also given. In accord with previous findings (Gardiner, Craik, & Bleasdale, 1973; Gruneberg, Smith, & Winfrow; 1973; Gruneberg & Sykes, 1978; Read & Bruce, 1982), the participants discriminated the likelihood of fluctuations quite well. More importantly for this research, the validity of predictions did not diminish significantly when tested after an interval of 1 month versus 2 hours, in accord with the finding obtained by Bahrick and Phelps (1998). Predictions are approximately equally valid for upward versus downward fluctuations; however, the paucity of downward fluctuations reduces the reliability of these data.

EASE OF LEARNING JUDGMENTS, JUDGENTS OF LEARNING AND PERFORMANCE OVER VERY LONG TIME INTERVALS

The 9-year longitudinal study (Bahrick et al., 1993) was undertaken in order to assess the effects of widely spaced practice on the acquisition and maintenance of knowledge. Although the spacing effect had been demonstrated in more than 300 previous investigations (Bruce & Bahrick, 1992), the earlier work involved short intervals between successive presentations, and the explanations (e.g., encoding variability and deficient processing theories) did not seem relevant to spacing effects obtained with time intervals of several weeks between learning sessions. This study was specifically intended to clarify the findings of a previous cross-sectional investigation of very long-term retention of Spanish learned in school (Bahrick, 1984). The results showed that when acquisition of the language extended over 2 to 3 years, a far greater proportion of original knowledge achieved the form of permastore knowledge than when acquisition was concentrated in a period of 1 year. The cross-sectional study confounded amount and distribution of practice because participants who took more Spanish courses engaged in more practice as well as more widely spaced practice. Therefore, the purpose of the longitudinal study was to sort out the effect of these two confounded variables.

The data of this study also provide information about the accuracy of long-term metacognitive predictions and some indications regarding the bases for these predictions. However, a few caveats are in order. First, the investigation was not designed for the purpose of exploring metacognition. Rather, it focused on spacing effects, and metacognitive ratings were used as a way of obtaining partial control over the difficulty of items assigned to various experimental conditions. As a result, the metacognitive data are not as complete or definitive as they might otherwise be. Second, the data are based on only four individuals, and this small number of participants precludes conventional assessment of the generality of the findings. Finally, because training and testing were carried out by four investigators working in different parts of the world over a 9-year period, there are instances of missing data and irregularities of procedure that can generally be avoided in a controlled laboratory environment.

A brief summary of the primary investigation (Bahrick et al., 1993) follows. Four individuals (aged 57, 57, 27, and 25 at the beginning of the investigation) learned and relearned 300 English–foreign language word pairs. Either 13 or 26 relearning sessions were administered at intervals of 14, 28, or 56 days. Fifty of the 300 word pairs were learned under each of these six learning conditions (13 or 26 relearning sessions by three intersession intervals). The learning sessions involved a series of alternating presentation and cued-recall test trials, combined with a dropout procedure. According to this procedure, only word pairs failed on a given test trial were included on the following presentation trial. Thus, at the end of each learning session, the participant had given a single correct response to each word pair. Paired associate recall was tested 1, 2, 3, and 5 years after learning terminated, with 12 or 13 of the 50 word pairs from each of the six learning conditions assigned to each of the four retention intervals. When assigning word pairs to retention intervals, word difficulty was controlled on the basis of the cumulative number of presentations of the word pair during all learning sessions. (More difficult words were recalled later in each learning session and received a larger number of presentations per session.)

As previously stated, the main purpose of the investigation was to establish the effect of the intersession interval on very-long-term maintenance of vocabulary. Although the 56-day interval between learning sessions required slightly more exposures during the early learning sessions than the 14-day and 28-day intervals, the longer intersession intervals yielded very large benefits in recall that persisted undiminished throughout the 5-year retention interval.

Two types of metacognitive data were collected in the investigation:

1. Prior to the first learning session, the participants rated the ease of learning (EOL) for each of the 300 word pairs on a 3-point scale, and these individual ratings were used to control difficulty level in the assignment of words to the six learning conditions.
2. At the end of the final learning session (several minutes after recall of the last-learned word pair), participants rated the probability that they would recall individual words on a retention test to be administered several years later. These judgment of learning (JOL) ratings were also given on a 3-point scale.

The data permit assessment of the validity of these metacognitive judgments, and they permit inferences regarding the cognitive basis for the judgments. The validity of the EOL ratings was assessed by calculating gamma correlations between the ratings and the number of presentation trials required to learn the words. We used two indicants of difficulty for each word pair: (a) an index of initial difficulty based on the number of presentations required during the first learning session to obtain a single correct response, and (b) an index of overall difficulty obtained from the cumulative number of exposures during the first 13 learning sessions (every word pair was included in a minimum of 13 sessions).

The mean gamma correlation for the four participants was .51 (SD = .12) for predicting initial difficulty and .43 (SD = .13) for predicting cumulative difficulty. The predictive validity was higher for the measure of initial difficulty than for the measure of cumulative difficulty for all four participants. The correlations with initial difficulty are somewhat higher than those reported by Leonesio and Nelson (1990) for the acquisition of noun–noun pairs.

We also calculated the gamma correlations between EOL ratings and JOL ratings given at the end of training, and between EOL ratings and ultimate recall. The mean correlation between EOL and JOL ratings for the same words was .48 (SD = .17), and the mean correlation of EOL ratings with final recall was .24 (SD = .16). Thus, the initial EOL ratings have considerable communality with predictions of recall made after extended training, but they have little communality with ultimate retention performance. Leonesio and Nelson (1990) also found that EOL and JOL ratings correlated. However, the correlation they reported (G = .19) is lower than the gamma values we obtained in spite of the fact that the time intervening between their EOL and JOL ratings was less than an hour, whereas the separation in this investigation averaged 2 years. In the Leonesio and Nelson (1990) study, higher gamma values were obtained for the correlation between EOL and JOL than for the correlation between EOL and final recall (G = .12). We also found that EOL ratings predict JOL ratings better than they predict ultimate recall, but our correlations are close to theirs only for the prediction of recall.

We assessed the validity of JOL ratings by the gamma correlations between these ratings and recall. We calculated validity separately for words tested after intervals of 1, 2, 3, and 5 years, and the results are shown in Fig. 2.1. There is no indication that the predictive validity of JOL ratings diminishes

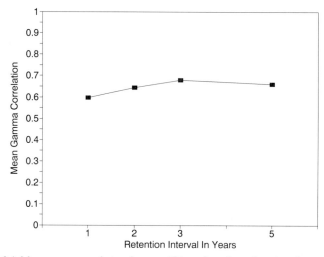

FIG. 2.1. Mean gamma correlations between JOLs and recall as a function of retention interval.

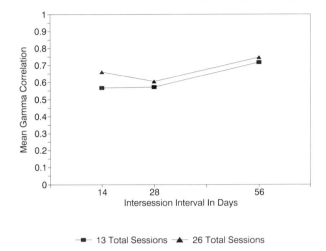

FIG. 2.2. Mean gamma correlations between JOLs and recall as a function of total number of learning sessions and intersession interval.

or systematically changes over the 5-year retention interval. The mean overall validity collapsed over the retention interval is .63 (SD = .05) for the four participants.

We analyzed the data based on the six separate learning conditions (intervals of 14, 28, or 56 days, and 13 or 26 learning sessions) and calculated gamma correlations between JOL ratings and recall for words learned in each of these conditions. Fig. 2. 2 shows the resulting mean gamma values. Words acquired in 26 learning sessions yield slightly higher mean gamma correlations than those learned in 13 sessions, and the longest intersession interval yields higher mean gamma values than the two shorter ones. Because the direction of differences is inconsistent among the four participants and because some data are missing from two participants for the longest interval, these conclusions are quite tentative.

To further explore the basis on which JOL ratings are formed, we calculated gamma correlations between these ratings and the difficulty of words (measured as the number of presentations prior to the first correct response) at various stages of training. Figure 2.3 shows gamma correlations between JOL ratings and word difficulty separately for learning sessions 1 to 5, for cumulative word difficulty during the first 13 sessions, and for word difficulty in the last session. The data are shown separately for the four participants and it is clear that exposures on the last learning session have the largest influence on JOL ratings, indicating a pronounced recency effect.

Finally, we calculated gamma correlations between word difficulty (again measured by the number of exposures during training) and ultimate recall.

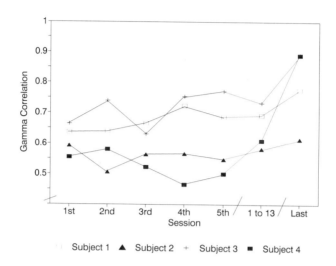

FIG. 2.3. Gamma correlations between JOLs and word difficulty as a function of learning session.

These correlations were obtained for the number of exposures on the first learning session (mean $G = .48$, $SD = .11$), on the last session (mean $G = .50$, $SD = .12$), and cumulatively for the first 13 learning sessions (mean $G = .53$, $SD = .12$). Thus, the best prediction of recall is based on the cumulative training record; however, this finding is consistent for only three of the four participants.

DISCUSSION AND INTERPRETATION

The Experiential Basis of Metacognitive Judgments

All four participants were able to predict long-term retention better than EOL. This was true even though the predictions of learning applied to performance only on the first learning trial (i.e., very soon after the ratings were given), and the predictions of retention applied to performance several years after the ratings were made. Apparently, the time interval separating judgment from relevant performance had less impact on the validity of the judgments than the available database for making the judgment. In the investigations reported here, JOLs were based on a record of experience with the specific words to be judged, a record that extended over at least 6 months and up to 4 years. In contrast, EOL judgments were made without a long record of experience with the individual words. Presumably, EOL ratings were based on immediate ease of encoding the foreign word, ease of forming an associative link between the foreign and the English word, or some combination of the two.

Both kinds of judgments are generally based on traces of experience (Koriat, 1993), but in this case, the experiential base for the EOL ratings was limited to a few seconds whereas the experiential basis for the JOL ratings extended over many months. Single-session list-learning experiments may not consistently show this result because the time base for JOL and EOL ratings is much more comparable in such studies than in this investigation. For this same reason, the gamma correlations obtained for predicting recall from JOL ratings were higher for our four participants than gammas typically reported in the literature for recently learned material. The extended training time yielded a better basis for predicting future recall, and it mattered little that the retention interval was 1 to 5 years rather than a few minutes. In contrast, EOL ratings were influenced by the time interval; they predicted early acquisition data somewhat better than later acquisition data. The participants were able to judge the immediate ease of encoding an association better than changes in encoding strategies developed during the course of extended training. These changes were necessitated when the initial methods failed to maintain retrieval of targets over long intersession intervals.

The record established during the long training process provided the basis for the JOL ratings. Individual gamma correlations based on early versus late learning sessions and on words learned under the three learning schedules permit inferences regarding the contributions these aspects of training made. Gamma correlations predicting JOL ratings were highest when they were based on the record of exposures during the final learning session. The fact that the correlations were lower when they were based on an early session or on the cumulative record from the first 13 sessions does not mean that early sessions are unimportant in regard to the judgments. Rather, the most recent training experience is weighed more heavily in forming the judgments. Optimum judgments would probably give the most recent experience somewhat less weight because the correlation between final recall and the training records is higher when it is based on the cumulative number of exposures over 13 learning sessions than when it is based only on the last learning session.

It is noteworthy that JOLs correlate more highly with ultimate recall than any indicant we examined from the objective training record. The mean correlation of JOLs with ultimate recall is .63; the highest gamma for predicting recall from the training record is .53 (based on cumulative exposures in the first 13 learning sessions). This finding suggests that some knowledge not reflected in the exposure record contributes to the validity of JOL ratings. Monitored information concerning the ease, the speed, or the subjective certainty of retrieval could be involved. Some aspects of such information (e.g., latency of retrieval) could be recorded and become a part of the objective training record, whereas other aspects (e.g., subjective ease or subjective certainty of recall) are inherently metacognitive. We can therefore only conclude that our metacognitive ratings are more valid predictors than the training criteria we examined, not that they are more valid predictors than those based on additional information that could potentially be extracted from the training record. Leonesio and Nelson (1990) reported significantly higher gamma correlations between trials to acquisition and criterion recall performance than between criterion performance and any metacognitive ratings. Whether the greatly extended practice conditions of this investigation account for the inverse relation we obtained remains an unanswered question.

Practical and Theoretical Implications

Research comparing the validity of metacognitive predictions of memory with predictions based on training data has important practical as well as theoretical implications. In the practical domain, it is important to identify aspects of training performance that are valid predictors of retention but are ignored or given inadequate weight in metacognitive judgments. Such information can be used to improve metacognitive monitoring, lead to more advantageous encoding strategies, and ultimately to superior maintenance of knowledge. Nelson, Dunlosky, Graf, and Narens (1994) described how metacognitive monitoring can be utilized to benefit multitrial learning. Comparing metacognitive predictions with computer-generated predictions of future performance also has theoretical importance. The comparison can help perfect models of artificial intelligence, identify significant individual difference variables, and contribute to understanding limitations in the human ability to monitor and update information obtained over extended time periods.

Research directed at optimizing learning on the basis of computer-generated analyses of training records has been conducted for many years (e.g., Atkinson, 1972; Groen & Atkinson, 1966). However, only recently have metacognitive data been included in such analyses (Nelson et al., 1994), and the results of this investigation are the first to suggest that metacognitive monitoring may yield predictors of maintenance of knowledge that are not available from the objective training record.

Metacognitive Ratings of Widespread Learning
and Long-Term Retention

Our data also show that previous investigations may have underestimated the potential validity and generality of metacognitive predictions of long-term retention. In the Bahrick and Phelps (1988) investigation, we obtained gamma correlations of .42 to .57 between FOK ratings (predictions of the likelihood of successful recognition) and recall performance 1 month later. These correlations were consistently higher than correlations between the same ratings and recognition performance following a 1-day retention interval. Because fewer participants contributed data that could be analyzed for the recall data, the increase in the correlations is impossible to interpret. Still, based on the data from Bahrick and Phelps (1988) and Bahrick and Hall (1991), it is safe to conclude that metacognitive ratings predict long-term recall of marginal semantic content with no less validity than they predict short-term recognition or recall.

In the Bahrick et al. (1993) investigation, we obtained gamma correlations approaching .70 for predicting retention over a period of several years. The accuracy of these predictions reflects the advantages of cumulative monitoring and storing of metacognitive information at long intersession intervals. The long intersession intervals not only yielded superior maintenance of knowledge over a 5-year period; the extended spacing effect may also have yielded more metacognitive knowledge as reflected in the high validity of metacognitive judgments.

ACKNOWLEDGMENTS

Preparation of this manuscript was supported by National Science Foundation Grant SBR9119800. We wish to thank Cathleen O'Toole and Tom Nelson for many helpful suggestions.

REFERENCES

Atkinson, R. C. (1972). Optimizing the learning of a second-language vocabulary. *Journal of Experimental Psychology*, 96, 124–129.

Bahrick, H. P. (1996). Synergistic strategies for memory research. In D. Herrmann, C. McEvoy, C. Hertzog, P. Hertel & M. K. Johnson (Eds.), *Basic and applied memory research: Theory in Context* (Vol. 1, pp. 51–62). Mahwah, NJ: Lawrence Erlbaum Associates.

Bahrick, H. P. (1984). Semantic memory content in permastore-50 years of memory for Spanish learned in school. *Journal of Experimental Psychology: General, 113,* 1 -29.

Bahrick, H. P., Bahrick, L. E., Bahrick, A. S., & Bahrick, P. E. (1993). Maintenance of foreign language vocabulary and the spacing effect. *Psychological Science, 4,* 316–321.

Bahrick, H. P., & Hall, L. K. (1991). Preventive and corrective maintenance of access to knowledge. *Applied Cognitive Psychology, 5,* 1–18.

Bahrick, H. P. & Phelps, E. (1988). The maintenance of marginal knowledge. In U. Neisser & E. Winograd (Eds.), *Remembering reconsidered: Ecological and traditional approaches to the study of memory* (pp. 178–192). New York: Cambridge University Press.

Bjork, R. A. (1994). Memory and metamemory considerations in the training of human beings. In J. Metcalfe & A. P. Shimamura (Eds.), *Metacognition: Knowing about knowing* (pp. 185–205). Cambridge, MA: MIT Press.

Bruce, D., & Bahrick, H. P. (1992). Perceptions of past research. Special Issue: The history of American psychology. *American Psychologist, 47,* 319–328.

Flavell, J. H. (1979). Metacognition and cognitive monitoring: A new area of cognitive-developmental inquiry. *American Psychologist, 34,* 906–911.

Gardiner, J. M., Craik, F. I. M., & Bleasdale, F. A. (1973). Retrieval difficulty and subsequent recall. *Memory and Cognition, 1,* 213–216.

Groen, G. J. & Atkinson, R. C. (1966). Models for optimizing the learning process. *Psychological Bulletin, 66,* 309–320.

Gruneberg, M. M., Smith, R. L., & Winfrow, P. (1973). An investigation into response blockaging. *Acta Psychologica, 37,* 187–196.

Gruneberg, M. M. & Sykes, R. N. (1978). Knowledge and retention: The feeling of knowing and reminiscence. In M. M. Gruneberg, P. E. Morris, & R. N. Sykes (Eds.), *Practical aspects of memory* (pp. 189–196). New York: Academic Press.

Hart, J. T. (1965). Memory and the feeling-of-knowing experience. *Journal of Educational Psychology, 56,* 208–216.

Hart, J.T. (1967). Memory and the memory-monitoring process. *Journal of Verbal Learning and Verbal Behavior, 6,* 685–691.

Koriat, A. (1993). Memory's knowledge of its own knowledge: The accessibility model of the feeling of knowing. In J. Metcalfe & A. P. Shimamura (Eds.), *Metacognition: Knowing about knowing* (pp. 115–135). Cambridge, MA: MIT Press.

Leonesio, R. J., & Nelson, T. O. (1990). Do different metamemory judgments tap the same underlying aspects of memory? *Journal of Experimental Psychology: Learning, Memory and Cognition, 16,* 464–470.

Metcalfe, J. (1994). Metacognitive processes. In R. A. Bjork, & E. L. Bjork (Eds.), *The handbook of perception and cognition,* (2nd Ed., pp. 381–407 San Diego, CA: Academic Press.

Metcalfe, J., & Shimamura, A. P. (Eds.). (1994). *Metacognition: Knowing about knowing.* Cambridge, MA: MIT Press.

Nelson, T. O. (1992). *Metacognition: Core readings.* Boston: Allyn & Bacon.

Nelson, T. O. & Narens, L. (1994). Why investigate metacognition? In J. Metcalfe & A. P. Shimamura (Eds.), *Metacognition: Knowing about knowing,* (pp. 1–25). Cambridge, MA: MIT Press.

Nelson, T. O., & Narens, L. (1990). Metamemory: A theoretical framework and new findings. In G. Bower (Ed.), *The psychology of learning and motivation* (Vol. 26, pp. 125–173). New York: Academic Press.

Nelson, T. O., Dunlosky, J., Graf, A., & Narens, L. (1994). Utilization of metacognitive judgments in the allocation of study during multitrial learning. *Psychological Science, 5,* 207–213.

Read, J. D. & Bruce, D. (1982). Longitudinal tracking of difficult memory retrievals. *Cognitive Psychology, 14,* 280–300.

Schmidt, R. A. & Bjork, R. A. (1992). New conceptualizations of practice: Common principles in three paradigms suggest new concepts for training. *Psychological Science, 3,* 207–217.

3

Control Processes Explored by the Study of Closed-Head-Injury Patients

Carlo Umiltà
Franca Stablum
University of Padova, Italy

THE NOTION OF CONTROL

With the term *cognitive control*, or simply, *control*, we mean the set of those cognitive processes that are not directly involved in the representation of cognitive states, but rather with the organization (e.g., selection and temporal sequencing) of such states toward attaining a specific goal. The basic idea is that a number of mental representations are normally active simultaneously and in parallel, but at any given time, only some of them guide action and thought. As Houghton and Tipper (1996) put it, the issue of control is concerned with the mechanism(s) by which "many are called but few are chosen" (p. 20).

Often control processes (also termed *control functions* or *executive functions*; we use these terms interchangeably) are thought to be related to the activity of a central system, which is called on when planning and decision making are required. Authors have made use of different terms to invoke the notion of such a central system: central executive store (Baddeley & Hitch, 1974), attention center (LaBerge, 1975), operating system (Johnson-Laird, 1983), executive system (Logan & Cowan, 1984), central executive (Baddeley, 1986), supervisory attentional system (Norman & Shallice, 1986), central processor (Umiltà, 1988), and anterior attention system (Posner & Petersen, 1990).

These and related formulations of the notion of control share the fundamental distinction between a separate controller and a multitude of processes that can be controlled by it. An essential feature of the controlled (or slave) processes is that they cannot initiate autonomously; that is, they are triggered either by external stimulation or by control processes. By contrast, the postulated controller would not be dependent on exogenous triggering. Its activity is thought to be initiated autonomously, from within the observer.

It must be pointed out, however, that the very notion of the existence of a controller was severely criticized by Allport (e.g., Allport, 1993; Allport, Styles, & Hsieh, 1994). In our view, Allport's criticism can be subdivided into two independent issues. The first concerns whether control is unitary. The second aspect concerns whether control processes can be isolated from the processes they control.

Recent computational models (e.g., Houghton, Glasspool, & Shallice, 1994; see Shallice, 1994, for a review) have shown that control need not depend on a unitary system. In fact, in these models, separable systems are responsible for the operations related to control processes. For example, in a competitive queuing model, item nodes compete for access to action by virtue of their activation level. However, this competition is not resolved at the level of the item nodes themselves. Rather, there is a sequence level (i.e., a separable network) in which sequence nodes generate control signals to the item nodes. These control signals activate a selected group of item nodes. The competition between the item nodes does not take place at the item node level either. It is devolved to a separate network, which is called *competitive filter*. In brief, computational models are based on distributed, rather than unitary control. However, control nodes and controlled nodes still belong to separable systems (i.e., separable networks).

One crucial issue for the notion of control is whether control systems can be separated from the systems they are held to control. This was the second of the issues we distinguished in Allport's criticism (Allport, 1993; Allport et al., 1994).

As of now, the major empirical evidence that control processes might involve separable systems is the effect of frontal lesions, which show that control processes can be selectively impaired. The idea that the frontal lobes are the seat of the highest level control operations and that lesions to the frontal lobes give rise to specific disorders of these functions goes back to the 19th century. More recently, Luria's (1966) position that the frontal lobes contain a system for the programming, regulation, and verification of

activity has been very influential in promoting neuropsychological research on control processes (see, e.g., reviews in Shallice, 1988; Stuss &
Benson, 1984).

VARIETIES OF CONTROL FUNCTIONS

It is generally accepted that control processes are characterized by common
properties, but it is also apparent that control processes play a role in a number
of rather dissimilar tasks (see, e.g., review in Shallice, 1994). The properties
that are common to all control processes are the following. Control processes
require attention, consist of a series of unitary operations, are limited by
short-term storage capacity, and are easily adapted and modified.

Resource allocation, sequencing of tasks, and task shifting are among the
best known circumstances in which control processes are involved. In the
case of attentional capacity allocation, the amount of allocated attention
depends on the information processing demands. The processing resources
are voluntarily allocated to a particular task or activity at the expense of
other tasks or activities (Wickens, 1984). When two or more tasks must be
executed, their execution sequence needs to be coordinated (Umiltà, Nicoletti, Simion, Tagliabue, & Bagnara, 1992). Shifts between tasks needs to
be controlled (Rogers & Monsell, 1995).

In addition, many other situations require controlled processing; for
example, confronting some forms of novelty, error correction or trou-
bleshooting, execution of ill-learned or novel sequence of actions, execution
of actions judged to be dangerous or technically difficult, and execution of
actions that require overcoming a strong habitual response (Shallice, 1994).

It has also been suggested that the inhibitory component of selective
attention belongs to control processes. As shown by the negative priming
phenomena, irrelevant information can be actively inhibited (Neill, Valdes,
& Terry, 1995). There is evidence that negative priming is a strategic effect,
in the sense that inhibition is used only for the most difficult selection tasks,
in which effortful deselection of previously selected items is required (i.e.,
the process of attentional disengagement and the correct sequencing of
responses). In these cases, control processes depend on selective inhibitory
mechanisms that attenuate the activation of potentially interfering representations (Houghton & Tipper, 1996).

Given the varieties of circumstances in which control processes play a
role, a natural question is whether the control system is internally equipotential or rather can be decomposed into more or less independent (i.e.,

modular) functional components. As mentioned earlier, computational models have shown that control is not necessarily unitary but can be distributed. That does not mean, however, that a distributed control system cannot be equipotential. To support nonequipotentiality, evidence must be obtained that the control system is subdivided into separable subsystems, that perform specialized functions.

In fact, there is evidence from animal studies that the frontal lobes, which are involved in tasks that specifically require control, are not equipotential (e.g., Fuster, 1980). In particular, it seems that an inability to deal with a prepotent response tendency and excessive distractibility arise from lesions in different areas of the frontal lobes.

As was already mentioned, most authors agree that in human beings the frontal lobes are involved in control functions (Shallice, 1988; Stuss & Benson, 1984). However, until now, these control functions have been relatively undifferentiated. More precise analysis of task performance is required to identify unique functions, as is replication of the dissociation pattern of such functions both within and between tasks.

An example of how the processes that are involved in higher levels of control can be differentiated comes from a study by Petrides (1991). Petrides showed that the subjective ordering task, which requires programming and online monitoring of voluntary actions, selectively depends on the activity of dorsolateral frontal areas (i.e., Areas 9 and 46), whereas a different area of the dorsolateral frontal convexity (i.e., Area 8) is selectively involved in conditional associative learning tasks. Yet another frontal region, the anterior cingulate, has been associated with selective attention (Posner & Petersen, 1990). In conclusion, there is the possibility that lesions located in different frontal areas cause dissociations between different processes within the overall rubric of what have come to be called control processes.

Also, it should be mentioned in this context that there appears to be a dissociation between test measures of control functions and real-life activities. Eslinger and Damasio (1985) described a patient with frontal lobe damage who performed well on a wide variety of neuropsychological tests, including some held to be sensitive to impairment of control functions, but had many severe practical difficulties in everyday life, which seemed to arise from lack of judgmental and organizational skills.

Shallice and Burgess (1991) described an analogous dissociation in three patients with frontal lobe damage. The patients performed within the normal range on many tests that tap control functions, but all three showed little spontaneous organization in everyday life. Two tests were devised to test their ability to schedule a number of relatively straightforward activities in a restricted period of time. It was found that the patients performed poorly on these tests.

It seems to us, however, that the dissociation between test measures and real-life situations is not particularly informative in showing a dissociation between different control operations. In fact, the dissociation could be explained simply by the insensitivity of the frontal test measures as compared to real-life demands on control functions.

CLOSED HEAD INJURY

Many studies have implicated frontal lobe damage, and especially damage to the prefrontal areas, which are held to subserve control processes (Shallice, 1988), as the main etiological factor in cognitive deficits after closed head injury (CHI; e.g., Levin, Goldstein, Williams, & Eisenberg, 1991).

The physical proximity of the sphenoid wing to the orbitofrontal region and marked shearing effects in this area predispose the frontal lobes to lesion after CHI. Magnetic resonance imaging has confirmed that the frontal region is the most common location of lesion after CHI. In addition, positron emission tomography scanning of CHI patients has shown zones of frontal hypometabolism extending beyond the boundaries of anatomical lesions.

These findings render it likely that CHI patients should manifest deficits presumably reflecting frontal dysfunctions, in particular deficits that are attributable to a selective impairment of control functions.

To study control functions in CHI patients, two approaches are available. One utilizes those tests that were developed to analyze frontal lobe functions, like the Tower of London, the Wisconsin Card Sorting test, the Cognitive Estimation Task, the Word Fluency test, and the Porteus Maze test (see, e.g., Ponsford & Kinsella, 1992). The other approach is based on the use of the reaction time (RT) procedure with experimental tasks that were devised to probe specific cognitive capabilities (see Stablum, Leonardi, Mazzoldi, Umiltà, & Morra, 1994; Stablum, Mogentale, & Umiltà, 1996).

Tests developed to analyze frontal lobe functions in focal lesions may be not sensitive enough to detect difficulties in CHI patients with more diffuse lesions. The lack of sensitivity of these "frontal" tests might be exacerbated further in patients who have suffered mild to moderate CHI.

In fact, behavioral changes are rarely apparent on standard neuropsychological tests, and there is also evidence that return of test scores to a normal level does not necessarily imply full recovery from trauma (Dikmen,

Temkin, & Armsden, 1989). The failure of neuropsychological batteries to detect cognitive deficits after CHI could be attributed to the fact that these batteries have been developed to detect focal and not diffuse brain damage (Gronwall, 1989). Another possible explanation is that the cognitive abilities are preserved, whereas it is the efficiency and the speed of processing that are damaged in CHI patients.

The RT methodology has instead proven to be particularly suitable to studying the cognitive deficits of CHI patients. It is precise, and sensitive and it allows microfunctional analysis of damaged cognitive components. By using this methodology, evidence of cognitive deficits in CHI has rapidly grown. In our studies (see the following), the CHI patients performed in RT paradigms that are known to tap different control processes.

TASK SEQUENCING AND COORDINATION

This was a variant of the dual-task paradigm, in which two tasks must be executed and their execution sequence has to be coordinated (Umiltà et al., 1992). The primary task is a speeded left–right discrimination of stimulus position. The unspeeded secondary task consists of reporting verbally whether the stimuli are the same or different. The primary task is performed either by itself or together with the secondary task. When both tasks are to be executed, participants are instructed to perform them according to a predetermined sequence: The speeded primary task must be executed first and the unspeeded secondary task must be executed second.

For normal participants, RT to the primary task is typically about 70 ms slower with the secondary task than without it. That is to say, normal participants show a dual-task interference effect (dual-task cost) of about 70 ms.

In a study (Stablum et al., 1994), a group of CHI patients and a control group of normal participants (individually matched for age, sex, and education) were tested. The CHI group selection criteria were an interval of 1 year or more from the trauma, a Glasgow Coma Scale score of 9 or less (which indicated severe CHI when the trauma occurred), no history of neurological or psychiatric disorders, and good neurological and motor recovery. The patients did not show any impairments on classical frontal lobe tests, including the Tower of London test, the Wisconsin Card Sorting test, and the Word Fluency test. In spite of apparently good recovery, all patients continued to have poorly defined complaints, such as difficulty in concentration and memory, fatigue, and irritability. In addition, some of them were not yet able to resume work.

The main finding was that the dual-task cost was significantly greater for the CHI group than for the control group (197 ms vs. 80 ms). This indicated that a year or more after the trauma, severe CHI patients still had problems in sequencing and coordinating the execution of two tasks, even in the face of nearly complete recovery, as assessed by classical frontal lobe tests.

In a subsequent study (Stablum, Mogentale, & Umiltà, in preparation) we correlated the dual-task cost shown by CHI patients (mild, moderate, and severe) with their scores on several neuropsychological tests. Significant correlations were found with the number of perseverative errors in the Wisconsin Card Sorting test ($r = .51$) and with performance in the Digit-Symbol Associations subtest of the Wechsler Adult Intelligence Scale ($r = .43$). In contrast, the dual-task cost did not correlate with scores obtained on the Raven test ($r = .13$), the Tower of London test ($r = -.10$), and the Word Fluency test ($r = -.04$). Taken together, these results suggest dissociations between control processes and other measures of cognitive capability, in accord with the results reported for patients with focal frontal lobe lesions (see Shallice & Burgess, 1991, for a review).

Stablum et al. (1996) tested mild CHI patients within the first 6 months after injury. Compared to control participants, the dual-task cost was much greater for participants with CHI. This was true, however, only for patients more than 30 years old and for patients who experienced loss of consciousness at the time of injury (247 and 240 ms, respectively).

Two years after injury, the patients more than 30 years old were retested with the dual-task paradigm. The results showed that the deficit was still present (i.e., the dual-task cost was 224 ms). This finding does not suggest recovery over time, and therefore provides evidence of persistent difficulties for control processes. The finding also disconfirms the widely held belief that the effects of a mild concussion are only temporary and that deficits spontaneously disappear. It is apparent that follow-up examinations are necessary after mild CHI, a practice very rarely adopted in the clinical neuropsychological examination.

Another study by Stablum, Umiltà, Mazzoldi, and Berrini (1996) was aimed at testing two possible models for explaining the greater dual-task cost found in CHI patients: the capacity sharing model (e.g., McLeod, 1977; Wickens, 1984) and the postponement model (e.g., Pashler & Johnston, 1989; Umiltà et al., 1992). The *capacity sharing model* maintains that each task draws on limited resources that are allocated between the tasks in a graded fashion. In a dual-task paradigm, RTs are slowed down because the execution of the two tasks partially overlaps, reducing the resources available to each. There are different versions of the capacity sharing model, some proposing a single resource pool and others proposing multiple resource pools. For every version of the model, however, the fundamental assumption is that cognitive operations can take place concurrently, but their speed and accuracy is limited by the proportion of resources, either general or specific in nature, they are allocated.

The *postponement model* maintains that execution of either task requires that a single mechanism, which thus constitutes a sort of bottleneck, is exclusively dedicated to one task for some period of time. When that mechanism is devoted to one task, those processing stages of the other task that also require it must be postponed. The postponement model also comes in different versions, depending on where the bottleneck is thought to occur. Proposals have included perceptual identification, decision making, response selection, response initiation, and response execution.

According to the version of the postponement model that was put forward by Umiltà et al. (1992), the lengthening of RT to the primary task occurs because the decision-making mechanism is occupied by the decision concerning the coordination of the two responses. The decision to perform the two tasks one after the other and the decision to execute the first response compete for access to the same processing stage. This common stage acts as a bottleneck, thus causing postponement of the response to the primary task.

To test which model better fits the data, we manipulated the difficulty of the first task (i.e., its resource load) by making incompatible the stimulus–response pairings for the left–right discrimination (i.e., the primary task). The capacity sharing model predicts that, if the two tasks compete for limited processing resources, then the dual-task cost should increase when the portion of resources needed to perform the primary task increases; that is, task difficulty should interact overadditively with task overlap. In contrast, the postponement model predicts either additivity or underadditivity when the primary task becomes more difficult (e.g., Pashler & Johnston, 1989; Umiltà et al., 1992). This is because the extra time that should have been spent waiting for the decision stage (i.e., the bottleneck) to become available passes in part while the more difficult primary task is being performed.

A group of severe CHI patients and a group of matched control individuals were tested. Patients were tested between 2 or 4 years after injury. Every participant performed in four conditions: single and double tasks with compatible and incompatible stimulus–response mappings. The dual-task cost was significantly greater for the CHI patients than for the control group (198 vs. 74 ms, respectively), replicating what had previously been found. Crucial to the purpose of the study was the interaction between group (CHI patients or controls), compatibility (compatible or incompatible stimulus–response mapping), and type of task (primary task only or primary task plus secondary task), which could index overadditivity, additivity, or underadditivity. The interaction did not reach significance (p = .303). In the CHI group, the dual-task costs were 219 and 176 ms for the compatible and incompatible stimulus–response mappings, respectively. In the control group, the dual-task costs were nearly identical for compatible and incompatible pairings (73 and 75 ms, respectively). This suggests additivity for the control participants and additivity or perhaps underadditivity for the CHI patients.

The results support the postponement model as an explanation of the dual-task cost that was found in either the CHI group or the control group. This outcome is in accord with the results obtained by Umiltà et al. (1992) with young normal individuals. Thus, the greater dual-task cost incurred by CHI patients cannot be explained by proposing that their processing resources are diminished. Rather, it would seem that the process of coordinating the execution of the two tasks is more time consuming in CHI patients than in control participants. Therefore, the competition for access to the stage that constitutes the bottleneck lasts longer and execution of the primary task is postponed for a longer time in CHI patients.

In a study we are presently conducting (Mogentale, Stablum, Umiltà, & Dal Sasso, 1996), a group of CHI patients was submitted to a treatment that consisted of five experimental sessions, in each of which the patients performed in the dual-task paradigm. The dual-task cost was assessed before the treatment (test), immediately after the treatment (retest), and 3 months after the treatment (follow-up). A significant reduction of the dual-task cost from test to retest was found. There was no significant difference between retest and follow-up, indicating that the beneficial effect of the treatment was still present 3 months after the treatment had been discontinued. This outcome suggests that rehabilitation of the ability to coordinate dual-task performance is possible (an optimistic note against the general pessimistic feelings on rehabilitation of control functions). What remains to be tested is whether the effect of the treatment generalizes to other control functions.

TASK SHIFTING

In everyday activity, people often shift rapidly from one intended set of cognitive operations to another. Shifts between sets of cognitive operations can be internally generated (i.e., they occur "at will") or externally generated (i.e., they occur in response to an external cue). Under different circumstances, instead, people can maintain activity of the same set of cognitive operations for an extended period of time.

An interesting question concerns the nature of the mechanisms that are responsible for implementing these intentional shifts of set. Considering that shifting set appears to be a prototypical control operation, an obvious possibility is that it is governed by control processes.

One attractively simple experimental approach to this problem is the shifting-task paradigm (e.g., Allport et al., 1994; Rogers & Monsell, 1995). For example, individuals are presented with lists of items (e.g., two-digit numbers). In the single-task condition, they are required to perform the same task throughout the list (e.g., adding 3s, or subtracting 3s). In the task-shifting condition, instead, they are required to alternately add 3 to and subtract 3 from successive items. Comparing the task-shifting condition with the single-task condition, one typically finds costs of task alternation.

In one of our studies (Stablum et al., 1994), we made use of an experimental situation that was first devised by Morra and Roncato (1986, 1988). In it, the individual has to perform two tasks; that is, recognizing by pressing a key where an arrow is pointing (i.e., left or right), or reading aloud a syllable. The type of stimulus (arrow or syllable) is a prompt for the correct task to be executed. Different stimuli require different responses, the participant having to switch from one task to the other. Series of 2 or 10 arrows and series of 2 or 10 syllables follow one another in a regular manner. Note that, unlike a prime or a cue, a prompt cannot be ignored because it is essential to responding appropriately to the stimulus. Thus, prompting results in controlled preparation for performing a specific task.

The results obtained with normal participants showed that in the long series (LS) condition, RT to the first stimulus of the series was about 150 ms slower than RTs to all the subsequent nine stimuli, whereas in the short series (SS) condition, the first-stimulus RT was only 20 ms slower with respect to the second stimulus. In other words, there was a cost, attributable to task shifting, for either list, but the cost was much greater for the LS condition than for the SS condition.

The greater cost for the LS condition suggests that in this condition the participant could not count the stimuli to prepare for the task shift (or, perhaps, found it to be inconvenient). In the SS condition, instead, it was easy to prepare for the task shift.

If one assumes that CHI patients have difficulties in loading the appropriate action schema, comparatively greater costs should be expected in the LS condition, in which preparation did not occur in anticipation of the task shift. In contrast, if CHI patients have difficulties in controlling changes of action schema (i.e., in deselecting the old schema and selecting the new one), they should face comparatively greater costs in the SS condition, in which the task shift could be anticipated.

By using this paradigm we demonstrated a significantly greater SS shifting cost in a severe CHI group in comparison with a matched control group (59 vs. 19 ms). In contrast, the LS shifting cost was not significantly different for patients and controls (154 vs. 137 ms).

In the SS condition, participants are likely to make a controlled decision to shift to the new task, whereas in the LS condition the shift is not prepared in advance and is triggered by the appearance of the new stimulus. Therefore, the extra cost showed by CHI patients indexes a specific deficit in control processes.

In our study the same patients performed in the task-sequencing and the task-shifting paradigms. Looking at the individual data, interesting double dissociations emerge. Remember that for the control group the mean dual-task cost was 80 ms and the mean SS shifting cost was 19 ms. For example, one patient showed a very small dual-task cost (27 ms) and a large SS shifting cost (38 ms). In contrast, another patient showed the opposite pattern: a large dual-task cost (162 ms) and an SS shifting cost within the normal range (21 ms). These double dissociations confirm that the control system is comprised of separable subsystems that perform specialized functions.

NEGATIVE PRIMING

Selective attention is concerned with how people select information to provide the basis for responding and with how information irrelevant to that response is dealt with. One possibility is that selective attention relies on inhibition of nontarget, "distracter" stimuli.

Distracter inhibition is often studied by the use of the negative priming paradigm (e.g., see Houghton & Tipper, 1996, for a review). This paradigm is based on the finding that, when a person is required to selectively respond to one (i.e., the target) of two simultaneously presented stimuli, then any inhibitory process acting on the ignored distracter (i.e., the nonselected stimulus) becomes manifest (often in longer RTs compared to a suitable control condition) if that distracter is subsequently re-presented as the target.

The slower RTs when previously ignored irrelevant information is presented subsequently as the relevant information has been explained by postulating inhibitory processing associated with internal representations of the to-be-ignored distracter(s). This would be a particularly clear instance of the fact that control processes often involve inhibitory mechanisms (Houghton & Tipper, 1996).

To explore how irrelevant information is processed in CHI patients, we carried out two experiments (Stablum, Mogentale, Mazzoldi, & Umiltà, in preparation). In the first, we used a negative priming paradigm with hierarchical stimuli (i.e. a large capital letter comprised of small capital letters; see Navon, 1977). These stimuli are either consistent, when the small capital letters are identical to the large one (e.g., a large H formed by small Hs), or conflicting, when the small letters are different from the large one (e.g., a large H formed by small Ss).

In the global attention condition, participants have to recognize the large letter, regardless of the identity of the small letters. In the local attention condition, participants have to recognize the small letters, regardless of the identity of the large letter. Typically, two effects are found: the global advantage effect and the interference effect (see, e.g., Kimchi, 1992, for a review). RTs in the global attention condition are faster than RTs in the local attention condition (global advantage effect) and RTs to conflicting stimuli are slower than RTs for consistent stimuli (interference effect).

With this paradigm, inhibition is found when, in two subsequent trials, the same letter acts first as the distracter and then as the target. For example, in the global attention condition, in the first trial the target large H is formed by small Ss, then, in the immediately following trial, the target large S is formed by small Es. Thus, the letter S is the distracter in the first trial and becomes the target in the second trial. Negative priming is indexed by slower RT to the large S of the second trial in comparison to a control condition in which the large S was preceded by a stimulus that did not contain Ss as distracters.

A group of CHI patients and a matched control group were tested. The results showed both the global advantage effect and the interference effect. More interestingly, there was a significant interaction between group and negative priming. The controls showed a negative priming effect (40 ms) in the local attention condition (i.e., the harder selection condition) and a facilitation effect (12 ms) in the global attention condition (i.e., the easier selection condition). The CHI patients had the reverse pattern, showing a negative priming effect (26 ms) in the global attention condition and a very small facilitation effect (5 ms) in the local attention condition.

The data for the controls are similar to those obtained in a study with normal young participants (Stablum, Ricci, & Umiltà, submitted for publication). They show that the negative priming effect occurs in the harder selection condition. In contrast, CHI patients manifested the negative priming effect only in the condition in which selection is easier. Thus, our results indicate that CHI patients have a specific deficit in separating relevant from irrelevant information, and, because of that, they inhibit the easier to select irrelevant information.

In the second experiment, we studied negative priming with Stroop stimuli (see MacLeod, 1991, for a review of the Stroop effect; and Neill & Westberry, 1987, for a similar paradigm). Participants had to respond to the color in which a color word was printed. The stimuli were either consistent (e.g., the word red printed in red color), conflicting (e.g., the word red printed in green color), or neutral (i.e., a series of colored Xs). Typically, RTs to conflicting stimuli are slower than RTs to consistent or neutral stimuli (interference effect). The negative priming effect occurs when a stimulus printed in red is preceded by a stimulus that contains the irrelevant word red. Therefore, the information "red" acts as a distracter in the first stimulus of the pair (i.e., the word red) and then becomes the target in the second stimulus (i.e., the color red).

A group of CHI patients was tested. The results showed the expected interference effect, RTs to conflicting stimuli being slower than RTs to either consistent or neutral stimuli. Also, an interesting significant interaction between severity of injury (mild, moderate, or severe) and negative priming was found. Whereas mild and moderate CHI patients showed some negative priming effect (10 ms), severe CHI patients showed a strong facilitatory effect (32 ms). That is to say, for severe CHI, the fact that the same information was first irrelevant (the distracter) and then relevant (the target) proved beneficial. This finding suggests that severe CHI patients are unable to inhibit the irrelevant information contained in the first stimulus.

CONCLUSION

In addressing the issue of control, we have taken into consideration two aspects that we believe to be crucial, as well as other aspects that may be related to the first two, but seem to us to be less fundamental. The two crucial aspects are whether control processes can be separated from other cognitive processes and whether control processes depend on the activity of specific brain structures.

Answering affirmatively to these questions is of paramount importance, because the very notion of control would be void if it could not be demonstrated that control processes are separable, both functionally and structurally, from other cognitive processes. It seems to us that the evidence obtained from neuropsychological studies convincingly shows that cognitive processes can be selectively impaired and depend on the specialized activity of the frontal, and especially prefrontal areas of the cerebral cortex. Thus, there is enough evidence to maintain that control is an isolable cognitive operation.

Other less crucial questions concern whether the control system is equipotential or can be decomposed into independent functional components, and whether, if there are independent components, they involve structurally distinct subsystems. Even though the neuropsychological evidence is not compelling, we are inclined to believe that there are different subsystems that subserve performance in tasks that require coordinating action schemata, deselecting old action schemata and selecting new action schemata, and suppressing irrelevant information.

In closing, we would like to note that many authors have also linked the phenomenal experience of consciousness with the contents and activities of the control system(s) (see review in Umiltà, 1988; but see also Velmans, 1991, for an opposite view). Therefore, another extremely interesting aspect of control, which was not considered in this chapter, concerns the possible relations between control and consciousness.

REFERENCES

Allport, D. A. (1993). Attention and control: Have we been asking the wrong questions? A critical review of twenty-five years. In D. E. Meyer & S. Kornblum (Eds.), *Attention and performance XIV:*

Synergies in experimental psychology, artificial intelligence, and cognitive neuroscience (pp. 183–218). Cambridge, MA: MIT Press.

Allport, D. A., Styles, E. A., & Hsieh, S. (1994). Shifting intentional set: Exploring the dynamic control of tasks. In C. Umiltà & M. Moscovitch (Eds.), *Attention and performance XV: Conscious and nonconscious information processing* (pp. 421–452). Cambridge, MA: MIT Press.

Baddeley, A. (1986). *Working memory.* Oxford, UK: Oxford University Press.

Baddeley, A., & Hitch, G. (1974). Working Memory. In G.H. Bower (Ed.), *The psychology of learning and motivation* (Vol. 8) (pp. 47-89). Hillsdale, N.J: Lawrence Erlbaum Associates.

Dikmen, S., Temkin, N., & Armsden, G. (1989). Neuropsychological recovery: Relationship to psychosocial functioning and postconcussional complaints. In H. S. Levin, H. M. Eisenberg, & A. L. Benton (Eds.), *Mild head injury* (pp. 229–241). New York: Oxford University Press.

Eslinger, P. J., & Damasio, A. R. (1985). Severe disturbance of higher cognition after bilateral frontal lobe ablation: Patient ERW. *Neurology, 35,* 1731–1741.

Fuster, J. M. (1980). *The prefrontal cortex: Anatomy, physiology, and neuropsychology of the frontal lobe.* New York: Raven.

Gronwall, D. M. A. (1989). Cumulative and persisting effects of concussion on attention and cognition. In H. S. Levin, H. M. Eisenberg, & A. L. Benton (Eds.), *Mild head injury* (pp. 153–162). New York: Oxford University Press.

Houghton, G., Glasspool, D. W., & Shallice, T. (1994). Spelling and serial recall: Insight from a competitive queueing model. In G. D. A. Brown & N. C. Ellis (Eds.), *Handbook of spelling research: Theory, process and intervention* (pp. 365–404). Chichester, UK: Wiley.

Houghton, G., & Tipper, S. P. (1996). Inhibitory mechanisms of neural and cognitive control: Applications to selective attention and sequential action. *Brain and Cognition, 30,* 20–43.

Johnson-Laird, P. N. (1983). *Mental models.* Cambridge, MA: Harvard University Press.

Kimchi, R. (1992). Primacy of wholistic processing and global/local paradigm: A critical review. *Psychological Bulletin, 112,* 24–38.

LaBerge, D. (1975). Acquisition of automatic processing in perceptual and associative learning. In P. M. A. Rabbitt & S. Dornic (Eds.), *Attention and performance V* (pp. 50–64). New York: Academic Press.

Levin, H. S., Goldstein, F. C., Williams, D. H., & Eisenberg, H. M. (1991). The contribution of frontal lobe lesions to the neurobehavioural outcome of closed head injury. In H. S. Levin, H. M. Eisenberg, & A. L. Benton (Eds.). *Frontal lobe function and dysfunction* (pp. 318–338). New York: Oxford University Press.

Logan, G. D., & Cowan, W. B. (1984). On the ability to inhibit thought and action: A theory of an act of control. *Psychological Review, 91,* 295–327.

Luria, A. R. (1966). *Higher cortical functions in man.* New York: Basic.

McLeod, P. (1977). A dual task response modality effect: Support for multiprocessor models of attention. *Quarterly Journal of Experimental Psychology, 29,* 651–667.

MacLeod, C. M. (1991). Half a century of research on the Stroop effect: An integrative review. *Psychological Bulletin, 109,* 163–203.

Mogentale, C., Stablum, F., Umiltà, C., & Dal Sasso, F. (1996). The rehabilitation of executive deficits in closed head injury patients. In J. Hoffman & A. Sebald (Eds.), Cognitive Psychology in Europe. *Preceedings of the Ninth Conference of the European Society for Cognitive Psychology* (pp. 126–127). Lengerich (Germany): Pabst Science Publishers.

Morra, S., & Roncato, S. (1986). Time required to unload irrelevant programs and to load the relevant ones. Paper presented at the *Joint Conference Experimental Psychological Society.* Rome, Italy.

Morra, S., & Roncato, S. (1988). Latenza della risposta in funzione del contenuto e dell'ordine di presentazione degli stimoli (l'effetto sorpresa). (Response latency as a function of content and stimulus presentation order: A surprise effect). *Giornale Italiano di Psicologia, 15,* 101–122.

Navon, D. (1977). Forest before trees: The precedence of global features in visual perception. *Cognitive Psychology, 9,* 353–385.

Neill, W. T., Valdes, L. A., & Terry, K. M. (1995). Selective attention and the inhibitory control of cognition. In F. N. Dempster & C. J. Brainerd (Eds.), *Interference and inhibition in cognition* (pp. 207–261). San Diego, CA: Academic Press.

Neill, W. T., & Westberry, P. L. (1987). Selective attention and the suppression of cognitive noise *Journal of Experimental Psychology: Learning, Memory and Cognition, 13,* 327–334.

Norman, D. A., & Shallice, T. (1986). Attention to action: Willed and automatic control of behavior.
   In R. J. Davidson & D. Shapiro (Eds.), *Consciousness and self-regulation: Advances in research* (pp.
   1-18). New York: Plenum.
Pashler, H., & Johnston, J. C. (1989). Chronometric evidence for central postponement in temporally
   overlapping tasks. *Quarterly Journal of Experimental Psychology, 41A*, 19–45.
Petrides, M. (1991) . Learning impairments following excisions of the primate frontal cortex. In H. S.
   Levin, H. M. Heisenberg, & A. L. Benton (Eds.), *Frontal lobe function and dysfunction* (pp. 256–272).
   New York: Oxford University Press.
Ponsford, J., & Kinsella, G. (1992). Attentional deficits following closed-head injury. *Journal of Clinical
   and Experimental Neuropsychology, 14*, 822–838.
Posner, M. I., & Petersen, S. E. (1990). *The attention system of human brain. Annual Review of Neuroscience,
   13*, 25–42.
Rogers, R. D. & Monsell, S. (1995). Costs of a predictable switch between simple cognitive tasks. *Journal
   of Experimental Psychology: General, 124*, 207–231.
Shallice, T. (1988). *From neuropsychology to mental structure.* Cambridge, UK: Cambridge University
   Press.
Shallice, T. (1994). Multiple levels of control processes. In C. Umiltà & M. Moscovitch (Eds.), *Attention
   and performance XV: Conscious and nonconscious information processing* (pp. 395–420). Cambridge,
   MA: MIT Press.
Shallice, T., & Burgess, P. (1991). Higher-order cognitive impairments and frontal lobe lesions in man.
   In H. S. Levin, H. M. Eisenberg, & A. L. Benton (Eds.), *Frontal lobe function and dysfunction* (pp.
   125–138). New York: Oxford University Press.
Stablum, F., Leonardi, G., Mazzoldi, M., Umiltà, C ., & Morra, S. (1994). Attention and control deficits
   following closed head injury. *Cortex, 29*, 603–618.
Stablum, F., Mogentale, C., Mazzoldi, M., & Umiltà, C., (in preparation). Interference and negative
   priming in closed head injury patients.
Stablum, F., Mogentale, C., & Umiltà, C. (1996). Executive functioning following mild closed head
   injury. *Cortex, 32*, 261–278.
Stablum, F., Mogentale, C., Umiltà, C. (in preparation). *Different measures of frontal lobe dysfunction in
   closed head injury patients.*
Stablum, F., Ricci, R., & Umiltà, C. (Submitted). *On the relation between interference and negative priming
   in visual selective attention.*
Stablum, F., Umiltà, C., Mazzoldi, M., & Berrini, G. (1996). Deficit esecutivi dopo trauma cranico chiuso:
   un problema di risorse o di accesso ai meccanismi decisionali? (Executive deficits following closed
   head injury: Lack of resources or difficulty in accessing decisional mehanisms? In L. Caldana & G.
   Zappalà (Eds.), *Traumi cranici: una sfida per gli anni 2000.* (pp. 367–370). Roma: Marabese Editore.
Stuss, D. F., & Benson, D. F. (1984). Neuropsychological studies of the frontal lobes. *Psychological Bulletin,
   95*, 3–28.
Umiltà. C. (1988). The control operations of consciousness. In A. J. Marcel & E. Bisiach (Eds.),
   Consciousness in contemporary science (pp. 334–356). Oxford, UK: Clarendon.
Umiltà, C., Nicoletti, R., Simion, F., Tagliabue, M. E., & Bagnara, S. (1992) . The cost of a strategy.
   European Journal of Cognitive Psychology, 4, 2 1–40.
Velmans, M. (1991). Is human information processing conscious? *Behavioral and Brain Sciences, 14*,
   651-726.
Wickens, C. D. (1984). Processing resources in attention. In R. Parasuraman & D. R. Davies (Eds.).
   Varieties of attention (pp. 63–102). New York: Academic Press.

4

Putative Functions of the Prefrontal Cortex: Historical Perspectives and New Horizons

Stephen Darling
Sergio Della Sala
Colin Gray
Cristina Trivelli
University of Aberdeen

Psychology has been said to have a short history, but a long past (Boring, 1957, ix). That is certainly true of cognitive neuropsychology, which, although "hardly a generation old", (Shallice, 1988, xxxiii), has a historical hinterland going back for several centuries. Moreover, some landmarks, such as the famous case of Phineas Gage, continue to be relevant because of the continuing challenge of the issues they raise.

In this chapter, we view current thinking about the functions of the frontal lobes within a historical perspective, beginning with a consideration of Gage's misfortune and following the threads of its implications into modern neuropsychology.

The Mind and the Brain

> Canst thou not minister to a mind diseas'd;
> Pluck from the memory a rooted sorrow;

Raze out the written troubles of the brain;
And with some sweet oblivious antidote
Cleanse the stuff'd bosom of that perilous stuff
Which weighs upon the heart? (Macbeth, Act V, scene 3).

The view that the brain (as opposed to the heart or any other bodily organ) is the basis of mental life, although advanced well over 2000 years ago, was slow to enter the canon of commonsense knowledge. Even by the middle of the 19th century, it had not yet gained universal acceptance. According to Boring (1957), "modern common sense, which identifies the mind with the brain, had not yet become the common view, and ... even the localization of the mind at or within the brain was a matter of some doubt" (p. 50).

Faculty Psychology

The 18th-century Scottish philosopher Thomas Reid (1785) held that the mind comprised a number of distinct abilities or *faculties*. According to Reid, there were 24 faculties, or "powers of the mind," some new ones being added later by his successor, Dugald Stewart. The faculties included what we now regard as biological drives such as hunger and sentiments like duty and pity, as well as the more obviously intellectual powers of judgment, memory, and conception.

In the 18th and early 19th centuries, Scottish philosophy had a strong influence on French psychology, a formative force in the system developed by Gall, which is described in the next section.

Phrenology

Within the general view that the brain is the seat of mental life, another strand of thought, also with a long past, can be discerned; namely, that specific mental functions are performed by specific regions and structures of the brain. For example, according to Boring, Albertus Magnus, in the 12th century, located feeling in the anterior ventricle of the brain and memory in the posterior ventricle. In the 17th century, Willis "placed memory and will in the convolutions of the brain, imagination in the corpus callosum, sense-perception in the corpus striatum, and certain emotions in the base of the cerebrum" (Boring, 1950, p. 50).

The system known as phrenology was devised by Gall, an anatomist, at the end of the 18th century. The term *phrenology*, however ("the science of the mind"), was not coined by Gall himself, but by his pupil Spurzheim, who did much to publicize and promulgate Gall's ideas (Spurzheim, 1815, 1826).

In phrenology, the brain structures in which Reid's powers of the mind resided were known as *organs*. For example, there was an organ of *amativeness* or physical love and an organ of *wit*. These organs were thought to correspond to the external contours of the skull. For example, Area 30 (see Fig. 4.1) was claimed to be the organ of comparison. The phrenologists, therefore, were perhaps the first to locate a mental function specifically in what is now regarded as the prefrontal area of the brain.

Phrenology has long since been dismissed in such derisive terms as "quackery", or "feeling the bumps." Indeed, most of its assumptions have since been falsified. Yet, Gall's early work was carried out in a scientific and painstaking manner. Moreover, the notion of mental faculties persists in the current notion of *modularity of mind* (Fodor, 1983), whereby functions such as language, numerical operations, and so on are regarded as relatively self-contained systems operating within the brain.

The Curious Case of Phineas Gage

On September 13, 1848, there occurred an accident, the spectacular and puzzling nature of which profoundly affected the subsequent development of brain science and the reverberations of which are still very much in evidence today.

FIG. 4.1. Illustration from Gall and Spurzheim's physiognomical system (Spurzheim, 1815) showing the alleged "bump" over area 30 (causality), clearly in the frontal cortex.

The victim of the accident was a railway construction worker named Phineas Gage. Gage was inserting an explosive charge when it detonated prematurely, propelling a cast iron tamping rod, some 3 cm in diameter and over 1 m long, through his skull, entering just below his left cheek and emerging from the top of his head. Our knowledge of the details of the case owes much to the painstaking work of Dr. John D. Harlow, to whom Gage was taken immediately after his accident (Harlow, 1848, 1868).

Despite the enormity of Gage's injury, it was noticed that although he had been momentarily stunned by the impact of the bar, he had regained consciouness by the time he was being taken to Harlow, and he made a full physical recovery from what, at that time, was the most serious open head injury ever to have been recorded (Barker, 1995).

Seven years after his death, Gage's skull was exhumed at Harlow's request. (The skull, with the tamping rod, is now preserved in the Warren Anatomical Medical Museum at Harvard University.) The tamping rod apparently had ablated both prefrontal lobes (H. C. Damasio, Grabowski, Frank, Galaburda, & A. R. Damasio, 1994).

Initially, as far as memory, reasoning, and language were concerned, Harlow saw no sign of any deterioration, which he found remarkable, considering how much brain tissue had been destroyed. Gage seemed to have no difficulty remembering everyday events, he was lucid and rational, and his language showed no obvious pathological features.

In other respects, however, Gage was a changed man. So dramatic was the change, in fact, that those who had known him before his accident concluded that: "he was no longer Gage" (Harlow, 1868, p. 340). Before the accident, Gage had been admired and respected for his dignity, competence, reliability and good judgment. Now, after his accident, he appeared to have been transformed into a different person, embodying the antitheses of those qualities. He was now impulsive and vacillating; moreover, his former politeness had given way to an uncharacteristic profanity:

> The equilibrium or balance, so to speak, between his intellectual faculties and animal propensities seems to have been destroyed. He is fitful, irreverent, indulging at times in the grossest profanity (which was not previously his custom), manifesting but little deference for his fellows, impatient of restraint or advice when it conflicts with his desires, at times pertinaciously obstinate, yet capricious and vacillating, devising many plans of future operation, which are no sooner arranged than they are abandoned in turn for others appearing more feasible. A child in his intellectual capacity and manifestations, he has the animal passions of a strong man (Harlow, 1868, pp. 339–340).

Robert Ellis Cahill(1983), a distinguished chronicler of New England folk-lore, documented the fact that Gage, having found it impossible to hold down a respectable job, was eventually reduced to exhibiting himself as a circus freak.

> To the doctor, his friends and relatives, who all were convinced that no man could live through such an experience, he chuckled and said, "I didn't have much of a brain before, but I only got half a brain now." He, of course, kept the crowbar, but because of the loss of his eye the railroad company would not rehire him. He left for Boston, where—on the common—he set up a tent and put himself and the crowbar on exhibition. P.T. Barnum then heard about Phineas and hired him for his New York museum, advertised as "The Only Living Man With a Hole in His Head." For those skeptics who visited Barnum's sideshow, they were allowed to peek through the top of Phineas' skull to watch his brain pulsate. Phineas was also displayed at Harvard University, before doubting doctors and scientists, who, after studying his well-healed wounds, doubted no more. (p. 34).

Gage's personality change was not the first to be reported in a head injured patient. Blumer and Benson (1974) reviewed a report (from 1835) of a patient who, having been a "morose" and "shut-in" character of "limited intellect", became, after his injury, one who was "gay", "vivacious," and "of jocular disposition" (Blumer & Benson, 1974, p. 152). For various reasons, however, it is the case history of Phineas Gage that has made the most impact.

The Impact of Phineas Gage

When Harlow's report was first published, the claims of phrenology were very much the center of attention in medical and scientific circles. It seems likely that Harlow, a distinguished graduate from a distinguished institution, would have been aware of phrenology and its implications . If so, however, there is little evidence of it in his report, which, it might be noted, contain no mention of the frontal lobes.

The participants in the debate about phrenology took a keen interest in Harlow's report, often finding in it evidence for their own different points of view. For example, Bigelow (1850) argued that because Gage had lost so much of the anterior part of his brain without impairment of his mental powers, this refuted the phrenologists' claim of localization of brain function. However, as we have seen, there were also some dramatic changes in Gage, and those changes could be viewed as damage to some of the higher mental functions described by the phrenologists and located in the frontal lobes of the brain. Harlow's report seems to have worked like a Rorschach inkblot, making it possible for those with varying viewpoints to find confirming evidence in his account.

In the discussion that followed the publication of Harlow's report, there were two concerns that have dominated neuropsychology ever since: the localization of brain function and the effects of damage to the frontal lobes.

Ferrier's Theory

Amongst those influenced by Harlow's reports was David Ferrier, who is regarded as having provided the first modern theory of frontal lobe function (Barker, 1995). Ferrier (1870) suggested that the role of the *prefrontal cortex* (the term was used by Ferrier) was the inhibition of motor responses. This was based on a sensory and motor associational model, which held that thought consisted of evoked associations between sensory and motor events that took place while actual motor output was inhibited. The organ of inhibition was, he claimed, the prefrontal cortex.

Ferrier (1876) explained the personality changes observed in frontal patients thus: " The removal of the frontal lobes causes no motor paralysis, or other evident physiological effects, but causes a form of mental degradation, which may be reduced in ultimate analysis to the loss of the faculty of attention" (p. 288).

Ferrier's (1876) ideas are prescient of modern cognitive theories: in fact, he even attributed an 'executive' function to the prefrontal lobes: "The centres of inhibition being thus the essential factor of attention, constitute the organic basis of all the higher intellectual faculties" (p. 287).

The core of Ferrier's idea recurs in modern theories such as those of A. R. Damasio, Tranel, & H. C. Damasio, (1990, 1991) and Norman and Shallice (1986).

THE HUMAN BRAIN

Progress in the Investigation of the Frontal Cortex

The structure and function of some cortical areas, such as the parietal, temporal, and occipital lobes, are now well mapped. There has also been progress in the investigation of the structure and function of some parts of the *frontal cortex*, the area lying anterior to the central sulcus. In the human brain, the frontal cortex amounts to as much as half of the total cortical area

(A. R. Damasio, 1985; H. C. Damasio, 1991; Grafman, 1995). If the cortex is "unfolded" using cartographic techniques, the proportion of frontal cortex in this "isometric cortex" may be even larger (James, 1992).

The frontal cortex contains a number of important structures, the functions of some of which are now well understood. For example, there are the (most dorsal) *motor area* and the (medially located) *supplementary motor area*, which are involved in motor action; *Broca's area*, which is important in the generation of speech; and *Brodmann's area 8*, which is involved in eye movements.

The Prefrontal Cortex

The prefrontal cortex is located at the anterior pole of the brain (see Fig. 4.2). Interest in this area is steadily increasing. Figure 4.3 compares the number of papers on the prefrontal lobes with the number on the occipital cortex over a period of several decades.

A major goal of this chapter is to review critically a representative sample of the most influential current theories of the function of the prefrontal cortex, identifying some of the difficulties they raise. We also attempt to identify what we believe to be the most promising lines of inquiry and to present a speculative scenario of the future theoretical landscape in this area.

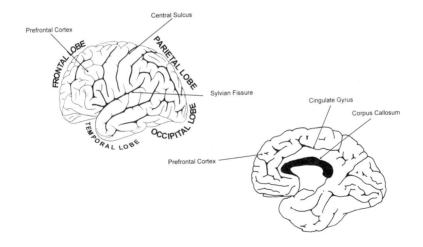

FIG. 4.2. The position of the prefrontal cortex.

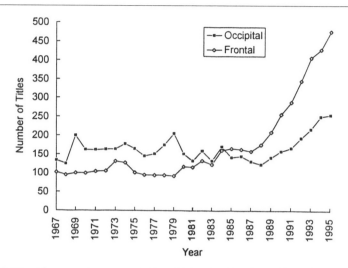

FIG. 4.3.   The surge of interest in the frontal lobes (based on the numbers of papers published on the frontal and occipital lobes).

The Evolution of the Prefrontal Cortex

The development of the prefrontal cortex in humans is, in evolutionary terms,
both recent and striking. Even in comparison with maraque monkeys and
chimpanzees, for example, the relative proportion of the cortex occupied by
the prefrontal region in humans represents an enormous increase (see Fig. 4.4).

The comparative recency of the development of the prefrontal cortex is
one of several factors have led many to regard the region as the seat of what
we believe to be our distinctive qualities of self-awareness and reflection
(Lezak, 1993).

Structure of the Prefrontal Cortex

There is, in this area, some potentially confusing terminology. Regrettably,
the term *prefrontal* is often used interchangeably with *frontal*, a practice that
brackets together, on the one hand, a number of areas, such as Broca's, the
functions of which are well known, with, on the other hand, an area of the
cortex, the function of which has continued to elude researchers after 125
years of research.

In studying the anatomy of the brain it is possible, by a process known as
cytoarchitectonic mapping, to divide the cortex into regions defined by their
cellular structure. Brodmann's (1909) mapping is still widely used. Under
his system, the prefrontal cortex is divided into (a) the *dorsolateral prefrontal
cortex* (Brodmann's Areas 9, 10, 44, 45, 46), (b) the *orbitofrontal cortex*
(Areas 11, 13, 47), and (c) the *frontal eye fields* (portions of Areas 8 and 9)

(Kolb & Whishaw, 1990). The dorsolateral prefrontal cortex is located above the orbitofrontal prefrontal cortex and these areas have different patterns of afferent and efferent connections, including different connec‐ tions with the thalamus (Goldman‐Rakic, 1987).

A distinctive feature of the human prefrontal cortex is the presence of large granular cells in Layer 4, which are to be found nowhere else. For this reason, the prefrontal cortex has also been described as the *frontal granular cortex*; indeed Warren and Akert's (1964) influential book bore the title *The Frontal Granular Cortex and Behaviour*. From this point of view, the frontal granular cortex is defined as the area with a distinctive pattern of granular cells in Layer 4.

Although the prefrontal and frontal granular cortex are often thought of as being identical, there are problems with the granular layer distinction. (Pandya & Yeterian, 1996). Although the granular cortex is present in most primate frontal regions, it is not present in all mammalian species, and therefore difficulties may arise with cross‐species comparison. Even more importantly, Pandya and Yeterian (1996) pointed out that of Brodmann's cytoarchitectonic areas routinely ascribed to the prefrontal cortex and its functions (i.e., 8, 9, 30, 45, and 46), only 8, 30, and 46 have the granular cells: Area 9 seems to be dysgranular and Area 45 is agranular in the composition of the prescient layer. For this reason, Pandya and Yeterian advocated the use of the connectional definition; namely, that the prefron‐ tal cortex is the set of areas in the frontal cortex that have high connectivity with the mediodorsal nucleus of the thalamus.

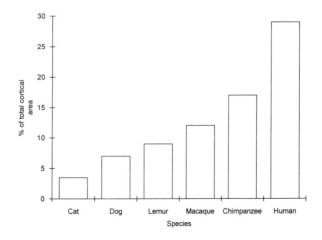

FIG. 4.4. Percentage of prefrontal cortex in the brains of different animals.

METHODOLOGY OF THE STUDY
OF THE FUNCTIONS OF THE PREFRONTAL CORTEX

Our present understanding of the functions of the prefrontal cortex is based upon four distinct kinds of inquiry:

1. Case studies.
2. The use of brain imaging techniques.
3. The psychometric approach.
4. The cognitive approach.

Case Studies

In neuropsychology, the traditional method of determining brain function is by studying patients with brain damaged. This practice has a cogent prima facie rationale: Should the behavior of a patient who has sustained a lesion in some area of the brain differ from the behavior of healthy controls, can we not conclude that the area concerned is at least implicated in the production of the behavior? There are, however, a number of serious difficulties with this argument, especially when it arises in connection with the prefrontal cortex.

Frontal Lobishness Is Not Specific to Frontal Lobe Damage

Over the years, a large number of cases of patients with prefrontal lesions have been reported. Despite the variety of symptoms and behavior observed in such patients, those with extensive experience of the sequelae of frontal lesions feel that there is a sufficient commonality among them to warrant the use of the term *frontal lobishness.* (Benson, 1994, p. 20). Among the symptoms of frontal lobishness given by Benson are tactlessness, disinhibition, moria (silliness), coarseness, and decreased attentiveness. Many of these characteristics appear to have been true of Phineas Gage after his accident.

Unfortunately, very similar manifestations have been reported in patients suffering from illnesses that had nothing to do with direct brain damage. For example, King George III displayed the symptoms of frontal lobishness to such a degree that he was thought to be mad (Macalpine & Hunter, 1993). There is, however, a condition known as *porphyria,* which causes sufferers to behave in a way very similar to those who have sustained lesions in their prefrontal lobes (British Medical Association, 1968). It would appear that King George III suffered from porphyria (Bennett, 1995; Macalpine &

Hunter, 1993). Porphyria is just one of several general metabolic disorders that can mimic prefrontal cortical damage.

Even when there has been demonstrable frontal damage, however, the interpretation of the presentation can still be highly problematic. One of our own patients, A. C., a retired policeman, had an operation to remove a meningioma (a benign tumor) that had invaded both frontal lobes. After his operation, he showed several of the manifestations of frontal lobishness, including a marked inattentiveness. However, he also showed a pronounced tendency to categorize people, and when he had assigned them to categories such as "gnome" or "weird priest," he would tell strange stories about them. A. C.'s condition was indistinguishable from a primary (i.e., psychiatric) obsessive-compulsive disorder, which may or may not have been activated by the lesions.

Some Difficulties With the Interpretation of Lesion Studies

A major problem with lesion studies is that the effects of the damage are rarely confined even to the frontal, let alone the prefrontal, cortex. There are several reasons for this:

1. In closed head injury, other areas of the brain are often abraded by the inner contours of the skull. It is therefore rare for lesions to be confined exclusively to the prefrontal cortex.
2. The distribution of the vascular system is neither homogeneous within the prefrontal cortex nor homologous in the different areas. Therefore the effects of bruising or diaschisis are likely to vary with the site of the lesion. On the other hand, one cannot conclude from this that different parts of the prefrontal lobes have different functions.
3. As with the vascular system, the nervous connections between the prefrontal and other areas are highly heterogeneous, leading to a corresponding heterogeneity of sequelae, that are difficult to interpret.
4. The supposed functions of the frontal lobes are complex and likely to involve a functional network extending widely over the various areas of the brain. The sequelae of lesions, therefore, throw little light on the precise role played by the prefrontal cortex.

Furthermore, in reference to 4 above, functions of such an overarching nature may be difficult to tap with tests of a relatively narrow range of functioning, such as conventional intelligence tests. This may explain a frequently reported sparing of everday functioning (Harlow, 1848, 1868) or performance on conventional intelligence tests (Sirigu et al. 1995), together with a diffuse symptomatology of other problems, such a those listed by Benson (1994).

Even in situations where a focal and circumscribed lesion is present solely in the prefrontal area, the implications for the function of other, predominantly posterior networks, may be significant.

Brain Imaging

The last decade has seen dramatic advances in the technology of brain imaging. Metabolism can be studied by measuring regional cerebral blood flow (rCBF) with techniques such as positron emission tomography (PET) and single photon emission computerized tomography (SPECT), together with increasingly advanced non-rCBF imaging techniques of functional magnetic resonance imaging (fMRI). These developments have made possible the *subtraction technique*, whereby it is possible to monitor differences between a resting, baseline condition and activation during the performance of a task (Parsons et al., 1995).

Such new techniques have demonstrated some frontal involvement in tasks requiring planning, such as the Tower of London and the Wisconsin Card Sorting test (Lenzi & Padovani, 1994). Neuroimaging analysis has one clear advantage over other approaches to neuropsychological function: The investigation can be conducted with healthy individuals, promising insights into normal brain functioning.

Unfortunately, the spatial resolution of rCBF techniques is, as yet, much inferior to that achievable with radiographic computerized tomography (CT) scans. Moreover, the temporal resolution is too slow for the rapid changes that can occur within the neural and metabolic systems. Also, rCBF techniques are very costly, which generally prohibits their use with healthy people.

The principle of the baseline can be difficult to implement in practice. Often a resting baseline is inappropriate when a task is complex and the experimenter wishes to ascertain the effects of some specific component.

The Psychometric Approach

In the 1960s, Milner (1963, 1964, 1971) carried out some seminal work on the mental capacities of patients who had undergone corticectomy to contain their epileptic seizures. By the time Milner began her work, the psychometrics movement had received an enormous boost from two world wars.

The tests used by Milner included card sorting, maze learning, delayed paired comparison, and word fluency tasks. The tasks were selected because they were available and there was a prima facie case for thinking that they might be sensitive to some of the most frequently reported cognitive symptoms of frontal lobishness.

One of the measures of frontal lobishness used by Milner was the Wisconsin Card Sorting Test (Berg, 1948; Grant & Berg, 1948), in which a participant is required to sort cards according to a given criterion, which then changes (Milner, 1964). She found her frontal patients too rigid to be able to adjust their sorting to meet the new criterion. Reports of perseveration, together with verbal statements indicating awareness that an error had been made, abound in the frontal literature and have been observed in many other testing paradigms (Milner, 1964; Shimamura, Janowsky, & Squire, 1991) and clinical examinations (Luria, 1966).

Despite the impact made by Milner's seminal work, it is difficult to interpret or to generalize from her results. On the one hand, the circumstances of her patients were such that the precise nature of the lesion was known, which conferred a considerable advantage over most reported cases of head injury; on the other, it is likely that a confounding variable was the additional damage caused by the disease process itself. For these (and other) reasons, it is difficult to attribute the changes in test performance reported by Milner unequivocally to prefrontal lobe damage. Another consideration is that Milner based her conclusions on studies of a very small sample of participants.

There is now a large body of evidence to show that the supposed frontal tests are certainly sensitive to brain damage; indeed, frontal patients have shown marked deficits on such tests. As Reitan and Wolfson (1994) observed, however, these tests appear to be as sensitive to damage in the nonfrontal areas of the brain as they are to frontal lesions. The Wisconsin Card Sorting Test has been demonstrated to be sensitive to brain damage in general but not specifically to frontal damage (Anderson, H. C. Damasio, Jones, & Tranel, 1991; Teuber, 1964).

The claim that perseveration is an indicator of specifically frontal damage is queried by Robinson, Heaton, Lehman, and Stilson (1980), who showed that patients with diffuse brain damage are also likely to show perseveration. The effects of frontal damage on verbal fluency are frequently confounded with aphasia or other expressive verbal disorders (Reitan & Wolfson, 1994).

The psychometric approach to the study of frontal functioning, therefore, has failed to produce a test that is sensitive specifically to frontal lobe damage.

Luria's Clinical Psychometric Approach

Luria (1966) followed a research strategy combining the clinical and psychometric approaches. According to Luria, the prefrontal cortex is concerned with the analysis and synthesis of the impulses of motor processes. The area is also concerned with the regulation of bodily functions:

> There are, therefore, important grounds for believing that the frontal lobes synthesise the information about the outside world received through the exteroceptors and the information about the internal states of the body and that they are the means whereby the behaviour of the organism is regulated in conformity with the effect produced by its actions. (Luria, 1966, p. 233)

In some of his patients with very large bilateral frontal lesions, Luria observed a condition, that he termed *frontal apraxia*, in which the patient has difficulty in initiating and terminating action sequences. The condition arises, Luria suggested, because the normal processes by which intentions are compared with actions are no longer available because of the frontal lobe damage. The problem does not lie in the drawing of individual circles, squares, or whatever the elements of the sequence may be: The difficulty seems to lie in selecting the correct sequence as a whole.

Luria believed that inner speech has an important regulatory function in program selection and explained various conditions in terms of a dysfunction of regulatory inner speech (Luria & Homskaya, 1964). This dysfunction may result in the sort of perseveration that Milner found with the Wisconsin Card Sorting Test.

The prefrontal cortex is one of the last regions of the central nervous system to mature. Interestingly, young (healthy) children show a perserveration similar to that found in Luria's adult patients (Luria, 1959, 1961).

The discrepancy between the frontal patient's correct verbal statement of what should be done and what is actually being done is explained in terms of a failure of the normal regulatory function of inner speech (Luria, 1966; Luria & Homskaya, 1964).

The Frontal "Syndrome"

For some years, following Hebb's (1939) claim (with apparently supporting evidence) that damage to the frontal cortex had relatively little effect, approaches to the study of prefrontal functioning (Brickner, 1936; Rylander,

1939; Zeigarnik, 1961) tended to be descriptive, or *syndromic*, rather than theory driven. In view of the great heterogeneity of symptoms in the supposedly unitary frontal "syndrome," however, a theory is clearly needed to drive the gathering of the sorts of data that are likely to cast further light on the perplexing question of frontal lobe functioning.

Table 4.1 shows a very substantial list of the features most commonly reported in frontal patients. Unfortunately, in no two patients are the sets of observable features likely to be completely overlapping; sometimes, indeed, there can be very little overlap, one patient being subdued and apathetic, another excitable and hyperactive.

EXECUTIVE FUNCTIONING

Cognitive Approaches

The early work on brain function derived its data exclusively from patients with damaged or dysfunctional brains. The past two decades, however, have seen, in the vigorous field of neuropsychology, a fruitful rapprochement between cognitive psychology, with data based on work with healthy individuals, and theories of brain function.

Executive Function and Dysexecutive Syndrome

Earlier, the limitations of a descriptive, syndromic approach were discussed, and the necessity for theory-driven research was demonstrated. The models of cognitive psychology offer the direction that is needed for further research.

A pervasive notion in cognitive psychology is that of the regulation of some processes by other higher processes, operating in a more managerial role. In the present context of neuropsychology, this is an attractive notion, because the systems of the brain are difficult to explain in terms of self-regulation.

Another central notion in cognitive psychology is that of the *schema*, a term introduced by Bartlett (1932) denoting an abstract plan, structure, or program that guides the processing of information. In cognitive psychology, there is widespread agreement that schemata, or knowledge-based programs, are stored in hierarchical assemblies that operate in an integrated manner, although there are important conceptual differences among these formulations (Baddeley, 1990; Baddeley, Bressi, Logie, Della Sala, & Spinnler, 1986; Baddeley & Hitch, 1974; Grafman, 1995; Norman & Shallice, 1986; Rumelhart & Norman, 1985; Schank, 1982; Schank &

TABLE 4.1

Sequelae of Lesions in the Prefrontal Cortex

List of Suggested Symptoms	Reference
Psychiatric or behavioral manifestations	
Tactlessness	Benson (1994)
Lack of behavioral restraint / failure of appropriate inhibition	Benson (1994), Harlow (1868)
Jocularity / facetiousness (*Witzelsucht* / *Moria*)	Jastrowitz (1888), Blumer and Benson (1974)
Boastfulness	Benson (1994)
Decreased initiative	Blumer and Benson (1974)
Memory impairments	Kolb and Whishaw (1990), Shimamura (1995), Goldman-Rakic (1987)
Apathy	Geschwind (1977)
Shallow affect / change of affect	A. R. Damasio et al. (1990), Eslinger and A. R. Damasio (1985), Harlow (1868)
Abulia	Benson (1994)
Akinesia	Benson (1994)
Irritability	Geschwind (1977)
Inappropriate sexual behavior / conversation	Benson (1994)
Euphoria	Geschwind (1977)
Capriciousness	Harlow (1868)
Perseveration of responses	Luria (1966)
Restlessness	Benson (1994)
Delusions: grandiosity, nihilism, paranoia,,	
Hypochondriasis	Benson (1994)
Apathy and indifference (*Pseudodepression*)	Blumer and Benson (1974)
Peurility and euphoria (*Pseudopsychopathy*)	Blumer and Benson (1974)
Loss of spontaneity	Kolb and Whishaw (1990), Luria (1966)
Neuropsychological deficits	
Utilization behavior	Lhermite (1983), Shallice et al. (1989), Brazzelli et al. (1994)
Wisconsin Card Sorting Test	Milner (1964)
Word fluency	Milner (1964), Ramier and Hécaen (1970)
Stroop task	Vendrell et al. (1995)
Ambiguous figures task	Ricci & Blundo (1990)
Visual search task	Poppelreuter (1917)

Self-ordered search tasks	Owen et al. (1990)
Design fluency	Jones-Gotman and Milner (1977)
Maze learning task	Milner (1964), Benton et al. (1963)
Delayed response	Jacobsen (1936), Goldman-Rakic (1987)
Risk taking in neuropsychological tasks	A. R. Damasio (1995)
Rule breaking in neuropsychological tasks	Milner (1964)
Poor performance on strategy tasks	Milner (1964)
Associative learning deficits	Petrides (1982)
Frequency estimation	Smith and Milner (1984)
Egocentric spatial relations	Semmes, Weinstein, Ghent, and Teuber (1963)
"Frontal" apraxia	Luria (1966)
General cognitive deficits	
Differential effects of release from proactive interference	Smith et al. (1994)
Spatial and motor planning	Brazzelli et al. (1994), Shallice et al. (1989)
Novel task completion	Luria (1966), Shallice and Burgess (1991b)
Attentional deficits; distractibility	Shallice et al. (1989), Harlow (1848, 1868)
Short-term memory / working memory	Goldman-Rakic (1987, 1994), Baddeley et al. (1997)
Strategy generation	Owen et al. (1990)
Modification of behavior to accommodate new information	Milner (1964)
Analysis of risk contingencies	A. R. Damasio (1995)
Temporal arrangement of behavior	Fuster (1989, 1995)
General planning	Shallice and Burgess (1991a, 1991b)
Prospective memory	Schwartz (1995)
Corollary discharge deficits	Teuber and Mishkin (1954), Teuber (1964)
Disturbances of voluntary movement	Teuber (1964), Kolb and Milner (1981a, 1981b)
Disturbances of the regulatory function of speech	Luria (1966)

Abelson, 1977; Shallice, 1982; Shallice & Burgess, 1991a, 1991b; Sirigu et al., 1995).

Computer modeling (Sussman, 1975) has shown that explanations based solely on interschema competition, at various levels, cannot account for the patterns of function found in humans and that it is therefore necessary to posit some system of control at a superordinate level. Most theorists, therefore, posit some form of *executive system*, concerned with the selection and deployment of lower level schemata.

For some years, cognitive psychologists, although producing elaborate block-and-tackle diagrams of mental functioning, were quite insouciant about the physical substrates of boxes with labels such as short-term memory, long-term memory, and iconic store, or about the physical mechanisms that could serve as feedback loops and achieve retrieval from storage. In recent years, however, the need to find such substrates has come to be seen as a most pressing one. It is this need that helped bring the discipline of cognitive neuropsychology into being.

Because the concept of executive functioning arose within psychology at a time when psychologists often had little interest in brain mechanisms, it is not synonymous with frontal functioning, although it is tempting to identify the two. Executive function is a cognitive description, derived from theoretical cognitive models. Frontal syndromes are clinical and neuropsychological descriptions. Models such as those of Baddeley (Baddeley, 1986, 1996; Baddeley & Hitch, 1974; Della Sala & Logie, 1993) do not specify the anatomical substrate of the central executive that they describe.

SOME THEORIES OF EXECUTIVE FUNCTIONING

We begin this section with a theory that, because of its breadth of scope, will serve as a framework within which to view the more specific formulations that follow.

Setting the Scene: The Theory of Stuss and Benson

According to Stuss and Benson (1986), the functioning of the human brain is hierarchical, as shown in Fig. 4.5. At the summit of the hierarchy is self-awareness. At the next level lie the four executive activities of anticipation, goal selection, preplanning, and monitoring. At the third level lie two major functional systems, which exert regulatory control over a set of processes (attentional, perceptual, linguistic, cognitive, and autonomic/emotional) that are generally regarded as being predominantly effected by nonfrontal or posterior regions of the brain. Of the two regulatory systems, one is concerned with drives, and the other with sequencing.

Drives (i.e., emotional states that lead to action) are attended, in humans, by a number of distinct functions: attention, alertness, visuospatial orientation, autonomic and emotional functions, and memory. The drive-regulation

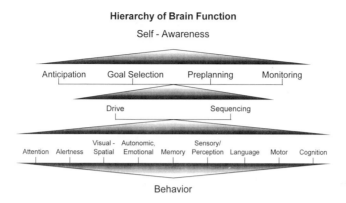

FIG. 4.5. The Hierarchical system of Stuss and Benson. Redrawn with permission from Stuss and Benson (1986), Raven Press. Used by permission of Lippencott-Raven Publishers.

system controls and coordinates those functions, so that the goal can be reached and the drive appeased. Drives and volition are regarded as forming a general set of what Stuss and Benson (1986) termed motivatory processes, the neologism motivatory being perhaps intended to embody simultaneously the ideas of drive, motivation and will.

Stuss and Benson (1986) suggested that damage to the orbital frontal cortex may result in inhibition of drive-action contingencies, whereas medial frontal damage may reduce the drives themselves.

The patterns of symptoms referred to by Blumer and Benson (1974) as pseudopsychopathy and pseudodepression are, in the system of Stuss and Benson (1986) interpreted as disturbances at the highest level of their hierarchy of functions.

Although the theory of Stuss and Benson (1986) is a comprehensive conceptualization of the problems and issues in this area and has great heuristic value, its lack of specification of the possible mechanisms by which the various layers of the hierarchy work could be viewed as a drawback.

Damasio's Somatic Marker Theory of Ventromedial Prefrontal Function

Eslinger and A. R. Damasio (1985) reported a patient, EVR, who, following bilateral ablation of the ventromedial frontal cortices in the course of surgical treatment for meningioma, displayed a peculiar pattern of deficits and preserved ability. Premorbidly, EVR was a highly intelligent, socially competent individual, able to hold down a steady skilled job. Following surgery, EVR achieved Wechsler Adult Intelligence Scale–Revised verbal and performance IQ scores at the 98th percentile.

According to A. R. Damasio et al. (1991), EVR has been unable to hold down a job since his surgery. He has social and financial difficulties and finds it especially difficult to make and carry out plans. Like Phineas Gage, EVR now shows marked indecisiveness and finds it difficult to make choices.

A. R. Damasio and his colleagues formulated a *somatic marker hypothesis* (Bechara, A. R. Damasio, H. C. Damasio, & Anderson, 1994; A. R. Damasio 1995; A. R. Damasio et al., 1991) that was intended to explain the postlesional behavior only of those patients with damage to the ventromedial frontal cortex. The hypothesis is that these patients cannot relate their cognition to their bodily states. In healthy individuals, such bodily states serve as triggers to prompt the next move in complex chains of action; although in skilled action, control can be directly from the cerebrum. The triggered bodily activations enable the healthy individual to make decisions by restricting the set of possible actions.

It is also suggested that certain somatosensory patterns act as boosters for working memory and attention. Logical reasoning itself, one of the most profound higher order activities, may perhaps depend on the establishment of such patterns.

In a series of experiments, Damasio and his colleages (Bechara et al., 1994; A. R. Damasio, et al., 1991; Tranel, 1994; Tranel, Anderson, & Benton, 1994; Tranel, H. C. Damasio, &, A. R. Damasio, 1995) have shown that when certain stimuli are presented to frontal patients, skin conductance responses (SCRs), an indicator of autonomic nervous system (ANS) activation, are diminished in comparison with nonfrontally brain damaged patients or with healthy controls. The difficulty does not arise from ANS dysfunction, because SCRs were elicited as normal in the frontal sample in situations where they are reliably elicited in normal individuals, such as the introduction of an unexpected loud noise, or the instruction to breathe deeply. It seems that at the reflex and simple levels, frontal patients evince normal autonomic activation. When introduced to stimuli that were emotionally charged (e.g., photographs of scenes of a disaster or bodily mutilation), the frontal patients, in contrast with the control groups, showed no increase in SCR response. Bechara et al. (1994) offered a similar analysis of frontal patients' difficulties in a gambling situation.

The somatic marker hypothesis holds that the sequencing problems arise because of the nonoccurrence of the somatic markers. This, however, is just one of several possible causal models of the situation. Another possibility is that both somatic markers and the sequencing and decision making depend on executive processing and are disrupted by impairment of the executive. Because correlation does not imply causation, the evidence adduced by Damasio and his colleagues cannot resolve the question of which model is appropriate.

Norman and Shallice's Supervisory Attentional Model

Norman and Shallice (1986) developed a general information-processing model predicting performance on nonroutine tasks (Shallice, 1982; Shallice & Burgess, 1991b). Their system is essentially a development of Luria's (1966) ideas, expressed in information-processing terms.

The model is based on Shiffrin and Schneider's (1977) claim that there are two kinds of task processing:

1. Fast, automatic, triggered by stimuli, but inflexible.
2. Slow, conscious, but independent of stimuli and flexible.

The former represent the processes underlying skilled actions and arise generally as a result of practice, whereas the latter are useful in novel situations.

The automatic processes are schemata, in the usual sense of the term, which are arranged hierarchically, in the manner of Stuss and Benson (1986). The schemata are in competition and among the factors affecting whether a given program will run are the nature of the stimulus and its present state of activation.

In addition there are two important control processes. First, there is contention scheduling that, through a mechanism of lateral inhibition, frees up bottlenecks in the information processing system, the most highly activated schemata being preferred. This idea is derived from the computerized information-processing model of Newell and Simon (1972). Contention scheduling, although economical of cognitive resources and usually reliable, fails in nonroutine situations.

The other major agent of control is the supervisory attentional system (SAS), which is concerned with schema selection in nonroutine situations and can override contention scheduling. Shallice (1988; Shallice & Burgess, 1991b) suggested that many of the features of the classic dysexecutive syndrome are explainable if it is hypothesized that the SAS is a frontal system, or a predominantly frontal one, and he offered some data from frontal patients to support this.

The main prediction from the location of the SAS in the frontal cortex is that frontal lesions should yield a pattern of unmodulated contention scheduling, leaving the patient at the mercy of environmental stimuli.

An example is the phenomenon of *utilization behavior* (UB; Brazzelli, Colombo, Della Sala, & Spinnler, 1994; Lhermite, 1983; Shallice, Burgess, Schon, & Baxter, 1989), which is the use by patients of objects that happen to be available, even when such use is quite irrelevant to the requirements of the situation. It could be argued that the UB observed by Lhermitte was induced by the situation. Shallice et al. and Brazzelli et al. (1994), however, demonstrated that UB can be spontaneous.

It is important to note that UB involves compulsive meaningful use of objects, rather than lower level tactile manipulation, as in Kluver and Bucy's (1937) syndrome, which can be observed in other pathologies.

The distinction between induced and incidental UB is an interesting one, for Wernicke (1906) suggested that spontaneous use of objects may occur, a phenomenon he termed *hypermetamorphosis*, which he described as part of a luetic *paralytic psychosis*, that produces widespread prefrontal neuronal damage. Subsequently, however, the term has often been used to denote the kind of oral manipulation of objects seen in patients with bilateral temporal lesions. The spontaneous UB described by Shallice (1988), however, seems to be characteristic of frontal patients.

The prediction that easy distractibility may be one consequence of frontal damage is supported by the appearance of patterns of UB amongst some (although by no means all) frontal patients. Moreover, the "stuck-in-set" perseveration patterns observed in frontal patients (Cicerone, Lazar, & Shapiro, 1983; Drewe, 1974; Milner, 1964; Nelson, 1976) are consistent with the prediction of unmodulated contention scheduling in the presence of strong trigger contingencies to produce inappropriate and inflexible responses arising from the capture of processing resources by some schemata. The fact that patients can often (wrongly) verbalize what they are doing may, under the theory, reflect differential bottlenecks in the processing system.

Shallice and his colleagues have also explored the role of the SAS in the solving of novel problems. In the cognitive estimation task (Shallice & Evans, 1978), individuals are asked to make realistic estimates of, say, the length of a man's spine. Kartsounis and Poynton, in an unpublished study cited in Shallice and Burgess (1991b), found that frontal patients performed poorly on the cognitive estimation task in comparison with nonfrontally brain-damaged controls.

Considerations of case histories create difficulties for the view that there is a unitary SAS. Patient EVR, studied by Eslinger and Damasio (1985), and patient PG, studied by Brazzelli et al. (1994)—see also the patients of Heck and Bryer (1986), A. R Damasio, et al., (1991) and Shallice and Burgess (1991a)—performed very well on standard tests of so-called executive functions, still showing many other problems of an emotional or social nature and having day-to-day orientation difficulties. Shallice and Burgess (1991a) developed the *multiple subgoal scheduling* and the *multiple errands* tasks, which are designed to achieve greater ecological validity than the usual tests. On the basis of such work, Shallice and his colleagues proposed a fractionation of the SAS.

Shallice and Burgess (1991b) divided supervisory functioning into at least four areas, including:

1.   Plan formulation and modification.
2.   Marker creation or triggering.
3.   Goal articulation.
4.   Memory organization packets.

Schwartz's Update of Luria's Frontal Apraxia

What Luria (1966) called *frontal apraxia*, interpreted as a breakdown of routine action, was reevaluated by Schwartz (1995), who viewed it within the framework of the Norman and Shallice (1986) model.

Any situation in which an error occurs in a routine action may be regarded as a slip of action (Norman, 1981). The occurrence of slips of action can be regarded as omissions of a given action in a sequence, exchanges of component parts of an action schema with others (e.g., putting a match in one's mouth and striking a cigarette against a matchbox), or as substitutions of inappropriate objects for intended target objects.

Schwartz's (1995) contention is that the occurrence within automatic processing of potential points in which such slips may arise is common, and it is one of the tasks of the supervisory system to monitor schema feedback from both the somatic and neural levels of the body in order to preempt action slips. Feedback of schemata to the SAS is a key process in the modern conception of the supervisor in terms of the SAS model (Stuss, Shallice, Alexander, & Pichon, 1995). If the SAS is indeed involved in such low-level monitoring, it may be necessary to concede that the routine–nonroutine difference is not dichotomous but a matter of degree.

Schwartz (1995) also has a working memory component in her formulation. Working memory is needed to maintain the focus on the task goal, despite (say) a person's relocation in physically different surroundings. These ideas are consistent with the formulations of Baddeley and Hitch (Baddeley, 1986, 1996; Baddeley & Hitch, 1974) and Goldman-Rakic, (1987, 1990, 1992, 1995; Wilson, O'Scalaidhe, & Goldman-Rakic, 1993), and Schwartz has been led by their influence to ascribe a more extensive role to moment-to-moment monitoring than the notion of an anterior SAS would usually imply (cf. Stuss et al., 1995).

From her theory, Schwartz hypothesized the occurrence of an *action disorganization syndrome* (ADS) in frontal patients, and provides evidence for its occurrence. There are, however, problems with Schwartz's approach. It is unclear whether the ADS is a specifically frontal pattern, one arising from damage to a fronto-posterior network, or has a multiple etiology. Second, ADS has yet to be observed in a patient with solely executive impairments: It is usually present as a complex pattern of pathologies and often resolves itself after a period of rehabilitation.

A Theory Linking Intelligence with Executive Functioning: Duncan's Goal Neglect

Since the influential work of Hebb (1939), a pervasive claim in the prefrontal literature has been that intelligence is unrelated to frontal function. There have been many other cases in which a patient has presented with marked postlesional behavioral and social difficulties, and yet still achieved a high score on a standard intelligence test (e.g., Shallice & Burgess, 1991b).

Three considerations are germane here:

1. Traditional intelligence tests may measure crystallized, not fluid, intelligence.
2. Because of their purpose and the manner in which they have been constructed, traditional intelligence tests are unlikely to be sensitive measures of executive functioning.
3. Intelligence as described by Spearman and others tends to emphasize only the attentional component of executive functioning. The traditional intelligence test engages the testee in some very short pieces of thinking, from which the forward-planning element is largely absent.

Drawing on Cattell's (1967) distinction between fluid and crystallized intelligence, Duncan (1995) argued that many supposed tests of general intelligence actually measure crystallized intelligence, which is relatively immune to brain damage. If so, tests designed to measure fluid intelligence should correlate more highly with other measures of frontal functioning than do traditional intelligence tests. In fact, Duncan, Johnson, Swales, and Freer (1997) found that Cattell's Culture Fair Test and Raven's Progressive Matrices (Raven, 1965) correlate more highly with a frontal index than do other intelligence tests.

Some investigators report low correlations among the traditional frontal tests, that are all supposedly measuring the same abilities. Della Sala, Gray, Spinnler, and Trivelli (in press), however, found that a group of traditional frontal tests correlated more highly with one another than they did with tests not generally regarded as frontal; moreover, a single general factor accounted for fully 50% of the shared variance among the frontal group of tests. Even when all the tests were included in the factor analysis, a general factor still accounted for over 40% of the variance. It is also noteworthy that no group factors were extracted, as might be expected on a fractionation hypothesis.

Duncan and his associates (Duncan et al.,1997), with a sample of head-injured patients (rather than postoperative patients with frontal lesions, as in the Della Sala et al. [in press] study), found small correlations among the tests they used. A factor analysis of their correlation matrix, however, also yielded a single general factor, and no group factors emerged.

According to Duncan (1990, 1995), the key to differences in intelligence is goal selection. This process, however, although reminiscent of the top-down executive function of Stuss and Benson (1986) may sometimes operate in a bottom-up manner (cf. Anderson, 1983; Grafman, 1995). In Duncan's view, frontal damage can cause a disruption of this process, which he termed *goal neglect*.

Duncan (1995) devised a measure of goal neglect that embodies some of the features of the dual-task paradigm. Frontally injured patients appear to find this task more difficult than do controls.

Cattell's (1967) distinction between fluid and crystallized intelligence maps nicely onto the automatic versus controlled view of processing that is at least implicit in most current formulations of frontal functioning (e.g., Norman & Shallice, 1986). In this view, crystallised intelligence is deployed in automatic processing, (i.e., well-established routine procedures controlled by relatively low-level schemata), whereas fluid intelligence is required for controlled processing, which is necessary for novel tasks, and may require intervention by the central executive in schema selection and execution.

Frontal Implications of Baddeley and Hitch's Working Memory Model

The term *working memory* was originally coined by Baddeley and Hitch (1974) to distinguish their own conception of brief storage from older interpretations, such as Atkinson and Shiffrin's (1968) *short-term memory*. In contrast with short term memory, which embodies the idea of the brief retention of some analog of material that has just been presented, working memory is active and selective, functioning as a system, rather than a monolithic, undiscriminating buffer.

The working memory theory has become highly influential in cognitive psychology (and in neuropsychology). In the model, two modality-specific slave systems operate as short term storage units with specific capacities, under the control of a general processing unit called the *central executive*, the role of which (especially in more recent formulations) is to carry out functions that require the online manipulation and processing of information, especially in situations where special monitoring is required (Della Sala & Logie, 1993).

So far, it has not been easy to unpack the central executive empirically (Della Sala & Logie, 1993), and it has even been suggested that its value is largely heuristic. Certainly, although the two slave systems have been thoroughly operationalized, the central executive itself still remains rather mysterious, although some progress has been made toward clarifying its function. A defining feature in most formulations of the central executive is its role in deploying cognitive resources.

There is a tendency for the terms *short-term memory* and *working memory* to be used interchangeably. The former store, however, merely retains information: It does not process it. There is, in fact, evidence for such passive storage in man (Baddeley, 1986; Oscar-Berman, McNemara, & Freedman, 1991) and in primates (see Goldman-Rakic, 1987; Petrides, 1995). The equation of short-term memory with working memory, however, does violence to the latter, because it identifies working memory with a slave component, rather than a system with its own distinct components.

More recently, the basis for the location of the central executive within the prefrontal cortex in humans has been strengthened by work that has used modern brain imaging techniques. D'Esposito, Detre, Shin, Atlas, and Grossman (1995) provided evidence from fMRI that the frontal cortex is involved in tasks that hypothetically involve the central executive. The tasks were two nonworking memory tasks that are suspected to load on largely posterior networks: semantic judgment and spatial rotation. It was further ensured that points of conflict between these tasks were minimized at lower (i.e., sensory) processing levels in order to prevent confounding by limitations of resources at those levels. It was found that dual-task performance caused increased metabolic activity in the prefrontal cortex, whereas performance of each single task alone did not cause this activation. Other dual-task experiments, with component memory tasks, have suggested that the central executive plays a significant role in the coordination of activity (Della Sala, Baddeley, Papagno, & Spinnler, 1995), and further evidence cited by these authors (Baddeley, Della Sala, Papagno, & Spinnler, 1997), suggests that, in frontal patients, there may be an impairment of this integrative function in other activities, particularly those involving the slave systems. The dual-task approach, using a tracking task and a digit span task, may discriminate successfully between executively impaired and executively nonimpaired samples of patients with frontal injuries.

Giving Working Memory a Purely Frontal Substrate:
The Comparative Neurophysiological Model
of Goldman-Rakic

On the basis of work with animals, Goldman-Rakic has advanced a theory of multiple working memory domains (Goldman-Rakic, 1987, 1990, 1992, 1994, 1995). Although Goldman-Rakic's theory utilizes the working memory notion of Baddeley and Hitch (1974), she questioned the separation of the central executive from the slave systems, arguing that storage and processing of a specific type of material are aspects of a unitary specialized executive system located entirely in the prefrontal cortex. Within each system, storage and processing are achieved by modality-specific local circuits.

Goldman-Rakic and her associates identified, in monkeys, two kinds of circuits, one for processing spatial information, and the other for visual patterns. The evidence is based on work using the delayed response (DR) paradigm (Jacobsen, 1936), in which an animal, having been shown which of two closed food wells contains a tasty morsel, is required, by the interposition of a screen, to retain this information until the screen is removed (see Fig. 4.6).

The Goldman-Rakic team have been using a modification of the classic DR paradigm, known as the oculomotor delayed response (ODR) paradigm, in which an appropriate saccadic eye movement replaces selection from the food wells, and the production of a directionally correct saccade brings a reward.

Goldman-Rakic (1993) reported that surgical lesions around the principal sulcus in monkeys had a deleterious effect on ODR performance in

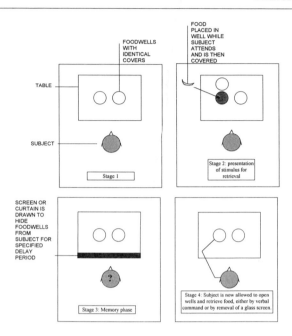

FIG. 4.6.   The classic delayed response paradigm.

localized areas of the visual field, indicating that the prefrontal cortex is involved in the short term retention of visual information. Goldman-Rakic, Funahashi, and Bruce (1990), using the ODR paradigm, have also identified cells around the principal sulcus in monkey brains that fire at specific phases during the performance of an ODR task: encoding, mnemonic, and responding. The cells are very close together, which is consistent with the interpretation that they are part of a single local circuit for short-term storage.

In a further study by Funahashi, Chaffee, and Goldman-Rakic (1993), monkeys learned a conditional rule for making saccadic responses in ODR: With one color of fixation point, the correct response was ipsilateral; with another, it was contralateral. (The second condition is known as the antisaccadic ODR). Once the rule had been learned, the monkey performed a random series of ODR and antisaccadic-ODR trials. It was found that during the mnemonic phase of the experiment, a neuron would fire for a particular presentation position irrespective of the direction of the correct response, indicating that it is information about position, rather than response, that is being stored (see Fig. 4.7).

Wilson et al. (1993), using similar methodology, found evidence for pattern-based circuits. In their experiment, in addition to a *spatial* delayed

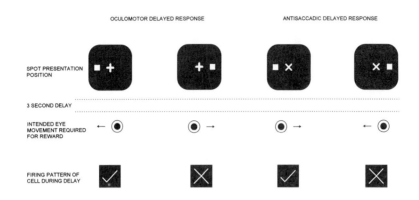

FIG. 4.7   The oculomotor delayed response paradigm used by Funahashi et al. (1993).

response (SDR) condition, there was also a *pattern* delayed response (PDR) condition. During the delay, cells in the dorsolateral prefrontal cortex fired under the SDR condition, but in the PDR condition, the firing was by cells in the inferior prefrontal convexity (see Fig. 4.8). It would appear therefore, that (in monkeys) some circuits are specialized for spatial storage, and others for pattern storage, and that their substrates differ both in location and at cellular level.

Goldman-Rakic's theory raises a number of questions, the most obvious being whether we can attribute structures and functions that have been demonstrated in monkeys to the human brain also. Moreover, the functions she has demonstrated are, in cognitive terms, rather rudimentary. It remains to be seen whether comparable units are found in the human brain.

Some Cognitive Informational Theories That Refer to Executive Function

A number of authors (Grafman, 1994, 1995; Stuss & Benson, 1986; Stuss et al., 1995) have proposed that one of the functions of frontal cortex is to modulate the activity of largely routine large-scale programs that are themselves arranged hierarchically. These approaches generally stem from cognitive psychology and artificial intelligence (Shank, 1982; Schank & Abelson, 1977).

Schank and Abelson (1977) published a highly influential book in which they applied an artificial intelligence approach to the use and understanding of language, which was implemented using their SAM computer package. Schank and Abelson configured a hierarchy of schemata, in which rela-

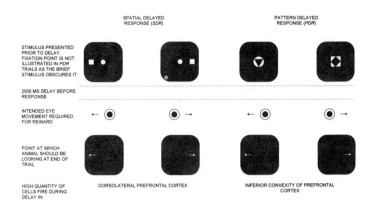

FIG. 4.8. Different frontal substrates for pattern and spatial image memory (Wilson et al. (1993).

tively high level control schemata known as *scripts* and *plans* coordinate lower level schemata which, according to Shallice (1988), differ from scripts in being specific to a given cognitive subsystem. Schank (1982) later modified his description of scripts and called them *memory organization packets*.

Grafman (1994, 1995) advanced a theory similar to that of Schank. He suggested that various *structured event complexes* are formed by chains of neural *events* (i.e., minor units of manipulation) and these accumulate into higher order *managerial knowledge units* (MKUs; see Fig. 4.9).

MKUs, which themselves can be ordered hierachically, serve at the highest levels of processing control;. Grafman (1995) viewed the SAS not as a separate entity, but as an emergent property of a collection of the highest level MKUs. He also suggested that in the brain, there is, in parallel with an anatomical posterior-to-anterior progression through the cortex, also a progression from atomistic functions to the highest level MKUs, the latter taking place in the prefrontal cortex. It is perhaps this last assertion that is the most questionable. Grafman provided no substantive evidence for it; although he did suggest how it might be put to the test. Sirigu et al. (1995), however, in an experiment in which frontally injured patients, posterior patients and normal controls were required to give details and evaluations of scripts, reported that the frontal group had most difficulty with the tasks. There would thus appear to be at least some frontal involvment in such cognitive processes. Among the theories we have considered so far, Grafman's is unique in being bottom-up: The notion of a separate central executive is rejected, such functioning being regarded as an emergent property of the MKUs.

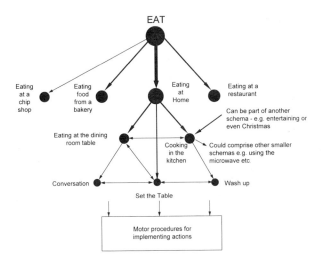

FIG. 4.9. An example of a managerial knowledge unit: An eating schema. Redrawn, with permission, from Grafman (1995).

SOME NEW DIRECTIONS FOR RESEARCH

Theory of Mind: A Frontal Function?

During the past decade, there has been a rapid growth in research examining children's understanding of what is known as theory of mind. According to Premack and Woodruff (1978), who, in the context of work with nonhuman primates, coined the phrase, *theory of mind* is the attribution of mental states to oneself and to others: "A system of inferences of this kind is properly viewed as a theory, first because such states are not directly observable, and second, because the system can be used to make predictions, specifically about the behaviour of other organisms". Theory of mind, then, means the awareness that a situation may not look the same to another person, together with the ability to view the scene from someone else's standpoint.

Autism is a specific developmental disorder with a range of sequelae that include delay in the acquisiton of theory of mind (Baron-Cohen, 1992; Leslie, 1991). There is also evidence that autistic children display some of the symptoms of frontal lobishness. For example, they are magnetized by salient objects and show repetitive behavior (Russell, Mauthner, Sharpe, & Tidswell, 1991), and have difficulty with classic frontal executive tasks such as the Tower of Hanoi (Prior & Hoffman, 1990), the Wisconsin Card Sorting Test (Ozonoff, 1991), and Milner's Maze Test (Hughes & Russell, 1993).

It is not being claimed here that autism is a frontal pathology, but the foregoing studies do suggest that autism may have some frontal aspects. Moreover, recent neuroimaging studies suggest that in normal people the frontal cortex is implicated in carrying out tasks that require theory of mind. Baron-Cohen et al. (1994) used SPECT to demonstrate a reciprocal activational change between left and right frontal polar regions when normal individuals carried out a recognition task for mental state items compared with items about body states. (Autistic children were already known to find this task difficult.) Goel, Grafman, Sadatov, and Hallet (1995) reported that adding a theory of mind component to an object labeling task (i.e., modeling the knowledge of another mind about objects) caused a relative activation increase in the left frontomedial cortex.

We suggest that this line of inquiry is well worth pursuing, because the reflective quality of theory of mind resonates strongly with the theories of the central executive in cognitive neuropsychology.

Measuring the Central Executive Experimentally

The central executive is the least understood component of working memory. Given that its role is supposed to be that of coordinating the two slave systems detailed in the model, the most obvious prediction is that dual-task performance should be particularly susceptible to impairment of the central executive. This possibility was first investigated by testing patients with dementia of the Alzheimer's type (AD), because this was the focus of interest at that time and because some encouraging pilot data seemed to demonstrate that the working memory impairment shown by AD patients was most readily attributable to a central executive deficit (Spinnler, Della Sala, Bandera, & Baddeley, 1988).

As predicted, it was found that when AD patients were required to perform two tasks simultaneously, one task tapping the resources of the phonological loop, and the other taxing the visuospatial sketchpad, their performance was impaired to an extent that cannot be accounted for in terms of the difficulty of the component tasks (Baddeley, Bressi, Della Sala, Logie, & Spinnler, 1991; Baddeley et al., 1986; Della Sala et al., 1995; Della Sala, Logie, & Spinnler, 1993). The results of the exploratory study, therefore, suggested that the ability to combine two tasks may be an executive process of some generality, and of potential practical, as well as theoretical, significance. For reviews see Baddeley (1996) and Baddeley and Della Sala (1996).

A further study (Baddeley & Della Sala, 1996) investigated the relation between dual-task performance and frontal lobe function. In this study, a group of patients with defined frontal lobe lesions were assigned to one of two subgroups on the basis of whether they were behaviorally normal or showed a behaviorally assessed dysexecutive syndrome. All participants were tested on a measure of central executive functioning based on dual-task performance, and on two tasks generally assumed to measure frontal lobe function, namely the Wisconsin Card Sorting Test and Word Fluency. The dysexecutive group found the dual task significantly more difficult. Interestingly, both groups scored similarly (and poorly) on the two frontal tests, suggesting that the dual task may prove to be a more sensitive measure to frontal lobe damage than the traditional tests.

This is not an isolated finding. Alderman (1996) demonstrated that patients with brain lesions who had failed to respond to a rehabilitation program based on a behavioral token economy rationale showed greater impairment on a dual task than did those who had benefited from the rehabilitation program. This result is particularly striking, given the often reported dissociation between performance on the so-called frontal tests and behavior in single case studies, where behaviorally dysexecutive patients have often performed adequately on the tests (Brazzelli et al., 1994; A. R. Damasio, 1995). We are tempted to conclude that dual-task performance is a potentially useful marker of dysexecutive behavior and damage to the prefrontal areas.

SOME GENERAL OBSERVATIONS AND CONCLUSIONS

From the time of the phrenologists (Spurzheim, 1815), many have argued that the basis of human mental life lies in the function of the frontal lobes of the brain. In support of this claim, there are several cogent considerations. There is, for example, the development of the human prefrontal cortex in comparison with nonhuman primates, a development that, in evolutionary terms, is both recent and marked. On the assumption that nonhuman primates lack the qualities of self-awareness and the powers of reflection and planning—but see Premack and Woodruff (1978)—it is reasonable to locate the substrate of those qualities in the region of the brain that shows the greatest interspecies difference.

There is indeed a considerable body of converging evidence for the view that the prefrontal cortex is concerned with the set of activities variously referred to as executive functioning, higher mental processes, and so on. Within this general framework, however, a variety of mechanisms have been advanced.

For example, Damasio's somatic marker hypothesis interprets executive functioning in terms of somatic and emotional states (A. R. Damasio, 1995). Other writers (Fernier, 1876; Luria, 1966) have focused on the inhibition of actions, a concept embodying the idea that, in general, there are dynamic hierarchical relations among functions and in particular that the prefrontal cortex achieves its control by inhibiting other functions where necessary. Grafman (1995) suggested that the scope and level of MKU processes progressively increase towards the anterior regions of the brain, and that the control processes at the highest level are to be found in the prefrontal cortex. Shallice (1988; Shallice & Burgess, 1991b) located the executive component of his model (the SAS) in the prefrontal cortex.

Baddeley (1996), although well aware of the difficulties with deriving localization arguments from cognitive models, suggested that the prefrontal cortex is a likely substrate for the central executive. In the theory of Goldman-Rakic (1995), which was derived almost entirely on the basis of animal data, the idea of frontal functioning, in the form of multiple working memory domains, has moved far beyond reflexive or sensorimotor functions and a long way toward the characteristics of executive functioning.

Despite this consensus, however, the data yielded by research on prefrontal lobe function are very difficult to interpret. At the outset, the search for a definitive frontal lobe syndrome in those who have sustained prefrontal lesions was impeded by reports of very similar presentations in patients with quite different illnesses that have nothing to do with brain lesions. (This is well illustrated by the case of King George III, who appears to have suffered from porphyria, a metabolic disease; and yet his symptoms strongly resemble many accounts of the sequelae of lesions in the prefrontal cortex.)

In most areas of scientific inquiry, there is the danger that observations may be truer reflections of the scientist's preconceptions than they are of nature. It is also important that the researcher, rather than simply trying to notch up confirming instances, should also be vigilant for data that do not support the theory. In this area, it has been argued, the researcher is more than usually at risk, because here (for obvious reasons) introspection exerts an especially powerful pull and there is the danger that the results of the research will turn out to be a self-fulfilling prophecy. It is natural for us to create a central executive in our own image, by analogy with our ineluctable experience of a continuous and unitary self.

The early work in this area, being based on case histories of those who had sustained prefrontal brain lesions, naturally followed an essentially syndromic paradigm. However, correlational, data-driven research of this kind tends to yield a vague sketch map of an unexplored landscape, rather than the Ordinance Survey that is required. To make further progress, research must be driven by theory. Moreover, the theory must be anchored in a bedrock of replicable empirical operations. A purely descriptive, atheoretical syndromic approach is, in any case, inevitably a fiction, because the choice of measures inevitably reflects ideas of a more or less theoretical nature. On the other hand, merely substituting a theoretically laden term such as executive for a descriptive one such as frontal is quite insufficient, without clear specification of the processes involved.

The search for a consistent pattern associated with lesions in the prefrontal lobes has yielded a disconcerting variety of results, including some patterns that seem contradictory. The view that there is a coherent and discoverable set of well-defined executive abilities and functions is belied by the numerous dissociations that have been reported in the literature. In part, such dissociations may well derive from the varying etiologies associated with prefrontal lesions, some of which invariably involve damage to nonfrontal areas also. There is also the possibility, however, that the notion of a single central executive, overseeing all manner of cognitive functions, may be false and that, in reality, there are several quite distinct aspects of executive functioning (Shallice & Burgess, 1991a). It has even been suggested that there are multiple executives in the prefrontal cortex, each concerned with the processing of information primarily from a specific posterior area of the brain (Goldman-Rakic et al., 1990).

There are also some important metatheoretical considerations. There is, for example, the danger of the homuncular fallacy which, to paraphrase Kenny (1991), is the attribution of whole-body predicates to parts that cannot have such predicates. A theorist commits the homuncular fallacy if, implicit in the theory is the suggestion that there is, somewhere within the brain, a little person, or gnome, monitoring what is going on and making whatever adjustments may be necessary. The positing of an implicit homunculus raises a worrying question: If there are gnomes within brains, are there not also brains within those gnomes, the workings of which themselves require explanation? The theorist is thus driven into an infinite regress. From the theoretical point of view, the concept of executive functioning is very attractive, because it seems to make sense of such a wide range of phenomena. Yet, despite its theoretical flexibility—perhaps because of it—there has always been cause for unease. For who supervises the super-visor or manages the manager? Is the concept of the central executive merely a homuncular theory, with all the attendant problems of circularity and infinite regress? Could it be said that Norman and Shallice's (1986) SAS or Baddeley and Hitch's (1974) central executive are homuncular theories?

It seems unwise to posit managing systems to account for various aspects of managerial thinking (planning, making decisions, etc.) without attempt-ing to make it clear precisely how and over which functions the control is exercised. It is essential to try to explain exactly how such supposed components govern the operation of cognitive subsystems.

One way of attempting to avoid the homunculus trap is to subdivide or fractionate the functions of the executive sytems, using cognitive and neuropsychological paradigms. Shallice and his associates (Shallice & Bur-gess, 1991a, 1993) and Stuss et al. (1995), have taken approaches of this kind and suggested a number of subfunctions. Advocates of fractionation argue cogently that concepts of executive functioning tend to be very general and difficult to operationalize. Several different kinds of fractiona-tion are being developed at present: cognitive or cognitive neuropsychologi-cal (Baddeley, 1996); neuroimaging (e.g., Stuss et al., 1995), and patient based and neuropsychological (Shallice & Burgess, 1991b).

The problem with the fractionation approach is that it tends to become data generated and increasingly difficult to relate to a coherent corpus of theory; in fact, it shares some of the difficulties that attach to the atheoreti-cal syndromic approach, and risks encountering a similar fate. Della Sala et al. (in press) suggested that, despite the foregoing cautions and caveats, the notion of a homuncular executive should be retained, at least in a metatheoretical or heuristic sense. In the past, the idea of executive coher-ence generated research that considerably clarified the manner in which the slave systems of the working memory system operated. More recently, Baddeley et al. (1997) described attempts to investigate that aspect of the central executive concerned with the deployment of attention as indicated by dual-task performance. The results of a factor analysis (Della Sala et al., in press) suggest some functional unity among frontal executive compo-nents. There would appear to be some merit in continuing to ascertain whether the various fractions studied really are components of the same coherent processing sytem, or are quite separate and independent activities.

So far, there have been a number of promising attempts to unify the various fractionation paradigms. For example, Grafman (1995) suggested that rather than being a separate component, the SAS may be a network of higher order MKU schemata. Schwartz (1995; Schwartz, Reed, Montgomery, Palmer, & Mayer, 1991), with her action-disorganization syndrome approach, is trying to integrate modern cognitive data with some of the observations reported in the clinical case histories.

The main goal of the lines of inquiry just described is the clarification of the cognitive subsystems that implement the various facets of executive (and, it is to be hoped, frontal) functioning. As yet, however, research into the component processes of executive functioning is still in its early stages, and important areas, such as problem solving, have not yet been approached in this way (Della Sala et al., in press).

Recent years have also seen a welcome rapprochement between the cognitive neuropsychological approaches just described and the neurophysiological anatomical formulations of those such as Goldman-Rakic, with its marriage of concepts from hitherto quite distinct disciplines.

Finally, the links between metacognition (Flavell, 1985) and executive functioning are obvious and important. The difference is that metacognition is an essentially conscious activity of self-monitoring, whereas those such as Shallice and Burgess made no claim that the operations they described are necessarily available to consciousness. Perhaps the promising convergence of these two quite distinct research traditions to a coherent view of high-level mental functioning may indicate that the gap between implicit and conscious functions may not be so great as has generally been supposed.

In locating the mentalistic concepts of self-awareness, self-monitoring, and excecutive functioning in the mechanisms of the prefrontal cortex, modern neuropsychology envisages what in Cartesian terms would be an unthinkable marriage of body and mind. Indeed, A. R. Damasio (1994) spoke of Descartes' error in creating such a sharp division between mind and body, which has drawn some trenchant responses (e.g., Dennett, 1995). It is certainly not our intention to enter that debate here; indeed, we accept that many apparently empirical questions are really epistemological or metaphysical questions in disguise and cannot be resolved by scientific inquiry. It is exciting, however, to consider that in the functioning of the prefrontal cortex may be found not only the interface between the mental and the physical but no less than the substrate (if not the substance) of thought itself.

REFERENCES

Alderman, N. (1996). Central executive deficit and response to operant conditioning methods. *Neuropsychological Rehabilitation*, 6 (3) 161–186.

Anderson, J. R. (1983). *The architecture of cognition*. Cambridge, MA: Harvard University Press.

Anderson, S. W., Damasio, H., Jones, R. D., & Tranel, D. (1991). Wisconsin Card Sorting Test as a measure of frontal lobe damage. *Journal of Clinical and Experimental Neuropsychology, 13*, 909–922.

Atkinson, R. C., & Shiffrin, R. M. (1968). Human memory: A proposed system and its control processes. In K. W. Spence (Ed.), *The psychology of learning and motivation: advances in research and theory* (Vol. 2, pp. 89–195). New York: Academic Press.

Baddeley, A. (1986). *Working memory*. Oxford, UK: Oxford University Press.

Baddeley, A. (1990). *Human memory: Theory and practice*. Hove, UK: Lawrence Erlbaum Associates.

Baddeley, A. (1996). Exploring the central executive. *Quarterly Journal of Experimental Psychology., 49A(1)*, 5–28.

Baddeley, A., Bressi, S., Della Sala, S., Logie, R., & Spinnler, H. (1991). The decline of working memory in Alzheimer's disease: A longitudinal study. *Brain, 114*, 2521–2542.

Baddeley, A., Bressi, S., Logie, R. H., Della Sala, S., & Spinnler, H. (1986). Dementia and working memory. *The Quarterly Journal of Experimental Psychology, 38A*, 603–618.

Baddeley, A., & Della Sala, S. (1996). Working memory and executive control. *Philosophical Transactions of the Royal Society Series B, 351*, 1346, 1397-1403.

Baddeley, A., Della Sala, S., Papagno, C., & Spinnler, H. (1997). Dual-task performance in dysexecutive and non-dysexecutive patients with a frontal lesion. *Neuropsychology, (11)*. 187–194.

Baddeley, A., & Hitch, G. (1974). Working memory. *The Psychology of Learning and Motivation, 8*, 47–89.

Barker, F. G. (1995). Phineas among the phrenologists: The American crowbar case and nineteenth century theories of cerebral localisation. *Journal of Neurosurgery, 82*, 672–682.

Baron-Cohen, S. (1992). The theory of mind hypothesis of autism: History and prospects of the idea. *The Psychologist: Bulletin of the British Psychological Society, 5*, 9–12.

Baron-Cohen, S., Ring, H., Moriarty, J., Schmitz, B., Costa, D., & Ell, P. (1994). Recognition of mental state terms: Clinical findings in children with autism and a functional neuroimaging study of normal adults. *British Journal of Psychiatry, 165*, 640–649.

Bartlett, F. C. (1932). *Remembering*. Cambridge, UK: Cambridge University Press.

Bechara, A., Damasio, A. R., Damasio, H., & Anderson, S. W. (1994). Insensitivity to future consequences following damage to human prefrontal cortex. *Cognition, 50*, 7–12.

Bennett, A. (1995). *The madness of King George*. London: Faber & Faber.

Benson, D. F. (1994). *The neurology of thinking*. New York: Oxford University Press.

Benton, A. L., Elithorn, A., Fogel, M. L., & Kerr, M. (1963). A perceptual maze task sensitive to brain damage, *Journal of neurology, neurosurgery and psychiatry, 26*, 540–544.

Berg, E. A. (1948). A simple objective test for measuring flexibility in thinking, *Journal of General Psychology, 39*, 15–22.

Bigelow, H. J. (1850). Dr. Harlow's case of recovery from the passage of an iron bar through the head. *American Journal of Medical Science, 20*, 1–22.

Blumer, D., & Benson, D. F. (1974). Personality changes with frontal and temporal lesions. In D. F. Benson & D. Blumer (Eds.), *Psychiatric aspects of neurologic disease* (pp. 151–169). New York: Grune & Stratton.

Boring, E. G. (1950). *A history of experimental psychology* (2nd ed.). Englewood Cliffs, NJ: Prentice-Hall.

Brazzelli, M., Colombo, N., Della Sala, S., & Spinnler, H. (1994). Spared and impaired cognitive abilities after bilateral frontal damage. *Cortex, 30*, 27–51.

Brickner, R. M. (1936). *The intellectual functions of the frontal lobes: Study based upon observation of a man after partial bilateral frontal lobectomy*. New York: Macmillan.

British Medical Association. (1968). *Porphyria—A royal malady*. London: Tavistock.

Brodmann, K. (1909). *Vergleichende Lokalisationlehre der Grosshirnrinde in ihren Prinzipien dargestellt auf Grand des Zellenbaues*. [Comparative principles of localisation of the cortex, organized on the basis of cellular structure] Leipzig, Germany: Barth.

Cahill, R. E. (1983). *New England's witches and wizards*. Peabody, MA: Chandler Smith.

Cattell, R. B. (1967). The theory of fluid and crystallised intelligence. *British Journal of Educational Psychology, 37*, 209–224.

Cicerone, K. D., Lazar, R. M., & Shapiro, W. R. (1983). Effects of frontal lobe lesions on hypothesis sampling during concept formation. *Neuropsychologia, 21*, 513–524.

Damasio, A. R. (1985). The frontal lobes. In K. M. Heilman & E. Valenstein (Eds.), *Clinical neuropsychology (2nd ed., pp. 339–376)*. New York: Oxford University Press.

Damasio, A. R. (1994). *Descartes' error: Emotion, reason and the human brain*. New York: Grosset/Putnam.

Damasio, A. R. (1995). On some functions of the human prefrontal cortex. *Annals of the New York Academy of Sciences, 769,* 241–252.

Damasio, A. R., Tranel, D., & Damasio, H. C. (1990). Individuals with sociopathic behavior caused by frontal damage fail to respond automatically to social stimuli. *Behavioral and Brain Research, 41,* 81–94.

Damasio, A. R., Tranel, D., & Damasio, H. (1991). Somatic markers and the guidance of behavior. In H. S. Levin, H. M. Eisenberg, & A. L. Benton (Eds.), *Frontal lobe function and dysfunction* (pp. 217–229). New York: Oxford University Press.

Damasio, H. C. (1991). Neuroanatomy of frontal lobes in vivo: A comment on methodology. In H. S. Levin, H. M. Eisenberg, & A. L. Benton (Eds.), *Frontal lobe function and dysfunction* (pp. 92–124). New York: Oxford University Press.

Damasio, H. C., Grabowski, T., Frank, R., Galaburda, A. M., & Damasio, A. R. (1994). The return of Phineas Gage: Clues about the brain from the skull of a famous patient. *Science, 264,* 1102–1105.

Della Sala, S., Baddeley, A., Papagno, C., & Spinnler, H. (1995). Dual task paradigm: A means to examine the Central Executive. *Annals of the New York Academy of Sciences, 769,* 161–172.

Della Sala, S., Gray, C., Spinnler, H., & Trivelli, C. (in press). Frontal lobe functioning: The riddle revisited. *Archives of clinical neuropsychology.*

Della Sala, S., & Logie, R. H. (1993). When working memory does not work: The role of working memory in neuropsychology. In F. Boller & H. Spinnler (Eds.), *Handbook of neuropsychology* (Vol. 8, pp. 1–62). Amsterdam: Elsevier.

Della Sala, S., Logie, R., & Spinnler, H. (1993). Is primary memory deficit of Alzheimer patients due to a "central executive" impairment? *Journal of Neurolinguistics, 7,* 325–346.

Dennett, D. C. (1995). Book review. Descartes' error: Emotion, reason and the human brain–Damasio, A. R., *Times Literary Supplement,* 4821, 3–4.

D'Esposito, M. D., Detre, J. D., Shin, R. K., Atlas, S., & Grossman, M. (1995). The neural basis of the central executive system of working memory. *Nature, 378,* 279–281.

Drewe, E. A. (1974). The effect of type and area of brain lesion on Wisconsin Card Sorting Test performance. *Cortex, 10,* 159–174.

Duncan, J. (1990). Goal weighting and the choice of behaviour in a complex world. *Ergonomics, 33,* 1265–1279.

Duncan, J. (1995). Attention, intelligence and the frontal lobes. In M. S. Gazzaniga (Ed.), *The cognitive neurosciences* (pp. 721–734). Cambridge, MA: MIT Press.

Duncan, J., Johnson, R., Swales, M., & Freer, C. (1997). Frontal lobe deficits after head injury: Unity or diversity of function? *Cognitive4 neuropsychology, 16* (5), 713–741.

Eslinger, P. J., & Damasio, A. R. (1985). Severe disturbance of higher cognition after bilateral frontal lobe ablation: Patient E.V.R. *Neurology, 35,* 1731–1741.

Ferrier, D. (1876). *The Functions of the Brain.* London: Smith & Elder.

Flavell, J. H. (1985). *Cognitive development.* Englewood Cliffs, NJ: Prentice-Hall.

Fodor, J. A. (1983). *The modularity of mind: An essay on faculty psychology.* Cambridge, MA: MIT Press.

Funahashi, S., Chaffee, M. V., & Goldman-Rakic, P. S. (1993). Prefrontal neuronal activity in monkeys performing a delayed anti-saccade task. *Nature, 365,* 753–756.

Fuster, J. M. (1989). *The prefrontal cortex.* (2nd ed.). New York: Raven.

Fuster, J. M. (1995). Temporal processing. *Annals of the New York Academy of Sciences, 769* 173–181.

Geschwind, N. (1977). *Lectures in Neurobehavior.* Boston: Harvard Medical School.

Goel, V., Grafman, J., Sadatov, N., & Hallet, M. (1995). Modeling other minds. *Neuroreport, 6*(13), 1741–1746.

Goldman-Rakic, P. S. (1987). Circuitry of the primate frontal cortex and regulation of behavior by representational memory. In F. Plum (Ed.), *Handbook of physiology. the nervous system: Higher functions of the brain* (Vol. 5, pp. 373–417). Bethesda, MD: American Physiological Society.

Goldman-Rakic, P. S. (1990). The prefrontal contribution to working memory and conscious experience. In J. C. Eccles & O. Creutzfeldt (Eds.), *The principles of the design and operation of the brain* (pp. 389–487). Berlin: Springer-Verlag.

Goldman-Rakic, P. S. (1992). Working memory and the mind. *Scientific American, 267,* 111–117.

Goldman-Rakic, P. S. (1994). The issue of memory in the study of prefrontal function. In A.-M. Thierry, J. Glowinski, P. S. Goldman-Rakic, & Y. Christen (Eds.), *Motor and cognitive functions of the prefrontal cortex* (pp. 112–121). New York: Springer-Verlag.

Goldman-Rakic, P. S. (1995). Architecture of the prefrontal cortex and the central executive. *Annals of the New York Academy of Sciences, 769,* 71–84.

Goldman-Rakic, P. S., Funahashi, S., & Bruce, C. J. (1990). Neocortical memory circuits. *Quarterly Journal of Quantitative Biology, 55,* 1025–1038.

Grafman, J. (1994). Alternative frameworks for the conceptualisation of frontal lobe functions. In F. Boller & J. Grafman (Eds.), *Handbook of neuropsychology,* (Vol. 9 pp. 187–202). Amsterdam: Elsevier.

Grafman, J. (1995). Similarities and distinctions among current models of prefrontal cortical functions. *Annals of the New York Academy of Sciences, 769,* 337–368.

Grant, D. A., & Berg, E. A. (1948). A behavioral analysis of degree of reinforcement and ease of shifting to new responses in a Weigl-type card sorting problem. *Journal of Experimental Psychology, 38,* 404–411.

Harlow, J. M. (1848). Passage of an iron rod through the head. *Boston Medical and Surgical Journal, 39,* 389–393.

Harlow, J. M. (1868). Recovery from the passage of an iron bar through the head. *Publications of the Massachusetts Medical Society, 2,* 327–347.

Hebb, D. O. (1939). Intelligence in man after large removals of cerebral tissue: Report of four left frontal lobe cases. *Journal of General Psychology, 21,* 73–87.

Heck, E. T., & Bryer, J. B. (1986). Superior sorting and categorising ability in a case of bilateral frontal atrophy: An exception to the rule. *Journal of Clinical and Experimental Neuropsychology, 8,* 313–316.

Hughes, C., & Russell, J. (1993). Autistic children's difficulty with mental disengagement from an object: Its implications for theories of autism. *Developmental Psychology, 21,* 498–510.

Institute for Personality and Ability Testing. (1973). *Measuring intelligence with the culture fair tests.* Champaign, IL: Institute for Personality and Ability Testing.

Jacobsen, C. F. (1936). Studies of cerebral function in primates. *Comparative Psychology Monographs, 13,* 1–68.

Jacobsen, C. F., Wolf, J. B., & Jackson, T. A. (1935). An experimental analysis of the frontal association area in primates. *Journal of Nervous and Mental Disorders, 82,* 1–14.

James, B. (1992). The unfolded shape of the brain. *Journal of the Royal Society of Medicine, 85,* 551–552.

Jastrowitz, M. (1888). Beitrage sur Localisation im Grosshirn und ueber deren praktische Verwerthung. [Contribution to lodcalisation in the brain and its practical implications] *Dtsch. Med. Wochenschrift, 14,* 81–83, 108–112, 125–128, 151–153, 172–175, 188–192, 209–211.

Jones-Gotman, M., & Milner, B. (1978). Design fluency: The invention of nonsense drawings after focal cortical lesions. *Neuropsychologia, 15,* 653–674.

Kenny, A. (1991). The homunculus fallacy. In J. Hyman (Ed.), *Investigating psychology: Sciences of the mind after Wittgenstein* (pp. 155–165). London: Routledge.

Kluver, H., & Bucy, P. C. (1937). Psychic blindness and other symptoms following bilateral temporal lobectomy in rhesus monkeys. *American Journal of Physiology, 119,* 352–353.

Kolb, B., & Milner, B. (1981a). Performance of complex arm and facial movements after focal brain lesions. *Neuropsychologia, 19,* 505–514.

Kolb, B., & Milner, B. (1981b). Observations on spontaneous facial expressions after focal cerebral excisions and after intracarotid injection of sodium amytal. *Neuropsychologia, 19,* 514–515.

Kolb, B., & Whishaw, I. Q. (1990). *Fundamentals of human neuropsychology* (3rd ed.). New York: Freeman.

Lenzi, G. L., & Padovani, A. (1994). The contribution of imaging techniques to current knowledge of the frontal lobes. In F. Boller & J. Grafman (Eds.), *Handbook of neuropsychology* (Vol. 9, pp. 83–124). Amsterdam: Elsevier.

Leslie, A. M. (1991). The theory of mind deficit in autism: Evidence for a modular mechanism of development. In A. Whiten (Ed.), *Natural theories of mind: Evolution, development and simulation of everyday mindreading* (pp. 63–78). Oxford, UK: Basil Blackwell.

Lezak, M. D. (1993). Newer contributions to the neuropsychological assessment of executive functions. *Journal of Head Trauma Rehabilitation, 8,* 24–31.

Lhermite, F. (1983). "Utilization behaviour" and its relation to lesions of the frontal lobes. *Brain, 106,* 237–255.

Luria, A. R. (1959). *The regulative role of speech in normal and abnormal behavior.* New York: Pergamon.

Luria, A. R. (1961). *The role of speech in regulation of normal and abnormal behavior.* London: Pergamon.

Luria, A. R. (1966). *Higher cortical functions in man.* New York: Basic Books.

Luria, A. R., & Homskaya, E. D. (1964). Disturbances in the regulative role of speech with frontal lesions. In J. M. Warren & K. Akert (Eds.), *The frontal granular cortex and behavior* (pp. 353–371). New York: McGraw-Hill.

Macalpine, I., & Hunter, R. (1993). *George III and the mad-business.* London: Penguin.

Milner, B. (1963). Effects of different brain lesions on card sorting. *Archives of Neurology, 9,* 90–100.

Milner, B. (1964). Some effects of frontal lobectomy in man. In J. M. Warren & K. Akert (Eds.), *The frontal granular cortex and behavior* (pp. 313–334). New York: McGraw-Hill.

Milner, B. (1971). Interhemispheric differences in the localization of psychological processes in man. *British Medical Bulletin, 27,* 272–277.

Nelson, H. E. (1976). A modified card-sorting test sensitive to frontal lobe defects. *Cortex, 12,* 313–324.

Newell, A., & Simon, H. (1972). *Human problem solving.* Englewood Cliffs, NJ: Prentice-Hall.

Norman, D. A. (1981). Categorisation of action slips. *Psychological Review, 88,* 1–15.

Norman, D. A., & Shallice, T. (1986). Attention to action: Willed and automatic control of behaviour. In G. E. Schwarts & D. Shapiro (Eds.), *Consciousness and Self-regulation: Advances in research and theory* (Vol. 4, pp. 1–18). New York: Plenum.

Oscar-Berman, M., McNemara, P., & Freedman, M. (1991). Delayed-response tasks: Parallels between experimental ablation studies and findings in patients with frontal lesions. In H. S. Levin, H. M. Eisenberg, & A. L. Benton (Eds.), *Frontal lobe function and dysfunction* (pp. 230–255). New York: Oxford University Press.

Owen, A. M., Downes, J. J., Sahakian, B. J., Polkey, C. E., & Robbins, T. W. (1990). Planning and spatial working memory following frontal lobe lesions in man. *Neuropsychologia, 28,* 1021–1034.

Ozonoff, S. (1991). Reliability and validity of the Wisconsin Card Sorting Test in studies of autism. *Neuropsychology, 9*(4), 491–500.

Pandya, D. N., & Yeterian, E. H. (1996). Comparison of prefrontal architecture and connection. *Philosophical Transactions of the Royal Society of London, Series B, 351.* No. 1346, pp. 1423–1432.

Parsons, L. M., Fox, P. T., Hunter Downs, J., Glass, T., Hirsch, T. B., Martin, C. C., Jerabek, P. A., & Lancaster, J. L. (1995). Use of implicit motor imagery for visual shape discrimination as revealed by PET. *Nature, 375,* 54–58.

Petrides, M. (1982). Motor conditional associative learning after selective prefrontal lesions in the monkey. *Behavioural and brain research, 5,* 407–413.

Petrides, M. (1995). Functional organisation of the human frontal cortex for mnemonic processing: Evidence from neuroimaging studies. *Annals of the New York Academy of Sciences, 769,* 85–96.

Poppelreuter, W. (1917). *Die psychischen Schädigungen durch Kopfschuss in Kriege 1914/1916.* [Psychological damage from head wounds in the 1914–1916 war,] Leipzig, Germany: Leopold Voss Verlag.

Premack, D., & Woodruff, G. (1978). Does the chimpanzee have a "theory of mind"? *Behavior and Brain Sciences, 1,* 516–526.

Prior, M., & Hoffman, W. (1990). Brief report: Neuropsychological testing of autistic children through an exploration with frontal lobe tests. *Journal of Autism and Developmental Disorders, 20,* 581–590.

Ramier, A-M., & Hecaen, H. (1970). Role respectif des atteintes frontales et de la lateralisation lesionnelle dans les deficits de la 'fluence verbale'. [The respective role of frontal injuries and lesion location in deficits of verbal fluency]. *Revue de la Neurologie, 123,* 17–22.

Raven, J. C. (1965). *Advanced progressive matrices. Sets I and II.* London: H. K. Lewis.

Reid, T. (1785). *Essays on the intellectual powers of man.* Edinburgh, UK: McLachlan & Stewart.

Reitan, R. M., & Wolfson, D. (1994). A selective and critical review of neuropsychological deficits and the frontal lobes. *Neuropsychology Review, 4,* 161–198.

Ricci, C., & Blundo, C. (1990). Perception of ambiguous figures after focal brain lesions. *Neuropsychologia, 28,* (11), 1163–1173.

Robinson, A. L., Heaton, R. K., Lehman, R. A. W., & Stilson, D. W. (1980). The utility of the Wisconsin Card Sorting Test in detecting and localising frontal lobe lesions. *Journal of Consulting and Clinical Psychology, 48,* 605–641.

Rumelhart, D. E., & Norman, D. A. (1985). Representation of knowledge. In A. M. Aitkenhead & J. M. Slack (Eds.), *Issues in cognitive modelling* (pp. 15–62). London: Lawrence Erlbaum Associates.

Russell, J., Mauthner, N., Sharpe, S., & Tidswell, T. (1991). The windows task as a measure of strategic deception in preschoolers and autistic subjects. *British Journal of Developmental Psychology, 9,* 331–349.

Rylander, G. (1939). *Personality changes after operations on the frontal lobes: A clinical study of 32 cases.* London: Oxford University Press.

Schank, R. C. (1982). *Dynamic memory*. New York: Cambridge University Press.

Schank, R. C., & Abelson, R. (1977). *Scripts, plans, goals and understanding*. Hillsdale, NJ: Lawrence Erlbaum Associates.

Schwartz, M. F. (1995). Re-examining the role of executive functions in routine action production. *Annals of the New York Academy of Sciences, 769,* 321–335.

Schwartz, M. F., Reed, E. L., Montgomery, W., Palmer, C., & Mayer, M. H. (1991). The quantitative description of action disorganisation after brain damage: A case study. *Cognitive Neuropsychology, 8,* 381–414.

Semmes, J. S., Weinstein, L., Ghent, L., & Teuber, H.-L. (1963). Impaired orientation in personal and extrapersonal space. *Brain, 86,* 747–772.

Shallice, T. (1982). Specific impairments of planning. *Philosophical Transactions of the Royal Society of London, B298,* 199–209.

Shallice, T. (1988). *From neuropsychology to mental structure*. Cambridge, UK: Cambridge University Press.

Shallice, T., & Burgess, W. P. (1991a). Deficits in strategy application following frontal lobe damage in man. *Brain, 114,* 727–741.

Shallice, T., & Burgess, W. P. (1991b). Higher order cognitive impairments and frontal lobe lesions in man. In H. S. Levin, H. M. Eisenberg, & A. L. Benton (Eds.), *Frontal lobe function and dysfunction* (pp. 125–138). New York: Oxford University Press.

Shallice, T., & Burgess, W. P. (1993). Supervisory control of action and thought selection. In A. Baddeley & L. Weiskrantz (Eds.), *Attention: Selection, awareness and control: A tribute to Donald Broadbent* (pp. 171–187). Oxford, UK: Clarendon.

Shallice, T., Burgess, W. P., Schon, F., & Baxter, M. D. (1989). The origin of utilisation behaviour. *Brain, 112,* 1587–1598.

Shallice, T., & Evans, M. E. (1978). The involvement of the frontal lobes in cognitive estimation. *Cortex, 14,* 294–303.

Shiffrin, R. M., & Schneider, W. (1977). Controlled and automatic information processing II: Perceptual learning, automatic attending and a general theory. *Psychological Review, 84,* 127–190.

Shimamura, A. P. (1995). Memory and the prefrontal cortex. *Annals of the New York Academy of Sciences, 769,* 151–160.

Shimamura, A. P., Janowsky, J. S., & Squire, L. R. (1991). What is the role of frontal lobe damage in memory disorders? In H. S. Levin, H. M. Eisenberg, & A. L. Benton (Eds.), *Frontal lobe function and dysfunction* (pp. 173–195). New York: Oxford University Press.

Sirigu, A., Zalla, T., Pillon, B., Grafman, J., Agid, Y., & Dubois, B. (1995). Selective impairment in managerial knowledge following pre-frontal cortex damage. *Cortex, 31*(2), 301–316.

Smith, M. L., Leonard, G., Crane, J., & Milner, B. (1994). The effect of frontal or temporal lesions on susceptibility to interference in spatial memory. *Neuropsychologia, 33*(3), 275–285.

Smith, M. L. & Milner, B. (1984). Differential effects of frontal lesions on cognitive estimation and spatial memory. *Neuropsychologia, 22,* 697–705.

Spinnler, H., Della Sala, S., Bandera, R., & Baddeley, A. (1988). Dementia, ageing and the structure of human memory. *Cognitive Neuropsychology, 5,* 193–211.

Spurzheim, J. C. (1815). *The physiognomical system of Drs. Gall and Spurzheim, founded on an anatomical and physiological examination of the nervous system in general, and of the brain in particular, and indicating the dispositions and manifestations of the mind*. London: Baldwin, Cruddock & Joy.

Spurzheim, J. C. (1826). *Phrenology, in connection with the study of physiognomy: Part I: Characters*. London: Baldwin, Cruddock & Joy.

Stuss, D. T., & Benson, D. F. (1986). *The frontal lobes*. (2nd ed.). New York: Raven.

Stuss, D. T., Shallice, T., Alexander, M. P., & Picton, T. W. (1995). A multidisciplinary approach to anterior attentional functions. *Annals of the New York Academy Of Sciences, 769,* 191–212.

Sussman, G. J. (1975). *A computational model of skill acquisition*. New York: American Elsevier.

Teuber, H-L. (1964). The riddle of frontal lobe function in man. In J. M. Warren & K. Akert (Eds.), *The frontal granular cortex and behavior* (pp. 410–444). New York: McGraw-Hill.

Teuber, H-L., & Mishkin, M. (1954). Judgement of visual and postural vertical after brain injury. *Journal of Psychology, 38,* 161–175.

Tranel, D. (1994). "Acquired sociopathy": The development of sociopathic behavior following focal brain damage. In D. C. Fowles, P. Sutker, & S. H. Goodman (Eds.), *Progress in experimental personality and psychopathology research* (Vol. 17, pp. 285–311). New York: Springer.

Tranel, D., Anderson, S. W., & Benton, A. (1994). Development of the concept of 'executive function' and its relationship to the frontal lobes. In F. Boller & J. Grafman (Eds.), *Handbook of neuropsychology* (Vol. 9, pp. 125–148). Amsterdam: Elsevier.

Tranel, D., Damasio, H. C., & Damasio, A. R. (1995). Double dissociation between overt and covert face recognition. *Journal of Cognitive Neuroscience, 7,* 425–432.

Vendrell, P., Junque, C., Pujol, J., Jurado, M. A., Molet, J., & Grafman, J. (1995). The role of prefrontal regions in the Stroop task. *Neuropsychologia, 33 (3),* 341–352.

Warren, J. M., & Akert, K. (Eds.). (1964). *The frontal granular cortex and behavior.* New York: McGraw-Hill.

Wernicke, C. (1906). *Grundrisse der Psychiatrie.* [Basics of psychiatry]. Leipzig, Germany: Verlag von George Thieme.

Wilson, F. A. W., O'Scalaidhe, S. P., & Goldman-Rakic, P. S. (1993). Dissociation of object and spatial processing domains in primate prefrontal cortex. *Science, 260,* 1955–1958.

Zeigarnik, B. (1961). *Pathology of thinking.* Moscow: Moscow University Press.

5

The Role of Metacognitive Processes in the Regulation of Memory Performance

Asher Koriat
Morris Goldsmith
University of Haifa

The increased interest in consciousness during the past two decades has opened once again the long-standing issue regarding the causal role of conscious experience in behavior. Is consciousness an inherent component of cognitive functioning, or is it merely an epiphenomenon that—from an information-processing standpoint—could just as well be done without. Among students of metacognition there is an implicit assumption that the subjective experience associated with monitoring one's own cognitive processing does in fact guide and regulate action. Thus, for instance, if we believe that we will not remember the name of a person who has just been introduced to us (a low *judgment of learning*), we may take special measures to commit the name to memory. When we fail to recall that name in a subsequent encounter with the person, we will probably spend more time searching for it if we have a strong gut feeling that we should know the name (a strong *feeling of knowing*). And if the name "George" finally does come to mind, we will still hesitate to burst out with "Hello George" if we are not quite sure that that really is his name (a low *confidence judgment*).

In this chapter, we focus on the last stage of the process of remembering and examine the conditions that make one act on a retrieved piece of information. In particular, we address the question of how the metamemory processes of monitoring and control affect people's performance in tasks intended to tap memory.

THE CONTRIBUTION OF METAMEMORY PROCESSES TO MEMORY PERFORMANCE: SOME ILLUSTRATIVE EXAMPLES

When attempting to assess memory performance—for example, memory for the material studied during an academic course, or memory for a witnessed event—we may not be aware of the fact that we are often also tapping metamemory processes that are utilized by the rememberer in the service of achieving certain goals. Although the effects of such metamemory processes on memory performance are perhaps most clearly seen in functionally rich, naturalistic settings, they undoubtedly exist in more sterile laboratory contexts as well.

To illustrate the potential contribution of metamemory processes to memory performance and highlight the dilemma created by this contribution, consider the following example. You are grading a course examination that includes a set of short-answer questions, and find that on the exam you are currently checking, the answer to a particular question has been crossed out. Presumably, the question should be scored as an omission. Nevertheless, being tempted to read the crossed-out answer, you find it to be perfectly correct (a situation that in our experience occurs more often than one might think). What should you do? Should you grant the student with full credit? After all, it appears that he or she "knows" the correct answer. Or should the student be penalized because he or she apparently does not "know that he or she knows" the solicited information? More generally, should poor monitoring and unwise strategic decision making be allowed to influence the student's grade on the test, and ultimately, success in the course?

This example illustrates the point that in many situations memory performance depends not only on what might be termed *memory*, but also on monitoring and control processes that fall under the rubric of *metamemory* (see also Barnes, Nelson, Dunlosky, Mazzoni, & Narens, in press; Nelson & Narens, 1990; and other chapters in this volume). In this case, the student apparently first thought that he or she knew the answer (monitoring) and wrote it down (control), but then changed his or her mind about the correctness of the answer (monitoring) and decided to cross it out (control). The monitoring aspect, then, involves the subjective assessment of how likely it is that an answer that comes to mind is correct, whereas the control aspect concerns the operational decision to write down the answer or withhold it, or to cross out an answer that one has just written or leave it for inclusion in the final scoring.

Note that in the situation just described there was no explicit penalty for a wrong answer, so the student would not have risked losing points by venturing an answer. Apparently other motivations were involved apart from the desire to get the highest score possible—perhaps the motivation to be accurate, not to make a fool of oneself, and so forth. In other cases, however, the test may be designed such that the student is explicitly required to make a strategic choice, and here metamemory processes will certainly contribute to the final score. For example, the student may be required to answer only a subset of questions of his or her choice, say, four out of six. Here it is clear that the scores will be affected by the student's ability to choose the right questions to answer, which in turn should depend on his or her ability to monitor the likelihood of providing a correct and complete answer to each question. Two students who have the same degree of knowledge can attain different scores if they differ in their monitoring ability.

Now consider a further example. Many of the standard psychometric tests of intelligence and scholastic aptitude (e.g., the Scholastic Aptitude Test and the Graduate Record Examination subject tests) use a multiple-choice format in conjunction with *formula scoring* procedures (Thurstone, 1919) that are designed to discourage guessing and also to correct for it by levying a greater penalty for incorrect answers than for omissions. It is not always clear to test administrators that performance on such tests also taps metacognitive ability; that is, the ability to make effective decisions about whether to risk providing an answer to a question or instead to omit (Budescu & Bar-Hillel, 1993). Thus, for instance, one test-taker may tend to guess on the basis of even a small amount of partial knowledge, whereas another may feel uncomfortable providing an answer about which he or she is unsure (Abu-Sayf, 1979; Gafni, 1990). One test-taker may be effective in distinguishing between answers that are more likely or less likely to be correct, whereas another test-taker may be less effective in discriminating between what he or she knows and does not know (Angoff, 1989; Budescu & Bar-Hillel, 1993). Should differences in the operation and effectiveness of the monitoring and control processes of these test-takers be allowed to influence their scores on these tests? Exactly what types of knowledge and abilities are these tests intended to measure?

Finally, turning to the many real-life situations in which people recount past events, the effects of metamemory processes on memory performance are even more apparent. In such situations, people generally have great freedom in deciding which pieces of information to report and which to omit, what perspective to adopt, what level of generality or detail to provide in reporting the various aspects of an event, and so on. Consider, for instance, an eyewitness to a crime. Here, too, the "scoring rule," so to speak, explicitly discourages commission errors and guessing. In fact, the oath taken by a person on the witness stand is "to tell the whole truth and nothing but the truth." Thus, the witness' testimony is likely to be mediated by metamemory processes in which he or she assesses the likelihood that various pieces of information that come to mind are correct, and decides whether or not to report them in accordance with the perceived functional incentives. When considering such testimony, we might be more inclined (than in the case of academic testing) to treat the underlying metamemory processes as being part and parcel of the person's "memory" itself. After all, the main concern in the courtroom is with the accuracy or dependability of the witness' report; that is, with the extent to which the testimony can be trusted (see Deffenbacher, 1991).

These examples bring to the fore two basic points. First, there are many situations in which memory reporting is mediated by the metamemory processes of monitoring and control, and little is known about how such processes operate or about the effects that such processes have on actual performance. Second, it is not generally realized by researchers and test administrators that a principled decision should be made regarding whether or not to include the effects of metamemory processes in the assessment of memory performance. In fact, it is a rather complicated matter to decide how metamemory processes should be treated when assessing memory performance. We now turn to a review of work we have done that addresses both of these points.

THE ROLE OF REPORT OPTION IN MEDIATING ACCURACY-BASED AND QUANTITY-BASED MEMORY PERFORMANCE

When considering the role of metamemory processes in memory reporting, it is important to distinguish between two properties of memory, its quantity and its accuracy. In fact, our initial interest in the performance conse- quences of metamemory processes derived from an examination of some basic differences between quantity-oriented and accuracy-oriented memory research (Koriat & Goldsmith, 1994, 1996a, 1996b). Traditionally, memory research has been guided by a *storehouse* metaphor of memory, leading to the evaluation of memory in terms of the amount of stored information that can be recovered. The more recent wave of naturalistic, "everyday" memory research, however, has inclined more toward a *correspondence* conception of memory, in which memory is evaluated in terms of its *accuracy* or faithfulness in representing past events. The ramifications of this shift for both memory research and memory assessment are complex and far reaching (Koriat & Goldsmith, 1996a), and in fact, the correspondence metaphor can lead to an accuracy-oriented assessment approach that is qualitatively different from the traditional, quantity-oriented approach. For present purposes, however, we restrict our attention to memory accuracy and memory quantity performance as they are typically evaluated in a standard item-based assessment context.

In item-based memory assessment, the memory test or report is segmented into discrete items or propositions that can be dichotomously evaluated as either right or wrong, and that are generally given equal weight in computing the overall memory score. This, for instance, is the approach taken in the vast amount of memory research based on the list-learning paradigm (Ebbinghaus, 1964; Puff, 1982), as well as in much psychometric and educational testing (Cronbach, 1984). In this context, quantity-based and accuracy-based memory measures can be distinguished in terms of *input-bound* and *output-bound* measures, respectively: Quantity measures, traditionally used to tap the amount of studied information that can be recovered, are input-bound, reflecting the likelihood that each input item is correctly remembered (e.g., the percentage of studied words recalled or recognized). Accuracy measures, in contrast, evaluate the *dependability* of memory—the extent to which remembered information can be trusted to be correct. Hence, these measures are output bound: They reflect the conditional probability that each *reported* item is correct (e.g., the percentage of reported words that actually appeared in the studied list). Essentially, then, whereas input-bound measures hold the person responsible for what he or she fails to report, output-bound measures hold the person accountable only for what he or she does report.

Despite the different definitions of quantity-based and accuracy-based memory measures, there are conditions in which the two types of measures are operationally equivalent: The critical factor is report option; that is, whether or not participants are required to answer all items. When memory is tested through a *forced-report* procedure, memory quantity and accuracy measures are necessarily equivalent, because the likelihood of remembering each input item (quantity) is equal to the likelihood that each reported item is correct (accuracy). Accuracy and quantity measures can differ substantially, however, under *free-report* conditions, in which participants are implicitly or explicitly given the option either to volunteer a piece of information or to abstain (e.g., respond "I don't know"; Neisser, 1988). Most everyday remembering is of this sort. Also, in memory research, the most common example is the standard free-recall task, in which reporting is essentially controlled by the participant. Under free-report conditions, people tend to provide only information that they believe is likely to be correct, so that their performance is mediated by a decision process employed to avoid incorrect answers (Klatzky & Erdelyi, 1985; Koriat & Goldsmith, 1994). Because the number of volunteered answers is generally smaller than the number of input items, the output-bound (accuracy) and input-bound (quantity) memory measures can vary substantially.

Report option is important however, not only because it allows memory accuracy to be operationally distinguished from memory quantity, but also because it has a substantial effect on memory accuracy performance. The contribution of report option was revealed in several experiments (Koriat & Goldsmith, 1994) that orthogonally manipulated report option (free vs. forced reporting), test format (open-ended or cued recall vs. multiple-choice recognition), and memory measure (accuracy vs. quantity). In one experiment (Koriat & Goldsmith, 1994, Experiment 1), we gave participants a 60-item general-knowledge test, in which all answers were either single-word terms (e.g., photosynthesis) or proper names (e.g., Mozart). In addition to the standard methods of free recall[1] and forced recognition, we also included the less common procedures of forced recall (in which the participants were required to answer all items) and free recognition (in which the participants were allowed to skip over items). Both quantity and accuracy scores were derived for all four methods. The results indicated that although test format was the critical factor affecting memory quantity performance, recognition superior to recall, it was report option that was the critical factor affecting memory accuracy: First, free-report accuracy performance was substantially better than forced-report performance for both the recall and the recognition test formats. Second, under free-report conditions, in which the recall and recognition participants had equal opportunity to screen their answers, the recognition and recall accuracy scores were virtually identical. This basic pattern was also obtained using a

---

[1]We use the term *free recall* in opposition to *forced recall*, in order to denote the option of *free report*. In traditional usage, however, the former term has been employed in opposition to serial recall, indicating only that the individual is free to choose the order in which items are to be recalled.

standard list-learning paradigm (Koriat & Goldsmith, 1994, Experiment 2) and when the participants were given a very strong incentive for accuracy (Koriat & Goldsmith, 1994, Experiment 3).

These results suggest that memory accuracy performance can be improved considerably when people are allowed to control their own memory reporting. Across the three experiments, the accuracy advantage of free over forced report ranged from 61% to 89% for recall and from 15% to 38% for recognition. Furthermore, given the option of free report, people can apparently adjust their memory accuracy in accordance with the operative level of accuracy incentive: When our free-report participants were given a very high accuracy incentive (receiving a monetary bonus for each correct answer, but forfeiting all winnings if even a single incorrect answer was volunteered), they improved their accuracy performance substantially compared to performance under a more moderate incentive (in which the penalty for each incorrect answer equaled the bonus for each correct answer). In fact, fully one fourth of the high-incentive participants succeeded in achieving 100% accuracy. The improved accuracy, however, was accompanied by a corresponding reduction in quantity performance (i.e., in the number of correct answers provided or selected).

What are the implications of such findings for the role of metamemory processes in mediating memory performance? Perhaps the most basic implication is that one cannot simply ignore the operation of these processes, particularly as far as memory accuracy is concerned.

Let us go back and consider some of the earlier memory examples. Clearly, to elicit accurate testimony from witnesses, they should be allowed to tell their story under free-report conditions; that is, they should be encouraged to say "I don't remember" if they feel they do not remember. As a matter of fact, this idea has been incorporated into most witness interview guidelines (e.g., Fisher & Geiselman, 1992; Flanagan, 1981; Hilgard & Loftus, 1979), in which interrogators are generally cautioned against putting words in the witness' mouth or pressing the witness for an answer. The advice is to allow the witness to tell his or her story first in a free narrative format before moving on to more directed forms of questioning, and even then to place greater faith in the accuracy of the former testimony than the latter[2]. In the early stages of an investigation, however, one might be interested primarily

---

[2]Actually, this recommendation regarding the use of free-narrative questioning stems from a great deal of eyewitness research that has focused on test format rather than on report option: Directed questioning and recognition tests are held to be more likely than open-ended questioning and recall tests to contaminate a person's memory with information contained in the questions themselves (see, e.g., Gorenstein & Ellsworth, 1980; Hilgard & Loftus, 1979; Loftus, 1979; Loftus & Hoffman, 1989).

in extracting as much information from the witness as possible (to obtain potential "leads"), even if some of that information turns out to be incorrect. In that case, it may be necessary to find ways to prevent witnesses from employing their natural memory screening processes (Fisher & Geiselman, 1992), because unless those processes are employed with perfect efficiency, the witness might unwittingly screen out correct (and crucial) information along with the incorrect answers (discussed later).

Similar concerns also arise in the more standard, quantity-oriented testing situations, such as in the academic, psychometric, and laboratory testing situations, discussed earlier. We considered one case, for instance, in which correct information was withheld (crossed out) due to faulty monitoring processes and apparently hidden motivations, such as the motivation to be accurate, that were ostensibly extraneous to the task. How much more so should memory performance be subject to the vicissitudes of the test-taker's monitoring and control processes in those cases in which the person is explicitly encouraged to employ such processes, as when the test-taker is allowed to choose which questions to answer (e.g., in academic testing), or to omit answers to items about which he or she is unsure (e.g., under formula scoring procedures)?

From both a theoretical and a practical standpoint, then, it is important to achieve a better understanding of the operation of metamemory processes under free-report conditions and their effects on both accuracy-based and quantity-based memory performance.

THE MONITORING AND CONTROL PROCESSES
UNDERLYING FREE-REPORT MEMORY PERFORMANCE

Figure 5.1 presents a simple model of how metamemory processes are used to regulate memory accuracy and quantity performance under free-report conditions (Koriat & Goldsmith, 1996b). Essentially, the model merges the logic of signal-detection theory (e.g., Banks, 1970; Green & Swets, 1966; Lockhart & Murdock, 1970) with concepts and tools from the study of metamemory. Thus, in addition to an unspecified memory retrieval mechanism, the model includes a *monitoring* mechanism that is used to subjectively

---

Unfortunately, however, report option and test format are generally confounded in both eyewitness and traditional laboratory research (see Koriat & Goldsmith, 1994). Thus, we should stress that in our research, in which test format and report option were orthogonally manipulated, report option was the critical factor affecting memory accuracy, and in fact, test format had no effect on memory accuracy at all (Koriat & Goldsmith, 1994, 1996b).

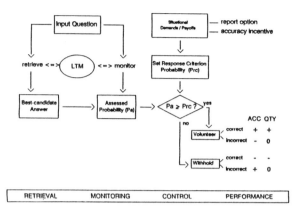

FIG. 5.1. A schematic model of how monitoring and control processes are used in the strategic regulation of memory performance. Effects on memory accuracy and memory quantity performance are signified by plus (increase), minus (decrease), and zero (no effect). From "Monitoring and Control Processes in the Strategic Regulation of Memory Accuracy, by A. Koriat and M. Goldsmith, 1996, *Psychological Review*. 103, (pp. 490–517. Copyright © 1996 by the American Psychological Association. Reprinted with permission.

assess the correctness of potential memory responses, and a control mechanism that determines whether or not to volunteer the best available candidate answer (see also Barnes et al., in press; Klatzky & Erdelyi, 1985). The control mechanism operates as a threshold on the monitoring output: The answer is volunteered if it passes the threshold, but is withheld otherwise. The threshold is set on the basis of the operative payoffs; that is, the gain for providing correct information relative to the cost of providing incorrect information.

Although the model's assumptions are quite simple, its implications for memory performance are not. Under the model, free-report memory performance can be shown to depend on several contributing factors:

1. Overall retention—The amount of correct information (i.e., the number of correct candidate answers) that can be retrieved.
2. Monitoring effectiveness—The extent to which the assessed probabilities successfully differentiate correct from incorrect candidate answers.
3. Control sensitivity —The extent to which the volunteering or withholding of answers is in fact based on the monitoring output.
4. Response criterion setting—The probability threshold that is set in accordance with the incentive to be accurate (e.g., payoff schedule).

Most previous treatments of the potential effects of selective reporting, borrowing from signal-detection theory, have focused on the first and fourth factors only (see, e.g., Bousfield & Rosner, 1970; Erdelyi, Finks, & Feigin-Pfau, 1989; Klatzky & Erdelyi, 1985; Roediger & Payne, 1985). Thus, the widely acknowledged prediction is for a quantity-accuracy trade-off: In general, raising the response criterion should result in fewer volunteered answers, a higher *percentage* of which are correct (increased output-bound accuracy), but a lower *number* of which are correct (decreased input-bound quantity). The assumption is that although people cannot increase the quantity of correct information that they retrieve (Nilsson, 1987), they can enhance the accuracy of the information that they report by withholding answers that are likely to be incorrect. Of course, the converse is also true, particularly in situations, such as in multiple-choice testing, in which there is a good chance of guessing the right answer. In such cases, by lowering the response criterion one should generally increase the number of correct (and incorrect) answers. Quite often, however, there will be explicit or implicit incentives for both quantity and accuracy. Therefore, because raising the response criterion generally increases accuracy at the expense of quantity, the strategic control of memory performance requires the rememberer to weigh the relative payoffs for accuracy and quantity in reaching an optimal criterion setting.

Notwithstanding the importance of the control policy, however, it has gone largely unnoticed that both the accuracy gains and the quantity costs of selective reporting are heavily dependent on the effectiveness of the monitoring mechanism. Consider again a person on the witness stand. Assuming that the witness is not motivated to lie, can we expect him or her to be able to tell the whole truth and nothing but the truth? The answer will depend primarily on the person's monitoring effectiveness, which, we stress, is distinct both from the amount of information remembered and from the adopted control policy (response criterion level). For instance, a witness might remember very little of what happened, but if monitoring effectiveness is perfect, he or she will be able to volunteer all of the (correct) information that he or she remembers while screening out any potentially false information, yielding low quantity performance but high accuracy performance, with no quantity–accuracy trade-off. Conversely, the witness might remember a large amount of information but be relatively unable to determine which facts are correct and which are false. In that case, employing a liberal response criterion will produce a lot of correct information, but a great deal of false information as well (high quantity but low accuracy performance) whereas employing a more strict criterion might yield more accurate testimony (or it might not; see the following), but at the expense of withholding a substantial amount of correct information.

Our model, then, implies that overt memory performance should depend on a complex interplay between underlying memory and metamemory processes. What is the evidence for this model? Do the monitoring and control processes in fact operate in the postulated manner? We examined the assumptions and implications of the model in two experiments using a special procedure that combines both free and forced reporting. In the first experiment (Koriat & Goldsmith, 1996b, Experiment 1), we gave participants a general-knowledge test in either a recall or a recognition format. Participants first took the test under forced-report instructions (Phase 1) and provided confidence judgments regarding the correctness of each answer. Immediately afterward, they took the same test again under free-report instructions (Phase 2) with either a moderate accuracy incentive (receiving a monetary bonus for correct answers, but paying an equal penalty for wrong answers) or a high accuracy incentive (in which the penalty was 10 times greater than the bonus).

This design enabled us to trace the links postulated by the model (see Fig. 5.1) between retrieval, monitoring, control, and memory performance (accuracy and quantity). The results accorded well with the model: First, the participants exhibited a good ability to monitor the correctness of their answers, as indicated by moderately high within-subject correlations between confidence and the correctness of the answer on the forced-report phase (.87 for recall and .68 for recognition). Second, there was a very high correlation between subjective confidence and whether or not an answer would be volunteered in the free-report phase (the gamma correlations averaged .97 for recall and .93 for recognition!). Third, participants who were given the high accuracy incentive were more selective in their reporting, adopting a stricter criterion than those given the more moderate incentive. Finally, by employing these monitoring and control processes, participants in both incentive conditions were able to enhance their free-report accuracy performance relative to forced-report (a 46% and 63% improvement in the moderate- and high-incentive conditions, respectively). However, because the participants' monitoring was less than perfect, the increased accuracy was achieved at the cost of withholding some correct answers as well. Thus, a quantity–accuracy trade-off was observed both in comparing free- and forced-report performance (a 23% quantity decrease in the moderate-incentive condition), and in comparing performance under the two incentive conditions (a further 12% quantity decrease for the high-incentive compared to the moderate-incentive condition, after adjusting for different levels of forced-report performance).

The experiment just described examined the operation and effects of monitoring and control processes under fairly typical conditions. What should happen, however, when monitoring effectiveness is quite poor? In a second experiment (Koriat & Goldsmith, 1996b, Experiment 2), we manipulated monitoring effectiveness by using two different sets of general-knowledge items: One set (the "poor" monitoring condition) consisted of items for which the participants' confidence judgments were generally not correlated with the correctness of their answers (see also Fischhoff, Slovic, & Lichtenstein, 1977; Gigerenzer, Hoffrage, & Kleinbolting, 1991; Koriat, 1995), whereas the other set (the "good" monitoring condition) consisted of more typical items for which the participants' monitoring was more effective. The results indicated that in both monitoring conditions the participants based their free-report control decisions on their monitoring output, but the consequences for memory performance were dramatically different in the two cases: Whereas in the good monitoring condition, the participants were able to increase their accuracy substantially when given the option of free report (75% under free report compared to 22% under forced report), in the poor monitoring condition the participants were able to attain only a very low level of free-report accuracy (21% under free report compared to 8% under forced report). Despite this difference in the free-report accuracy improvement, the quantity cost of the improved accuracy was about the same for both monitoring conditions (about a 5 percentage-point drop when comparing free and forced report). Thus, as expected, a much more severe quantity–accuracy trade-off was observed in the poor monitoring condition.

Monitoring effectiveness, then, emerges as a critical determinant of memory performance in the many situations in which people have the option of providing or withholding information. When rememberers' confidence judgments are reasonably diagnostic of the correctness of their answers, the option of free report can allow them to achieve high levels of accuracy. At the extreme, when monitoring is perfect, completely accurate performance can be achieved with no quantity cost at all. Consider again a student who wants to avoid the embarrassment of providing incorrect answers on a test, preferring to omit the answer altogether when he or she feels that he or she does not know the answer. The extent to which this inclination will impair the student's quantity score (or indeed, improve accuracy performance) will depend on his or her monitoring ability. If the student is able to discriminate effectively between what he or she knows and what he or she does not know, the student might not lose any points at all by employing such a strategy.

In other situations, however, people's monitoring may sometimes be undiagnostic to the point of being useless. They will still control their memory reporting according to their monitoring output (for lack of any better basis), but the attained level of free-report accuracy may be little better than when they are denied the option of deciding which answers to volunteer. Documented cases of poor monitoring are more common than one might think. Cohen (1988), for example, found that although participants were quite accurate in monitoring the recallability of studied words, their judgments of the recallability of self-performed tasks had no predictive validity whatsoever. Koriat (1995), using deceptive items such as those used here (see also Fischhoff et al., 1977), found that feeling-of-knowing (FOK) judgments after unsuccessful recall were either not correlated or even negatively correlated with subsequent recognition memory performance. Weingardt, Leonesio, and Loftus (1994) found exposure to postevent misinformation to impair the relation between confidence and the accuracy of people's answers (see also Chandler, 1994). Finally, there is evidence that monitoring abilities may be relatively poor in certain special populations, for example, young children (e.g., Pressley, Levin, Ghatala, & Ahmad, 1987), Korsakoff patients (e.g., Shimamura & Squire, 1986; 1988) and patients with frontal lobe lesions (e.g., Janowsky, Shimamura, & Squire, 1989). Clearly, in all of these cases, the impaired monitoring is likely to have devastating consequences for free-report memory performance.

Of course, even when monitoring abilities are not actually impaired, differences in monitoring effectiveness may still contribute substantially to the variance in observed memory performance. Importantly, this contribution is independent of what might be called memory retention. In the experiment just described, for instance, we performed an additional comparison in which the good monitoring and poor monitoring items were matched on retention, so that forced-report quantity performance was equivalent. The basic pattern of results remained unchanged: The participants were able to attain a far superior joint level of free-report accuracy and quantity performance in the good monitoring condition than in the poor monitoring condition.

Findings from several other studies also suggest a dissociation between monitoring and retention. For instance, Kelley and Lindsay (1993) observed that advance priming of potential answers to general-information questions increased the ease of access to these answers, raising subjective confidence regardless of whether those answers were right or wrong. Similarly, research investigating the cue-familiarity account of the feeling of knowing indicates that FOK judgments can be enhanced by advance priming of the cue, again even when such priming has no effect on actual memory quantity performance (e.g., Reder & Ritter, 1992; Schwartz & Metcalfe, 1992). Finally, Chandler (1994) found that exposing participants to an additional set of pictures similar to the studied set increased their confidence ratings on a subsequent forced-choice recognition test, whereas in fact their actual performance was impaired.

Such dissociations highlight a basic difference between our proposed framework for conceptualizing the strategic regulation of memory reporting and the signal-detection approach to memory. Because the application of the signal-detection methodology is essentially limited to forced-report recognition memory (Lockhart & Murdock, 1970), the signal-detection framework does not address the separate contributions of memory retention (or memory strength) and monitoring effectiveness to memory performance. In that framework, subjective confidence and memory strength are generally treated as synonymous (Chandler, 1994), and in fact, confidence is often used to index memory strength (see, e.g., Lockhart & Murdock, 1970; Parks, 1966). By contrast, in our proposed framework for conceptualizing free-report performance, monitoring and retention (as well as control) are given a separate standing: One may have effective monitoring, yet very poor retention, or vice versa. Furthermore, poor free-report memory performance, for instance, could derive from poor retention, poor monitoring, an inappropriate control policy, or any combination of these three factors.

The conceptual separation of these components of free-report performance has important implications. At the theoretical level, it calls for more serious efforts to incorporate monitoring and control processes—as well as encoding, storage, and retrieval processes—into our theories and models of memory. At the same time, however, an acknowledgment of the potential effects of metamemory processes on memory performance poses a troubling policy issue: How should such effects be handled when assessing memory performance?

INCORPORATING MONITORING AND CONTROL PROCESSES INTO THE ASSESSMENT OF MEMORY

How have the effects of monitoring and control processes during memory reporting typically been treated in the evaluation of memory? In general, experimental psychologists have shied away from tackling the implications of subject-controlled processes in memory reporting, presumably because of the perceived conflict between the operation of these processes and the desire to maintain strict experimental control (see Nelson & Narens, 1994). Thus, one approach has been to take control away from the participant, for instance by using forced-report testing techniques (Erdelyi & Becker, 1974). Another alternative is to allow participants some degree of control, but then to attempt to "correct" for it by applying such techniques as those provided by the signal-detection methodology (Banks, 1970) or formula scoring (Budescu & Bar-Hillel, 1993). A third approach has been simply to ignore subject control altogether, assuming that it does not have much effect on performance anyway (see Roediger, Srinivas, & Waddil, 1989).

None of these approaches, however, seems completely satisfactory. First and foremost, they are all designed primarily to circumvent the contribution of subject-controlled processes to memory performance, treating this contribution as a nuisance variable rather than an integral aspect of memory functioning that should be assessed and studied. Such a strategy misses the point that metamemorial monitoring and control processes constitute a principal means by which people regulate their memory performance, and it is important to gain a better understanding of that regulation. Furthermore, it is questionable to what extent the aforementioned methods do in fact manage to yield a "pure" measure of memory performance that is untainted by the effects of metamemory processes.

Consider formula scoring, for example. This technique is usually applied in order to achieve an estimate of the test-taker's actual knowledge, cleansed from the contribution of guessing. Hence, on a 5-item multiple-choice test, for instance (in which there is a 20% baseline chance of guessing the correct answer), the test-taker might be awarded 1 point for each correct answer, but penalized one quarter point for each incorrect answer (commission error), with omissions simply ignored[3]. Using such a procedure, have the potential contributions of monitoring and control processes been effectively neutralized? Seemingly not. First, there are possible differences in the interpretation of the instructions that can lead to the adoption of different control policies. This may be particularly true when the test-taker is not informed of the exact scoring formula, but instead is given vague guidelines that encourage him or her to guess on the basis of partial knowledge but to

---

[3]This example assumes what is perhaps the most common formula scoring rule: $S = R - W / (k - 1)$, where S is the formula score, R is the number of right answers, W is the number of wrong answers (commission errors), and k is the number of response options. The basic property of this rule is that one's expected score is the same whether one guesses the answer to an item at random or whether one omits it (see Budescu & Bar-Hillel, 1993).

avoid guessing wildly (Abu-Sayf, 1979; Budescu & Bar-Hillel, 1993). In this case, the control policy that is adopted will depend to a large extent on what the person considers to be "enough" partial knowledge, and perhaps also on a variety of personality or other factors that may influence the tendency to guess, such as gender or culture (Gafni, 1990), or risk preferences (Budescu & Bar-Hillel, 1993). Furthermore, even when test-takers are informed of the precise scoring formula, this does not necessarily enable them to adopt the optimal control strategy for that formula (see Abu-Sayf, 1979; Koriat & Goldsmith, 1996b), nor does it preclude the possibility that extraneous motivations might also affect people's control decisions (as when people omit answers under forced-report instructions even though there is no objective advantage in doing so; cf. earlier example, and see Grandy, 1987). Yet both empirical studies and simulation analyses indicate that different control policies can yield substantially different levels of performance on such tests (e.g., Albanese, 1988; Angoff & Schrader, 1984; Cross & Frary, 1977; Frary, 1980; Slakter, 1968).

Second, even when the control policy is held constant, differences in monitoring effectiveness can also have a substantial effect on the test-taker's formula score. Metacognitive research has distinguished two distinct aspects of monitoring effectiveness, resolution and calibration (see, e.g., Koriat & Goldsmith, 1996b; Lichtenstein, Fischhoff, & Phillips, 1982; Nelson, 1984, 1996; Yaniv, Yates, & Smith, 1991). Resolution, or discrimination accuracy, is the aspect that we have considered so far, the extent to which the person is able to distinguish between answers that are more likely or less likely to be correct. Calibration, on the other hand, refers to the absolute correspondence between a person's confidence in his or her answers and the actual likelihood that they are correct. This measure relates to over- or underconfidence: A person would be overconfident, say, if most of his or her subjective probability assessments are exaggerated. Clearly resolution is important: As we saw before, it is this aspect of monitoring that enables the person to choose the right answers to volunteer and to withhold. In addition, calibration may also affect the person's performance. To illustrate, assume that a test-taker decides that it is worth volunteering any answer that has a better than 25% chance of being correct, but to withhold it otherwise. This person therefore sets his or her subjective response-criterion probability at the .25 level. If this person's probability assessments are miscalibrated, however, her control policy may actually be more liberal (if overconfident) or more conservative (if underconfident) than he or she intended, and this may affect his or her ultimate score on the test.

Of course, with different testing or scoring methods, some of these contributions of metamemory processes to test performance could perhaps be neutralized. The primary issue, however, is not merely methodological. The main question that we must ask ourselves in any assessment situation is precisely what aspect or aspects of the person's performance or ability are we interested in evaluating. Rarely is the quantity of information that a person can reproduce of interest in itself. In evaluating eyewitness testimony, for instance, the quantity of information is surely important, but the accuracy of the testimony may be even more crucial. Can we depend on most or all of what the witness says to be true? Of course, if the testimony is inaccurate, we also want to know why: Is the inaccurate reporting due to a deficiency in monitoring, or in control? Although perhaps less obvious, similar questions need to be asked in the context of scholastic and psychometric testing. Is the ability to monitor one's own knowledge, for instance, to be included among those aspects of the test-taker's aptitude or achievement that the test is intended to tap? Would we want to certify (or hire the services of) a doctor, lawyer, psychologist, or engineer who was deficient in discriminating between what he or she knows and does not know? Finally, in the context of cognitive neuropsychological testing, what are the critical aspects of impaired memory functioning associated with certain forms of brain damage? To what extent does the impaired performance stem from deficient retention, deficient monitoring or deficient control (see Schacter, chapter 6, this volume)?

In order to address such questions, it would be helpful to have available measurement techniques that incorporate metamemory processes into the assessment of memory performance, still allowing a separate evaluation of their independent contributions. One such method that we proposed (Koriat & Goldsmith, 1996b) involves the derivation of *quantity–accuracy profiles* (QAPs). Rather than attempt to provide a single point-estimate of memory performance, QAPs provide information regarding the potential memory quantity and memory accuracy performance that can be achieved by the person under given conditions. To illustrate the method, Fig. 5.2 presents the QAPs for two participants who took the general-knowledge (recall) test in the study we described earlier (Koriat & Goldsmith, 1996b, Experiment 1). For each participant, confidence data from the initial forced-report phase were used to compute the input-bound quantity scores and the output-bound accuracy scores (plotted on the y-axis) that would result from the application of 11 different response-criterion levels (plotted on the x-axis), ranging from 0 (forced report) to 1.0. In addition, the

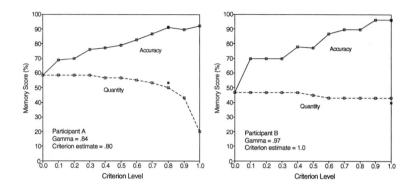

FIG. 5.2. Two illustrative quantity–accuracy profiles (QAPs). (Adapted from "Monitoring and Control Processes in the Strategic Regulation of Memory Accuracy, by A. Koriat and M. Goldsmith, 1996, *Psychological Review.* 103, (pp. 490–517. Copyright © 1996 by the American Psychological Association. Adapted by permission.

correlation between confidence and actual correctness of the answers on the forced-report phase (Kruskal–Goodman's gamma) was computed as a measure of monitoring effectiveness.

Finally, by examining the relation between confidence on the forced-report phase and volunteering or withholding answers on the free-report phase, a "best fit" estimate of the control policy (response criterion) adopted by the participant on the free-report phase was derived (for details, see Koriat & Goldsmith, 1996b). The actual quantity and accuracy scores achieved by the participant in the free-report phase are plotted as bullets above the estimated criterion level.

What type of information can be gleaned from these QAPs? If we were to look only at forced-report performance as a measure of retention (or knowledge), then Participant A's performance would be superior to Participant B's. The profiles, however, offer a much more complete picture than this. First, looking at the participant's actual free-report performance, we see that although A's quantity performance is still superior to B's, B's performance is more accurate than A's. Is B's superior accuracy due simply to the use of a stricter control policy? (Both participants operated under a 10:1 penalty-to-bonus payoff scheme.) The estimated response criterion for Participant B (1.0) is indeed higher than for Participant A (.80). However, even if A had adopted the same criterion as B, B's accuracy would still be higher. Even more noticeable, however, is the substantial price in quantity performance that A would pay by raising her criterion any further. Thus, pressing A to be "absolutely sure" about what she knows before venturing an answer would markedly impair her performance. These differences between A and B in potential accuracy performance and in the degree of trade-off between quantity and accuracy performance are reflected in the different levels of monitoring effectiveness they exhibit (gamma correlations of .84 and .97, respectively). So, who has better general knowledge, Participant A or Participant B? Although A appears to have more knowledge, B seems to be better able to discriminate between what she knows and what she does not know, yielding a higher level of potential accuracy. Also, B seems to be more cautious than A in her responding. Clearly, then, our ultimate appraisal will need to take into account the relative importance of these different aspects for the task at hand. For example, as a contributor to a brainstorming session we might prefer Participant A, with her greater amount of potential information (and her greater tendency to volunteer it), but as a key witness in a capital trial we would probably prefer Participant B, because of the high priority given to accurate testimony in that situation. An important advantage of this assessment procedure, then, is not only its ability to provide separate indices for the various aspects of memory performance (i.e., retention, monitoring, and control), but also that it forces one to make an explicit and thoughtful decision about the weight to be attached to each of these aspects in the overall performance evaluation.

Of course the QAP procedure has its own limitations. First, various aspects of the procedure, such as giving people the same test twice under both forced-report and free-report instruction or the elicitation of confidence judgments, may not always be feasible. Second, in many practical situations (e.g., university admissions), one is interested in a single index on which to compare people's performance, and the QAP procedure complicates the derivation of such an index. This complication, however, is the price of taking the contributions of subject-controlled metamemory processes seriously, rather than simply ignoring them.

CONCLUDING REMARKS

In this chapter, we focused on some of the metamemory processes that operate during memory reporting, and showed how these processes can have substantial effects on memory performance in a variety of situations. Although a great deal of work has been directed toward an understanding of metacognitive processes and their determinants in the last decade, clearly more needs to be done to uncover and address the performance consequences of these processes. The work we have reviewed here (see also Goldsmith & Koriat, in press) reveals some of the complexities that arise

116   KORIAT AND GOLDSMITH

when metamemory processes are allowed to operate during memory reporting, and poses the question of how such complexities should be handled. Memory researchers, neuropsychologists, and test administrators alike will need to grapple with the issue of whether, when, and how metamemory processes should be taken into account in the assessment of people's performance.

REFERENCES

Abu-Sayf, F. K. (1979). The scoring of multiple-choice tests: A closer look. *Educational* Technology, 19, 5–15.

Albanese, M. A. (1988). The projected impact of the correction for guessing on individual scores. *Journal of Educational Measurement, 25,* 149–157.

Angoff, W. H. (1989). Does guessing really help? *Journal of Educational Measurement, 26,* 323–336.

Angoff, W. H., & Schrader, B. W. (1984). A study of hypotheses basic to the use of rights and formula scores. *Journal of Educational Measurement, 21,* 1–17.

Banks, W. P. (1970). Signal detection theory and human memory. *Psychological Bulletin, 74,* 81–99.

Barnes, A. E., Nelson, T. O., Dunlosky, J., Mazzoni, G., & Narens, L. (in press). An integrative system of metamemory components involved in retrieval. In D. Gopher & A. Koriat (Eds.), *Cognitive regulation of performance: Interaction of theory and application: Attention and performance XVII.* Cambridge, MA: MIT Press.

Bousfield, W. A., & Rosner, S. R. (1970). Free vs. uninhibited recall. *Psychonomic Science, 20,* 75–76

Budescu, D., & Bar-Hillel, M. (1993). To guess or not to guess: A decision-theoretic view of formula scoring. *Journal of Educational Measurement, 38,* 277–291

Chandler, C. C. (1994). Studying related pictures can reduce accuracy, but increase confidence, in a modified recognition text. *Memory and Cognition, 22,* 273–280.

Cohen, R. L. (1988). Metamemory for words and enacted instructions: Predicting which items will be recalled. *Memory and Cognition, 16,* 452–460.

Cronbach, L. J. (1984). *Essentials of psychological testing.* New York: Harper & Row.

Cross, L. H., & Frary, R. B. (1977). An empirical test of Lord's theoretical results regarding formula scoring of multiple-choice tests. Journal of Educational Measurement, 14, 313–321.

Deffenbacher, K. A. (1991). A maturing of research on the behavior of eyewitnesses. *Applied Cognitive Psychology, 5,* 377–402.

Ebbinghaus, H. E. (1964). *Memory: A contribution to experimental psychology.* New York: Dover. (Original work published 1895)

Erdelyi, M. H., & Becker J. (1974). Hypermnesia for pictures: Incremental memory for pictures but not words in multiple recall trials. *Cognitive Psychology, 6,* 159–171.

Erdelyi, M. H., Finks, J., & Feigin-Pfau, M. B. (1989). The effect of response bias on recall performance, with some observations on processing bias. *Journal of Experimental Psychology: General, 118,* 245–254.

Fischhoff, B., Slovic, P., & Lichtenstein, S. (1977). Knowing with certainty: The appropriateness of extreme confidence. *Journal of Experimental Psychology: Human Perception and Performance, 3,* 552–564.

Fisher, R. P., & Geiselman, R. E. (1992). *Memory enhancing techniques for investigative interviewing: The cognitive interview.* Springfield, IL: Thomas.

Flanagan, E. J. (1981). Interviewing and interrogation techniques. In J. J. Grau (Ed.), *Criminal and civil investigation handbook* (Pt. 4, pp. 3-24). New York: McGraw-Hill.

Frary, R. B. (1980). The effect of misinformation, partial information, and guessing on expected multiple-choice test item scores. *Applied Psychological Measurement, 4,* 79–90.

Gafni, N. (1990). *Differential tendencies to guess as a function of gender and lingual-cultural reference group* (Rep. No. 115). Jerusalem, Israel: National Institute for Testing and Evaluation.

Gigerenzer, G., Hoffrage, U., & Kleinbolting, H. (1991). Probabilistic mental models: A Brunswikian theory of confidence. *Psychological Review, 98,* 506–528.

Goldsmith, M., & Koriat, A. (in press). The strategic regulation of memory reporting: Mechanisms and performance consequences. In D. Gopher & A. Koriat (Eds.), *Cognitive regulation of performance: Interaction of theory and application: Attention and performance XVII*. Cambridge MA: MIT Press.

Gorenstein, G. W., & Ellsworth, P. C. (1980). Effect of choosing an incorrect photograph on a later identification by an eyewitness. *Journal of Applied Psychology, 65*, 616–622.

Grandy, J. (1987). *Characteristics of examinees who leave questions unanswered on the GRE general test under right-only scoring* (Rep. No. 87–38). Princeton, NJ: Educational Testing Service.

Green D. M., & Swets, J. A. (1966). *Signal detection theory and psychophysics*. New York: Wiley.

Hilgard, E. R., & Loftus, E. F. (1979). Effective interrogation of the eyewitness. *The International Journal of Clinical and Experimental Hypnosis, 27*, 342–357.

Janowsky, J. S., Shimamura, A. P., & Squire, L. R. (1989). Memory and metamemory: Comparisons between frontal lobe lesions and amnesic patients. *Psychobiology, 17*, 3-11.

Kelley, C. M., & Lindsay, D. S. (1993). Remembering mistaken for knowing: Ease of retrieval as a basis for confidence in answers to general knowledge questions. *Journal of Memory and Language, 32*, 1–24.

Klatzky, R. L., & Erdelyi, M. H. (1985). The response criterion problem in tests of hypnosis and memory. *International Journal of Clinical and Experimental Hypnosis, 33*, 246–257.

Koriat, A. (1995). Dissociating knowing and the feeling of knowing: Further evidence for the accessibility model. *Journal of Experimental Psychology: General, 124*, 311–333.

Koriat, A., & Goldsmith, M. (1994). Memory in naturalistic and laboratory contexts: Distinguishing the accuracy-oriented and quantity-oriented approaches to memory assessment. *Journal of Experimental Psychology: General, 123*, 297–316.

Koriat, A., & Goldsmith, M. (1996a). Memory metaphors and the real-life/laboratory controversy: Correspondence versus storehouse conceptions of memory. *Behavioral and* Brain Sciences, 19, 167–188.

Koriat, A., & Goldsmith, M. (1996b). Monitoring and control processes in the strategic regulation of memory accuracy. *Psychological Review, 103*, 490–517.

Lichtenstein, S., Fischhoff, B., & Phillips, L. D. (1982). Calibration of probabilities: The state of the art to 1980. In D. Kahneman, P. Slovic, & A. Tversky (Eds.), *Judgment under uncertainty: Heuristics and biases* (pp. 306–334). Cambridge, UK: Cambridge University Press.

Lockhart, R. S., & Murdock, B. B. (1970). Memory and the theory of signal detection. *Psychological Bulletin, 74*, 100–109.

Loftus, E. F. (1979). *Eyewitness testimony*. Cambridge MA: Harvard University press.

Loftus, E. F., & Hoffman, H. G. (1989). Misinformation and memory: The creation of new memories. *Journal of Experimental Psychology: General, 118*, 100–104.

Neisser, U. (1988). Time present and time past. In M. M. Gruneberg, P. Morris, & R. Sykes (Eds.), *Practical aspects of memory: Current research and issues* (Vol. 2, pp. 545–560). Chichester, UK: Wiley.

Nelson, T. O. (1984). A comparison of current measures of the accuracy of feeling-of-knowing predictions. *Psychological Bulletin, 95*, 109–133.

Nelson, T. O. (1996). Gamma is a measure of the accuracy of predicting performance on one item relative to another item, not of the absolute performance on an individual item: Comments on Schraw (1995). *Applied Cognitive Psychology, 10*, 257–260.

Nelson, T. O., & Narens, L. (1990). Metamemory: A theoretical framework and new findings. In G. Bower (Ed.), *The psychology of learning and motivation* (pp. 125–173). New York: Academic Press.

Nelson, T. O., & Narens, L. (1994). Why investigate metacognition? In J. Metcalfe & A. P. Shimamura (Eds.), *Metacognition: Knowing about knowing* (pp. 1–25). Cambridge, MA: MIT Press.

Nilsson, L.-G. (1987). Motivated memory: Dissociation between performance data and subjective reports. *Psychological Research, 49*, 183–188.

Parks, T. E. (1966). Signal detectability theory of recognition-memory performance. *Psychological Review, 73*, 44–58.

Pressley, M., Levin, J. R., Ghatala, E. S., & Ahmad, M. (1987). Test monitoring in young grade school children. *Journal of Experimental Child Psychology, 43*, 96–111.

Puff, C. R. (Ed.) (1982). *Handbook of research methods in human memory and cognition*. New York: Academic Press.

Reder, L. M., & Ritter, F. E. (1992). What determines initial feeling of knowing? Familiarity with question terms, not with the answer. *Journal of Experimental Psychology: Learning. Memory and Cognition, 18*, 435–451.

Roediger, H. L., & Payne, D. G. (1985). Recall criterion does not affect recall level or hypermnesia: A puzzle for generate/recognize theories. *Memory and Cognition, 13*, 1–7.

Roediger, H. L., Srinivas, K., & Waddil, P. (1989). How much does guessing influence recall? Comment on Erdelyi, Finks, and Feigin-Pfau. *Journal of Experimental Psychology: General, 118*, 253–257.

Schwartz, B. L., & Metcalfe, J. (1992). Cue familiarity but not target retrievability enhances feeling-of-knowing judgments. *Journal of Experimental Psychology: Learning. Memory. and Cognition, 18*, 1074–1083.

Shimamura, A. P., & Squire, L. R. (1986). Memory and metamemory: A study of the feeling-of-knowing phenomenon in amnesic patients. *Journal of Experimental Psychology: Learning. Memory. and Cognition, 12*, 452–460.

Shimamura, A. P., & Squire, L.R. (1988). Long-term memory in amnesia: Cued recall, recognition memory and confidence ratings. *Journal of Experimental Psychology: Learning, Memory and cognition, 14*, 763–770.

Slakter, M. (1968). The penalty for not guessing. *Journal of Educational Measurement, 5*, 141–144

Thurstone, L. L. (1919). A method for scoring tests. *Psychological Bulletin, 16*, 235–240.

Weingardt, K. R., Leonesio, R. J., & Loftus, E. F. (1994). Viewing eyewitness research from a metacognitive perspective. In J. Metcalfe & A. P. Shimamura (Eds.), *Metacognition: Knowing about knowing* (pp. 157–184). Cambridge, MA: MIT Press.

Yaniv, I., Yates, J. F., & Smith, J. E. K. (1991). Measures of discrimination skill in probabilistic judgment. *Psychological Bulletin, 110*, 611-617.

6

Illusory Memories: A Cognitive Neuroscience Analysis

Daniel L. Schacter
Harvard University

Memory is essential to a wide variety of cognitive functions and everyday activities. Because our well-being and even survival may depend on access to reliable information about the past, it is not surprising that memory is often accurate. Nonetheless, memories are not always accurate and under some conditions they may be grossly distorted. When people misremember past experiences the consequences can be serious, as in cases of mistaken eyewitness identification (Loftus, 1979). Memory distortions and illusions have long been of interest to cognitive psychologists, dating to the classic study by Bartlett (1932) on the reconstructive nature of memory (for historical review, see Roediger, 1996; Schacter, 1995, 1996). Three decades later, Neisser (1967) put forward similar ideas. His monograph stimulated intensive interest on the part of cognitive psychologists in questions concerning memory distortions, resulting in many striking demonstrations of erroneous remembering in laboratory studies (e.g., Bransford & Franks, 1971; Loftus, Miller, & Burns, 1978). Cognitive studies concerning memory distortion continued through the 1980s (e.g., Dywan & Bowers, 1983; Jacoby & Whitehouse, 1989; Johnson, Foley, Suengas, & Raye, 1988) and have grown dramatically during the 1990s, inspired in part by controversies over the accuracy of memories retrieved in psychotherapy (cf., Kihlstrom, in press; Lindsay & Read, 1994; Loftus, 1993; Schacter, Norman, & Koutstaal, 1997) and effects of suggestive questioning on the reliability of childrens' recollections (e.g., Ceci, 1995).

Memory distortions are highly relevant to issues of metacognition, because they often involve failures of monitoring processes. Although memory distortions and illusions have been studied extensively in psychology, cognitive neuroscientists concerned with brain mechanisms of memory have paid relatively little attention to them. There are exceptions, of course, such as empirical and theoretical observations concerning confabulations about past events that are sometimes observed in patients with lesions to the ventromedial frontal lobes and nearby regions in the basal forebrain, patients who have dramatic failures of metacognition (Johnson, 1991; Moscovitch, 1995). However, the relative absence of cognitive neuroscience research on illusory remembering is notable (for a comprehensive review, see Schacter, Norman, & Koutstaal, 1998).

The main thesis of this chapter is that a cognitive neuroscience analysis of illusory recollections, combining observations of memory disorders produced by neurological dysfunction and studies of normal remembering with recently developed functional neuroimaging techniques, can provide important insights into the constructive nature of memory processes in the brain. A key point of agreement between cognitive and biological theories is that memories do not preserve a literal representation of the world; they are constructed from fragments of information that are distributed across different brain regions, and depend on influences operating in the present as well as the past (cf., Damasio, 1989; McClelland, 1995; Neisser, 1967; Schacter, 1996; Squire, 1992; Tulving, 1983). By studying memory distortions and illusions from a cognitive neuroscience perspective, it should be possible to gain useful insights into the neural underpinnings of this constructive process.

In this chapter I sketch the outlines of a cognitive neuroscience approach to constructive memory processes by considering recent research conducted in our own and others' laboratories. I begin by discussing evidence from neuroimaging research that highlights a distinction between strategic effort and conscious recollection in memory retrieval, which in turn provides a foundation for understanding brain systems that are relevant to memory distortion. I then use this distinction to examine memory distortions in a case of frontal lobe dysfunction, patients with amnesia produced by damage to the medial temporal lobes, normal aging, and healthy young volunteers. Converging evidence from these studies highlights that illusory memories depend on a dynamic interplay among dissociable component processes that contribute to the constructive nature of remembering.

RECOLLECTION AND EFFORT
IN MEMORY RETRIEVAL

As noted earlier, both cognitive psychologists and neuroscientists agree that memory retrieval is constructive. What component processes contribute to constructive retrieval? This question is brought into sharp focus by neuroimaging studies of memory. Research on memory processes using positron emission tomography (PET), and to a lesser extent functional magnetic resonance imaging (FMRI) has progressed rapidly in recent years (for reviews, see Buckner & Tulving, 1995; Ungerleider, 1995). Studies concerning retrieval of recently encountered words, pictures, and other kinds of episodic information have consistently revealed activations in the frontal lobes, particularly in right anterior prefrontal regions (Tulving et al., 1994). These extensive retrieval-related frontal lobe activations were intially surprising, because frontal lobe lesions do not usually produce severe amnesia (Schacter, 1987; Squire, 1987), although they are associated with a variety of memory impairments that are considered later. An important question concerns what exact role specific frontal regions play in retrieval of episodic memories. Similarly, questions concerning the role of the hippocampal formation have also arisen in neuroimaging research. Although the hippocampus and related medial temporal lobe structures have long been implicated in memory (Milner, Corkin, & Teuber, 1968; Squire, 1992), and early PET evidence showed hippocampal activation during retrieval (Squire et al., 1992), a number of subsequent PET studies of episodic memory retrieval failed to detect hippocampal activations, in contrast to extensive activity in prefrontal cortex and posterior cortical regions (e.g., Andreason et al., 1995; Shallice et al., 1994; Tulving et al., 1994).

When a blood flow increase is observed in a specific brain region during memory retrieval, it could be attributable to either of two distinct processes: the effort involved in attempting to remember target information, or the successful recollection of that information (Kapur et al., 1995; Nyberg et al., 1995; Schacter, Alpert, Savage, Rauch, & Albert, 1996). To tease apart these two contributors to retrieval activations, we manipulated the manner in which participants studied target words prior to scanning (Schacter, Alpert, et al., 1996). Words in the high recall condition were presented four times, and during each presentation participants engaged in a "deep" or elaborative encoding task (they rated the number of meanings associated with the target word; Craik & Tulving, 1975). We reasoned that participants would successfully recall many of these words on a subsequent test. Words in the low recall condition were presented only once, and participants engaged in a "shallow" encoding task (rating the number "t-junctions" in the word). We reasoned that participants would recall few of these words despite expending considerable retrieval effort as they attempted to think back to the study list. Participants were later given cued recall tests during separate 1-minute scans for high recall and low recall words in which the first three-letters of target words were presented, and they tried to retrieve appropriate list items. In a separate baseline condition, three letter word beginnings were presented that could not be completed with study list items, and participants responded with the first word that came to mind.

As expected, behavioral data revealed that participants remembered many more words in the high recall condition than in the low recall condition. Analysis of blood flow changes in the different conditions revealed a consistent pattern of results. Compared to the baseline condition, the low recall condition was associated with extensive bilateral blood flow increases in the prefrontal cortex, but there were no blood flow increases in the vicinity of the hippocampal formation. In contrast, the high recall minus baseline comparison yielded bilateral flow increases in the hippocampal formation, but no significant increases in prefrontal regions (we did observe trends for increases in the right prefrontal region). The high recall minus low recall comparison revealed blood flow increases in the right hippocampus, whereas the low recall minus high recall condition revealed blood flow increases in the left prefrontal cortex (see Schacter, Alpert, et al., 1996, for discussion of findings in other brain regions).

We also conducted the same experiment with a group of elderly adults, observing strong evidence of normal hippocampal blood flow increases during the high recall condition in our older participants (Schacter, Savage, Alpert, Rauch, & Albert, 1996). In contrast, however, elderly adults exhibited abnormal patterns of blood flow in prefrontal cortex during the low recall condition. Specifically, elderly adults did not show significant anterior prefrontal blood flow increases in the low recall condition. These findings are consistent with other data linking altered frontal lobe functioning with age-related memory changes (e.g., Craik, Morris, Morris, & Loewen, 1990; Glisky, Polster, & Routhieaux, 1995), and suggest that elderly adults did not engage in the same kinds of strategic or effortful retrieval processes in the low recall condition that young participants did.

The results from both young and old participants suggest that blood flow increases in the hippocampal formation during the stem cued recall test are primarily associated with the successful recollection of previously studied words. It remains to be determined whether and to what extent these observations generalize to other tasks and materials. However, Nyberg, McIntosh, Houle, Nilsson, and Tulving (1996) recently reported strong positive correlations between retrieval success and blood flow increases in left medial temporal regions on a recognition memory task. Schacter et al., (1995) reported blood flow increases in the right hippocampal formation during episodic recognition of novel possible objects, which were well remembered, but not during episodic recognition of novel impossible objects, which were more poorly remembered. Taken together, these studies provide converging evidence that blood flow increases in the hippocampal formation during episodic memory retrieval are associated with some aspect of the conscious recollection of a recent event. Failures to detect hippocampal activations in conditions that yield high levels of remembering may be related to difficulties in imaging this region or to the possibility that the hippocampal formation is engaged to some degree in all experimental conditions, thereby making it difficult to detect blood flow increases in particular conditions (for discussion, see Buckner & Tulving, 1995; Schacter, Alpert, et al. 1996; Ungerleider, 1995).

The pattern of frontal lobe activations in the Schacter, Alpert, et al. (1996) study suggest a rather different role for prefrontal regions and are consistent with the idea that specific regions within the left and right prefrontal cortices, respectively, play different roles in memory retrieval (Buckner & Petersen, 1996; Tulving et al., 1994). We found that right anterior prefrontal cortex (Area 10) was activated in the low recall minus baseline comparison, but not in the low recall minus high recall comparison. This observation suggests that right anterior prefrontal cortex may play an important role in processes that are involved in switching from lexical retrieval to episodic retrieval. One problem with this suggestion is that we failed to observe significant right prefrontal blood flow increases in the high recall minus baseline comparison. This finding is especially puzzling because Squire et al. (1992) reported right prefrontal activation in a condition that is quite similar to our high recall condition. However, the high recall minus baseline comparison did indeed yield a notable trend for a blood flow increase in right anterior prefrontal cortex, although it failed to meet the statistical threshold for significance used in the study.

Further consideration of Squire et al.'s (1992) findings and of the possible role of right prefrontal cortex in memory retrieval, provides some insight into why we observed only a trend for right prefrontal activation in the high recall minus baseline condition. In one condition of their experiment,

Squire et al. examined blood changes when participants were instructed to provide the first word that came to mind in response to a three-letter cue. Although this condition was designed to examine the implicit form of memory known as *priming* (Tulving & Schacter, 1990), participants produced almost as many words from the study list when they were instructed to write down the first word that came to mind as when they were instructed to try to remember study list words. By contrast, in most studies levels of priming are considerably lower than levels of explicit memory. When considered in light of the fact that Squire et al.'s participants were shown short study lists, engaged in deep or semantic encoding, and viewed the study lists twice, the nearly equivalent levels of priming and recall suggest that priming was "contaminated" by some form of explicit memory. Although participants were probably following instructions and writing down the first word that came to mind, they may have involuntarily remembered the study list words.

Consistent with the preceding ideas, and with data described earlier linking the hippocampal formation with conscious recollection, Squire et al. (1992) observed hippocampal activation during primed stem completion. Schacter, Alpert, et al., 1996, demonstrated that the priming-related hippocampal blood flow increase could be abolished by eliminating explicit memory contamination.) Importantly, however, Squire et al. did not observe right anterior frontal lobe activation in this "involuntary" explicit memory condition. This finding suggests that right prefrontal activation is, at least in part, associated with switching from involuntary retrieval into a voluntary or intentional retrieval mode. Perhaps Schacter, Alpert, et al. (1996) did not observe a robust right prefrontal activation in the high recall condition (even though intentional memory instructions were given) because after four exposures to the study list, participants often relied on an automatic, involuntary retrieval process to complete test stems. These suggestions are consistent with the results of two other PET studies of recognition memory in which right anterior prefrontal activity was associated with entering the voluntary or intentional retrieval mode (Kapur et al., 1995; Nyberg et al., 1995). However, in a related study of recognition memory, Rugg, Fletcher, Frith, Frackowiak, and Dolan (1996) found that right anterior frontal activations were also associated with increasing numbers of successful retrievals.

Although the exact nature of the right anterior prefrontal contribution to retrieval is not yet known, one possibility is that it is involved in reconstructing the general context of a recent event—focusing in on the target episode and filtering out or inhibiting irrelevant information (see Norman & Schacter, 1996; see Rugg et al., 1996, for a related suggestion). Thus, activation of this region may depend in part on the extent to which a particular task requires participants to filter irrelevant information and focus on specific episodes. By this view, the right prefrontal region should be activated whenever participants initiate voluntary or intentional retrieval and, depending on task demands and materials, may also show additional activation associated with successful retrieval. In contrast, the left prefrontal region that was activated in Schacter, Alpert, et al.'s (1996) low recall minus high recall comparison (in which there was no sign of activation of the right prefrontal region) may be involved in such strategic processes as generating candidate responses when it is difficult to recall target items. Future studies will be necessary to explore these and other possibilities.

Despite the fact that much remains to be learned about the generality of the foregoing observations, the contrasting roles of prefrontal cortex and hippocampal formation in episodic memory retrieval can help to conceptualize a variety of memory distortions and illusions that I now consider.

FALSE RECOGNITION AND THE RIGHT FRONTAL LOBE: PATIENT BG

A number of neuropsychologists have noted that damage to the ventromedial aspects of the frontal lobes and basal forebrain are often associated with the memory distortion known as *confabulation*, in which patients describe detailed recollections of events that never happened (cf., Dalla Barba, 1993; Johnson, 1991; Moscovitch, 1995). Moscovitch (1995) contended that confabulation arises as a result of impairment to strategic retrieval and monitoring processes that depend on frontal regions.

We have recently studied a 65-year-old man, BG, who suffered an infarction restricted to the right frontal lobe (Schacter, Curran, Galluccio, Milberg, & Bates, 1996). BG does not spontaneously generate extensive confabulations about events that never happened, shows no signs of amnesia, and is generally alert, attentive, and cooperative. He does, however, exhibit a striking pattern of false recognitions that provides useful clues concerning the role of prefrontal regions in illusory memories.

To investigate recognition memory in BG, we showed him a list of familiar words and later gave him a yes–no recognition test for old and new words. In addition to asking BG to indicate whether a word had appeared previously on a study list, we also probed the nature of his recollective experience by using the remember/know technique (Gardiner & Java, 1993; Tulving, 1985). Participants are instructed to indicate that they remember having encountered a word on the study list when they possess a specific recollection of something that they perceived or thought when they studied the word, whereas participants say they know that the word appeared on the study list when it seems familiar, but they do not recollect any specific details about it. Although remember and know responses are to some extent correlated with high-confidence and low-confidence responses, respectively, the evidence also shows that remember/know judgments are not entirely accounted for by differences in confidence (see Gardiner & Java, 1993). Results revealed that even though BG's memory for previously studied words (i.e., hit rate) was relatively normal, he made many more false alarms than did any of the eight control participants. Moreover, BG claimed to remember nearly 40% of new words that had not been on the study list, whereas control participants made remember responses to approximately 5% of new words. Both BG and control participants provided know responses to about 10% of new words.

Inspection of BG's performance revealed that many of the new words he claimed to remember were associatively related to words that had appeared in the study list. For example, BG claimed to remember seeing the new word *cellar* on the study list, when in fact he had studied *basement*. Cognitive research has shown that normal individuals are more prone to false recognition when new words are associatively related to previously studied words than when they have no associative relation to studied items (Roediger & McDermott, 1995; Underwood, 1965). BG's high rate of false recognitions may indicate that he was was unduly influenced by semantic or associative similarity when deciding whether he remembered a particular item.

In a follow-up experiment, some of the lure items on the recognition test were associatively related to a word that had appeared on the study list, and others were unrelated to the study list words. The key result was that BG provided many more remember responses to both related and unrelated lure items than did control participants, although he did so more frequently for related than unrelated lures. Thus, BG exhibited false recollections even when a nonstudied lure item had no relation to a previously studied item.

Another possibility is that BG's tendency to remember nonstudied words is attributable to the fact that all of the words in our experiments were familiar to him on the basis of preexperimental knowledge—that is, all of the words were represented in his long-term memory prior to the experiment. Perhaps BG mistakenly took the preexperimental familiarity of a word as evidence that it appeared on the study list, and hence claimed to remember nonstudied words. To test this hypothesis, we exposed BG to novel pseudowords (e.g., *brap, spafe*) that would not have been familiar to him on the basis of preexperimental knowledge. Results indicated that BG still exhibited the same false recognition phenomenon as in previous experiments, claiming to remember nonstudied pseudowords much more often than did control participants. In follow-up experiments in which we asked BG to write down what he remembers to words that he believes were on the list (Curran, Schacter, Norman, & Galluccio, 1997), we found that BG's explanations of his pseudoword false alarms almost always made reference to real words he believed were on the list. Thus, preexperimental familiarity likely plays some role in BG's illusory recollections of pseudowords.

Schacter, Curran, et al. (1996) were able to nearly eliminate BG's false recognition responses with a simple manipulation. We showed BG pictures of inanimate objects from various categories (e.g., furniture, articles of clothing). On a subsequent recognition test, some of the nonstudied lure items came from these categories, other lure items came from miscellaneous categories of inanimate objects that were not represented on the study list, and still other lure items were animate objects (i.e., animals). BG claimed to remember many of the lure items that were drawn from previously studied categories of inanimate objects. However, he almost never claimed to remember the lure items that were not members of previously studied categories.

BG's pattern of false alarms provides an interesting puzzle. On the one hand, BG exhibits considerable false recognition even for lure words that have no associative relation to words that appeared on the study list. On the other hand, he does not exhibit false recognition to lures from nonstudied categories. To understand this puzzle, Schacter, Curran, et al. (1996) suggested that BG relies excessively on information about the general correspondence between a test item and previously studied words when making a recognition decision. Control participants typically claimed to remember that a word or picture had appeared on a study list only when they retrieved specific information about a particular word or picture. BG, by contrast, relied inappropriately on a match between a test item and general characteristics of the study episode when making his recognition decisions.

In follow-up experiments with BG (Curran et al., 1997), we used signal detection analyses to separate out sensitvity and bias and BG's recognition performance. Not surprisingly, we found that BG consistently used excessively liberal response criteria compared to control participants. In addition, however, we also found evidence of impaired sensitivity. BG's impaired retention of specific information about individual items on the list likely contributed to his overreliance on general features of the study episode. Indeed, in one experiment, we increased BG's ability to recollect specific details about presented words via the use of a deep or semantic encoding task. Under these conditions, BG made predominantly know false alarms instead of remember false alarms, as in previous experiments. These observations suggest when BG has access to high-quality recollective information about specific items he has actually studied, he can use this information to oppose his usual overreliance on general similarity between study and test items.

Although overreliance on general similarity can account for BG's high false alarm rate, it does not explain why he claims to remember nonstudied items. As noted earlier, in the recent experiments by Curran et al. (1997), we analyzed exactly what BG claims to recall when he makes a remember false alarm. We found that he tends to provide associations to other words or sometimes to events in his life—specific information from an inappropriate context. Given previous evidence implicating the frontal lobes in memory for source or contextual information (Janowsky, Shimamura, & Squire, 1989; Schacter, Harbluk, & McLachlan, 1984), it seems likely that a source memory deficit contributes to the character of BG's false recollections.

The foregoing observations raise the possibility that frontal cortex, and perhaps right frontal regions in particular, play a role in effortful retrieval processes that are necessary to gain access to specific information about particular list items. We do not yet know whether and to what extent the processes that are defective in BG are related to the processes subserved by the right anterior prefrontal regions activated in PET studies of intact participants. Our findings are consistent with data from split-brain patients indicating that the left hemisphere is more prone to false recognition based on general similarity between study and test items than is the right hemisphere (Metcalfe, Funnell, & Gazzaniga, 1995; Phelps & Gazzaniga, 1992). In contrast, Parkin, Bindschaedler, Harsent, and Metzler (1996) reported a patient with left frontal lobe damage who makes excessive numbers of false alarms and resembles patient BG in a number of respects. Nonetheless, Norman and Schacter (1996) noted that BG's deficits may be related to problems generating a specific, focused representation of a study episode and filtering out irrelevant information—processes that, as I suggested earlier, may depend importantly on right frontal regions.

ILLUSORY RECOGNITION IN ELDERLY
AND AMNESIC INDIVIDUALS

One striking feature of our experiments with BG is that some normal elderly control participants occasionally exhibited surprisingly high levels of false recognition. In view of the apparent contribution of frontal lobe dysfunction to false recognition in BG and other patients, and in view of the previously mentioned evidence on age-related changes in frontal lobe function, it seems plausible to suppose that older adults would be more susceptible than younger adults to false recognition and other memory illusions. A number of experiments have provided evidence that supports this suggestion (Bartlett, Strater, & Fulton, 1991; Dywan & Jacoby, 1990; Rankin & Kausler, 1979).

We (Norman & Schacter, 1997) recently examined illusory memories in older adults using a method for inducing false recognition recently described by Roediger and McDermott (1995). Their procedure is based on an earlier study by Deese (1959) in which people were exposed to lists of semantically associated words, such as *bitter, taste, chocolate, cake, candy, eat, pie,* and others, and were then asked to recall the presented words. Deese found that participants frequently intruded a nonpresented associate of the targets, such as *sweet.* Roediger and McDermott (1995) replicated this result and also found that on a remember/know recognition test, participants made extraordinarily large numbers of false alarms (i.e., 70%–80%) to nonstudied associates such as *sweet*. Moreover, participants' false alarms were frequently accompanied by remember responses. Although false recognition is a well-established phenomenon in experimental psychology (Underwood, 1965), the magnitude of the effect is usually rather modest, with the false alarm rate typically less than half of that observed by Roediger and McDermott (1995). Participants in Roediger and McDermott's experiments were behaving much like patient BG, claiming to possess specific recollections of words that were never presented.

In our experiments, older and younger adults listened to a series of 15-word lists, each comprised of strong associates of a nonpresented semantic associate such as *sweet.* After each list, participants were given 1 minute in which they either performed arithmetic problems or recalled words from the just presented list. After all lists had been presented, participants were given a remember/know recogniton test for studied words (true targets), nonstudied semantic associates (false targets; e.g., *sweet)*, and nonstudied words that were unrelated to study list items (true target controls and false target controls, respectively). In addition, half of the older and younger participants were instructed to write down a brief explanation of what they recollected about an item when they made a remember response to provide some clues concerning the kind of information that people access when they make false recognition responses.

The experiment yielded three main results. First, on the free recall test, older adults produced fewer study list words than younger adults, yet produced more intrusions of critical lures. Second, on the recognition test, elderly adults correctly recognized fewer studied words than did younger adults, yet falsely recognized slightly more false targets than did younger participants. Both older and younger adults frequently claimed to remember critical lures; young adults made somewhat fewer remember responses to false targets than to true targets, whereas elderly adults actually made more remember responses to false targets than to true targets. Third, requiring participants to provide explanations of their false recognition responses had no effect on the magnitude of the effect. Explanations typically consisted of semantic associations to target words (e.g., for the false target *needle*, one participant said "This word came in the same list as thread").

In a second experiment, we followed up on this finding by probing more formally the characteristics of older and younger adults' accurate and illusory recognition responses. To do so, we used a technique developed by Johnson and her colleagues (Johnson et al., 1988) in which people are asked to rate various characteristics of their memories on a 7-point scale, ranging from *1 no memory of a particular characteristic* to 7 *(vivid memory)*. Thus, when participants indicated that a word had appeared on the list, they were asked to rate their memory for the sound of the word, its serial position in the list, associations they made to the word at the time of study, and so forth. The main data concerning recall and recognition replicated the outcome of the previous experiment: participants frequently falsely recalled and recognized nonpresented semantic associates, and older adults were more relatively susceptible to these memory illusions than were younger adults. Analysis of participants' ratings showed that false recognition, like veridical recognition, was based largely on retrieval of associative and semantic information. However, whereas accurate and illusory recognition did not differ in terms of rated vividness of associative and semantic information, veridical recognition of studied words was accompanied by higher ratings of memory for the sound of the word and other contextual information than was false recognition. These patterns were observed in both older and younger adults, although they were somewhat less pronounced in the elderly participants.

Why are elderly adults more susceptible to illusory recognition than younger participants? In view of previous demonstrations of impaired frontal lobe functioning in older adults, and older adults' documented problems remembering specific information about particular presented items, such as their source, we think it is likely that their false recognition is based on a similar, although much less severe, impairment as that observed in BG. False targets in the Roediger and McDermott (1995) paradigm are semantically similar to numerous previously studied words. Thus, preserved memory for general or gist information, together with impaired memory for specific information, would generate the pattern of results observed in the elderly. Likewise, if older adults generated a false target as an associative response to target words during list presentation, they may have been less able than younger people to carry out the kinds of source monitoring activities necessary to determine whether they had actually heard the word or only thought of it (e.g., Craik et al., 1990; Johnson, Hashtroudi, & Lindsay, 1993; Schacter, Osowiecki, Kaszniak, Kihlstrom, & Valdiserri, 1994). Older adults appear to be unable to engage in the kinds of effortful retrieval or monitoring processes needed to oppose the strong feeling of recollection or familiarity associated with general similarity between false targets and previously studied targets.

We have also examined false recognition of semantic associates in patients with organic amnesia (Schacter, Verfaellie, & Pradere, 1996). The amnesic syndrome typically results from damage in the medial temporal lobes, including the hippocampal formation, or in diencephalic structures such as the mamillary bodies (e.g., Parkin & Leng, 1993; Squire, 1992). Amnesic patients have great difficulty remembering recent events and new information, despite preserved intelligence, perception, and language. Our experiment included eight amnesic patients with damage primarily in the medial temporal lobes as a result of anoxia or encephalitis, and four with damage to the diencephalic region asociated with Korsakoff's syndrome. Amnesics and 12 matched control participants heard lists of associates of critical lures; they were later tested for studied words, critical lures, and unrelated words that had not been studied. Not surprisingly, amnesic patients showed much less accurate recognition of previously presented words than did control participants. More interestingly, amnesic patients were also much less susceptible to false recognition of semantic associates than were control participants. Schacter, Verfaellie, and Anes (1997) recently replicated these results with a different set of semantic associates and extended them to the domain of perceptual false recognition. After studying lists of perceptually related words (e.g., fade, fame, mate, hate), amnesics made fewer false recognition responses than did controls to a perceptually related false target (e.g., fate). These results suggest that illusory recognition of false targets depends on some of the same underlying neuroanatomical substrate as does veridical recognition of words that were actually studied—the medial temporal/diencephalic regions that are damaged in amnesia.

Our previously mentioned PET study of older and younger adults by Schacter, Savage, et al. (1996) is consistent with this observation. As noted earlier, older adults showed normal patterns of hippocampal activation in the high recall condition despite abnormal patterns of frontal lobe activation in the low recall condition. Thus, if false recognition depends in some way on medial temporal activation during retrieval, it would make sense that older adults exhibit such effects.

NEUROANATOMICAL CORRELATES OF ACCURATE AND VERIDICAL RECOGNITION: A PET STUDY

To examine further the neural substrates of illusory recognition, Schacter, Reiman, et al. (1996) conducted a PET study using an adaptation of the Roediger and McDermott (1995) paradigm. Prior to scanning, participants listened to a long list of words grouped into semantic categories that each included 20 associates of a nonpresented false target. We then administered yes–no recognition tests in separate 60-second scans for old words that had appeared on the study list; false targets that had not appeared but were related to previously presented words and new words that had not appeared and were not systematically related to previously presented words (true target controls and false target controls, respectively). In a separate passive fixation scan, participants simply looked at a crosshair for 60 seconds.

Compared to the passive fixation condition, both accurate recognition of studied words and false recognition of semantic associates were accompanied by significant blood flow increases in many of the same brain regions, including frontal lobes bilaterally, precuneus, and the left medial temporal lobe, in the vicinity of the parahippocampal gyrus. This latter observation is intriguing in light of previously mentioned findings that amnesic patients with medial temporal damage exhibited little false recognition of critical lures (Schacter, Verfaellie, & Pradere, 1996), and that medial temporal blood flow increases are associated with successful recollection (Nyberg et al., 1996; Schacter, Alpert, et al., 1996).

We observed mainly similarities between accurate and illusory recognition, with direct comparison between the two yielding little evidence of differences. Nonetheless, we did observe some evidence for differential brain activity during accurate and illusory recognition. Veridical recognition was accompanied by significant blood flow increases in a temporoparietal region that was not observed during false recognition. These differences were most pronounced in the vicinity of supramarginal gyrus and superior temporal gyrus. Previous PET and lesion studies have implicated these regions in the processing and storage of phonological information (cf. Déemonet et al. 1992; Paulesu, Frith, & Frackowiak, 1993; Petersen, Fox, Posner, Mintun, & Raichle, 1989; Roeltgen & Heilman, 1985). In light of these observations, we hypothesized that temporoparietal increases associated with veridical recognition may reflect participants' recollections of having heard or rehearsed the target words at the time of study; no such auditory and phonological information was available for critical lures. Although this idea is a preliminary one, it does fit well with the previously mentioned finding reported by Norman and Schacter (1997) and also by Mather, Henkel, and Johnson (1997) that people report more extensive memories of having heard or thought about true targets than false targets. However, we must be cautious regarding interpretation of this preliminary finding until further evidence is available from additional experiments.

One further suggestive finding from the PET study relates to the previously mentioned observations of a link between frontal lobe impairments and heightened susceptibility to false recognition. We found that false recognition was associated with more extensive activation in inferior frontal regions (orbitofrontal cortex) bilaterally and right anterior prefrontal cortex than was veridical recognition. One possible intepretation of this finding is that participants were trying to oppose or inhibit the sense of familiarity or recollection associated with the critical lures. That is, when participants were deciding whether a critical lure had appeared previously, they likely experienced a strong feeling that it did. At the same time, knowing that many associatively related items were on the list, they may have engaged in effortful retrieval processes as they tried to remember specific information about the test item's appearance in the study list. These are the kinds of processes that we suggested are deficient in patient BG, who exhibited extensive false recognition after a right frontal lobe lesion (Curran et al.,

1997; Schacter, Curran, et al., 1996), and are impaired to a lesser degree in elderly adults, who are especially susceptible to false recognition and show signs of frontal lobe dysfunction. These ideas lead to the prediction that older adults would show less evidence of blood flow increases in frontal regions during false recognition than younger adults.

Johnson et al. (1997) recently examined brain activity during false recognition of semantic associates using event-related potentials (ERPs), which provide a measure of averaged brain electrical activity in response to external stimuli. Although ERPs do not yield the kind of fine-grained spatial resolution of brain activity that PET provides, they do have one important advantage over PET techniques. Standard PET designs require blocking of stimuli according to experimental condition. Thus, for example, in the Schacter, Reiman, et al. (1996) PET study, all of the true targets were presented during one 1-minute scan, false targets were presented in a separate scan, and true target controls and false target controls were presented in two additional separate scans. By contrast, when using ERPs, it is possible to randomly intermix various types of items during test presentation, and then compare averaged waveforms for the various item types (e.g., true targets, false targets, etc.).

When test stimuli were blocked into different item types, as in the PET study, Johnson et al. (1997) observed a roughly similar pattern of results as had been observed with PET: There were significant differences between waveforms associated with true and false recognition at frontal electrode sites, and some evidence for differences at a left parietal electrode site. However, when the various item types were randomly intermixed during test presentation, Johnson et al. found no significant differences in ERP waveforms during true and false recognition.

Although the exact relation of these ERP results to the PET data is not entirely clear, the results indicate that test format influences brain activity during veridical and illusory recognition. Johnson et al. (1997) suggested that in blocked presentation conditions, where all the words within a block may seem equally familiar (or unfamiliar) to participants, they may focus on the presence or absence of sensory information (i.e., auditory and phonological details about what was heard during the study phase of the experiment). By contrast, in mixed test conditions, where some words seem highly familiar and others seem unfamiliar, participants may base their recognition decisions more heavily on a general sense of semantic familiarity with the test item, thus yielding largely similar patterns of brain activity during true and false recognition. These results indicate that conclusions about similarites and differences in brain activity during true and false recognition will likely depend importantly on how memory is tested, as well as on other features of experimental paradigms (e.g., materials, mode of study presentation, etc.), and perhaps on the imaging procedures that are used (for a recent fMRI study of true and false recognition, see Schacter, Buckner, Koutstaal, Dale, & Rosen, 1997).

CONCLUDING COMMENTS

Our knowledge of the neural systems and processes involved in illusory memories is still meager, and relevant empirical studies are just beginning. Nonetheless, the preliminary findings described in this chapter suggest that a cognitive neuroscience analysis is likely to provide important new insights into errors and distortions of remembering, which in turn can serve as a useful window on the nature of constructive processes in human memory. By comparing and contrasting different kinds of memory illusions, it should be possible to delineate the component processes involved in each of them. For example, the study by Schacter, Verfaellie, and Pradere (1996) discussed earlier shows that amnesic patients are less susceptible to false recognition of critical lures than are normal controls. By contrast, other recent evidence indicates that amnesics are more susceptible than controls to false recognitions based on illusory memory conjunctions, where people claim to have encountered a stimulus previously when in fact they only saw its component features separately (Kroll, Knight, Metcalfe, Wolf, & Tulving, 1996; Reinitz, Verfaellie, & Milberg, 1996). Illusory memory conjunctions appear to be attributable to inadequate binding of features at the time of encoding, a process that likely depends on the hippocampal formation (Kroll et al., 1996). Taken together, these studies highlight the different ways in which medial temporal brain regions may contribute to constructive aspects of remembering. Although concern with constructive processes has long been restricted to investigators taking a purely psychological approach, it seems likely that the analytic tools of modern cognitive neuroscience will enable us to penetrate more deeply into some of the most enigmatic yet revealing aspects of human memory.

REFERENCES

Andreason, N. C., O'Leary, D. S., Arndt, S., Cizadlo, T., Hurtig, R., Rezai, K., Watkins, G. L., Boles Ponto, L. L., & Hichwa, R. D. (1995). Short-term and long-term verbal memory: A positron emission tomography study. *Proceedings of the National Academy of Sciences, 92,* 5111–5115.

Bartlett, F. C. (1932). *Remembering*. Cambridge, UK: Cambridge University Press.

Bartlett, J. C., Strater, L., & Fulton, A. (1991). False recency and false fame of faces in young adulthood and old age. *Memory & Cognition, 19,* 177–188.

Bransford, J. D., & Franks, J. J. (1971). The abstraction of linguistic ideas. *Cognitive Psychology, 2,* 331–350.

Buckner, R. L., & Petersen, S. E. (1996). What does neuroimaging tell us about the role of prefrontal cortex in memory retrieval? *Seminars in the Neurology, 8,* 47–55.

Buckner, R. L., & Tulving, E. (1995). Neuroimaging studies of memory: Theory and recent PET results. In F. Boller & J. Grafman (Eds.), *Handbook of neuropsychology* (Vol. 10, pp. 439–466). Amsterdam: Elsevier.

Ceci, S. J. (1995). False beliefs: Some developmental and clinical considerations. In D. L. Schacter, J. T. Coyle, G. D. Fischbach, M.-M. Mesulam, & L. E. Sullivan (Eds.), *Memory Distortion* (pp. 91–128). Cambridge, MA: Harvard University Press.

Craik, F. I. M., Morris, L. W., Morris, R. G., & Loewen, E. R. (1990). Relations between source amnesia and frontal lobe functioning in older adults. *Psychology and Aging, 5,* 148–151.

Craik, F. I. M., & Tulving, E. (1975). Depth of processing and the retention of words in episodic memory. *Journal of Experimental Psychology: General, 104,* 268–294.

Curran, T., Schacter, D. L., Norman, K. A., & Galluccio, L. (1997). False recognition after a right frontal lobe infarction: Memory for general and specific information. *Neuropsychologia, 35,* 1035–1049.

Dalla Barba, G. (1993). Confabulation: Knowledge and recollective experience. *Cognitive Neuropsychology, 10,* 1–20.

Damasio, A. R. (1989). Time-locked multiregional retroactivation: A systems-level proposal for the neural substrates of recall and recognition. *Cognition, 33,* 25–62.

Deese, J. (1959). On the prediction of occurrence of particular verbal intrusions in immediate recall. *Journal of Experimental Psychology, 58,* 17–22.

Démonet, J.-F., Chollet, F., Ramsay, S., Cardebat, D., Nespoulous, J.-L., Wise, R., Rascol, A., & Frackowiak, R. (1992). The anatomy of phonological and semantic processing in normal subjects. *Brain, 115,* 1753–1768.

Dywan, J., & Bowers, K. S. (1983). The use of hypnosis to enhance recall. *Science, 222,* 1184–1185.

Dywan, J., & Jacoby, L. L. (1990). Effect of aging and source monitoring: Differences in susceptibility to false fame. *Psychology and Aging, 3,* 379–387.

Gardiner, J. M., & Java, R. I. (1993). Recognising and remembering. In A. F. Collins, S. E. Gathercole, M. A. Conway, & P. E. Morris (Eds.), *Theories of memory* (pp. 163–188). Hove, UK: Lawrence Erlbaum Associates.

Glisky, E. L., Polster, M. R., & Routhieaux, B. C. (1995). Double dissociation between item and source memory. *Neuropsychology, 9,* 229–235.

Jacoby, L. L., & Whitehouse, K. (1989). An illusion of memory: False recognition influenced by unconscious perception. *Journal of Experimental Psychology: General, 118,* 126–135.

Janowsky, J. S., Shimamura, A. P., & Squire, L. R. (1989). Source memory impairment in patients with frontal lobe lesions. *Neuropsychologia, 27,* 1043–1056.

Johnson, M. K. (1991). Reality monitoring: Evidence from confabulation in organic brain disease patients. In G. P. Prigatano & D. L. Schacter (Eds.), *Awareness of deficit after brain injury: Clinical and theoretical issues* (pp. 176–197). New York: Oxford University Press.

Johnson, M. K., Foley, M. A., Suengas, A. G., & Raye, C. L. (1988). Phenomenal characteristics of memories for perceived and imagined autobiographical events. *Journal of Experimental Psychology: General, 117,* 371–376.

Johnson, M. K., Hashtroudi, S., & Lindsay, D. S. (1993). Source monitoring. *Psychological Bulletin, 114,* 3–28.

Johnson, M. K., Nolde, S. F., Mather, M., Kounios, J., Schacter, D. L., & Curran, T. (1997). The similarity of brain activity associated with true and false recognition memory depends on test format. *Psychological Science, 8,* 250–257.

Kapur, S., Craik, F. I. M., Jones, C., Brown, G. H., Houle, S., & Tulving, E. (1995). Functional roles of prefrontal cortex in retrieval of memories: A PET study. *NeuroReport, 6,* 1880–1884.

Kihlstrom, J. F. (in press). Exhumed memory. In S. J. Lynn & N. P. Spanos (Eds.), *Truth and memory.* New York: Guilford.

Kroll, N. E. A., Knight, R. T., Metcalfe, J., Wolf, E. S., & Tulving, E. (1996). Cohesion failure as a source of memory illusions. *Journal of Memory and Language, 35,* 176–196.

Lindsay, D. S., & Read, J. D. (1994). Psychotherapy and memories of childhood sexual abuse: A cognitive perspective. *Applied Cognitive Psychology, 8*, 281–338.

Loftus, E. F. (1979). *Eyewitness testimony.* Cambridge, MA: Harvard University Press.

Loftus, E. F. (1993). The reality of repressed memories. *American Psychologist, 48*, 518–537.

Loftus, E. F., Miller, D. G., & Burns, H. J. (1978). Semantic integration of verbal information into a visual memory. *Journal of Experimental Psychology: Human Learning and Memory, 4*, 19–31.

Mather, M., Henkel, L. A., & Johnson, M. K. (1997). Evaluating characteristics of false memories: Remember/know judgments and Memory Characteristics Questionnaire compared. *Memory and Cognition, 25*, 826–837.

McClelland, J. L. (1995). Constructive memory and memory distortions: A parallel-distributed processing approach. In D. L. Schacter, J. T. Coyle, G. D. Fischbach, M.-M. Mesulam, & L. E. Sullivan (Eds.), *Memory distortion: How minds, brains and societies reconstruct the past* (pp. 69–90). Cambridge, MA: Harvard University Press.

Metcalfe, J., Funnell, M., & Gazzaniga, M. S. (1995). Right-hemisphere memory superiority: Studies of a split-brain patient. *Psychological Science, 6*, 157–164.

Milner, B., Corkin, S., & Teuber, H. L. (1968). Further analysis of the hippocampal amnesic syndrome: Fourteen year follow-up study of H. M. *Neuropsychologia, 6*, 215–234.

Moscovitch, M. (1995). Confabulation. In D. L. Schacter (Ed.), *Memory distortion: How minds, brains, and societies reconstruct the past* (pp. 226–254). Cambridge, MA: Harvard University Press.

Neisser, U. (1967). *Cognitive psychology.* New York: Appleton-Century-Crofts.

Norman, K. A., & Schacter, D. L. (1996). Implicit memory, explicit memory, and false recollection: A cognitive neuroscience perspective. In L. M. Reder (Ed.), *Implicit memory and metacognition* pp. 229–257. Mahwah, NJ: Lawrence Erlbaum Associates.

Norman, K. A., & Schacter, D. L. (1997). False recognition in young and older adults: Exploring the characteristics of illusory memories. *Memory and Cognition, 25*, 838–848.

Nyberg, L., McIntosh, A. R., Houle, S., Nilsson, L.-G., & Tulving, E. (1996). Activation of medial temporal structures during episodic memory retrieval. *Nature, 380*, 715–717.

Nyberg, L., Tulving, E., Habib, R., Nilsson, L.-G., Kapur, S., Houle, S., Cabeza, R., & McIntosh, A. R. (1995). Functional brain maps of retrieval mode and recovery of episodic information. *NeuroReport, 6*, 249–252.

Parkin, A. J., Bindschaedler, C., Harsent, L., & Metzler, C. (1996). Verification impairment in the generation of memory deficit following ruptured aneurysm of the anterior communicating artery. *Brain & Cognition, 32*, 14–27.

Parkin, A. J., & Leng, N. R. C. (1993). *Neuropsychology of the amnesic syndrome.* Hillsdale, NJ: Lawrence Erlbaum Associates.

Paulesu, E., Frith, C. D., & Frackowiak, R. S. J. (1993). The neural correlates of the verbal component of working memory. *Nature, 362*, 342–345.

Petersen, S. E., Fox, P. T., Posner, M. I., Mintun, M. A., & Raichle, M. E. (1989). Positron emission tomographic studies of the processing of single words. *Journal of Cognitive Neuroscience, 1*, 153–170.

Phelps, E., & Gazzaniga, M. S. (1992). Hemispheric differences in mnemonic processing: The effects of left hemisphere interpretation. *Neuropsychologia, 30*, 293–297.

Rankin, J. S., & Kausler, D. H. (1979). Adult age differences in false recognitions. *Journal of Gerontology, 34*, 58–65.

Reinitz, M. T., Verfaellie, M., & Milberg, W. P. (1996). Memory conjunction errors in normal and amnesic subjects. *Journal of Memory and Language, 35*, 286–299.

Roediger, H. L., III. (1996). Memory illusions. *Journal of Memory and Language, 35*, 76–100.

Roediger, H. L., III, & McDermott, K. B. (1995). Creating false memories: Remembering words not presented in lists. *Journal of Experimental Psychology: Learning, Memory, and Cognition, 21*, 803–814.

Roeltgen, D. P. & Heilman, K. M. (1985). Review of agraphia and a proposal for an anatomical-based neuropsychological model of writing. *Applied Psycholinguistics, 6*, 205–229.

Rugg, M. D., Fletcher, P. C., Frith, C. D., Frackowiak, R. S. J., & Dolan, R. J. (1996). Differential response of the prefrontal cortex in successful and unsuccessful memory retrieval. *Brain, 119*, 2073–2083.

Schacter, D. L. (1987). Memory, amnesia, and frontal lobe dysfunction. *Psychobiology, 15*, 21–36.

Schacter, D. L. (1995). Memory distortion: History and current status. In D. L. Schacter (Ed.), *Memory distortion: How minds, brains and societies reconstruct the past* (pp. 1–43). Cambridge, MA: Harvard University Press.

Schacter, D. L. (1996). *Searching for memory: The brain, the mind, and the past.* New York: Basic Books.

Schacter, D. L., Alpert, N. M., Savage, C. R., Rauch, S. L., & Albert, M. S. (1996). Conscious recollection and the human hippocampal formation: Evidence from positron emission tomography. *Proceedings of the National Academy of Sciences, 93*, 321–325.

Schacter, D. L., Buckner, R. L., Koutstaal, W., Dale, A., & Rosen, B. (1997). Late onset of anterior prefrontal activity during true and false recognition: An event-related fMRI study. *NeuroImage, 6*, 259–269.

Schacter, D. L., Curran, T., Galluccio, L., Milberg, W., & Bates, J. (1996). False recognition and the right frontal lobe: A case study. *Neuropsychologia, 34*, 793–808.

Schacter, D. L., Harbluk, J. L., & McLachlan, D. R. (1984). Retrieval without recollection: An experimental analysis of source amnesia. *Journal of Verbal Learning and Verbal Behavior, 23*, 593–611.

Schacter, D. L., Norman, K. A., & Koutstaal, W. (1997). The recovered memory debate: A cognitive neuroscience perspective. In M. A. Conway (Ed.), *False and recovered memories* (pp. 63–99. New York: Oxford University Press.

Schacter, D. L., Norman, K. A., & Koutstaal, W. (1998). The cognitive neuroscience of constructive memory. *Annual Review of Psychology, 49*, 289–318.

Schacter, D. L., Osowiecki, D. M., Kaszniak, A. F., Kihlstrom, J. F., & Valdiserri, M. (1994). Source memory: Extending the boundaries of age-related deficits. *Psychology and Aging, 9*, 81–89.

Schacter, D. L., Reiman, E., Curran, T., Yun, L. S., Bandy, D., McDermott, K. B., & Roediger, H. L., III. (1996). Neuroanatomical correlates of veridical and illusory recognition memory: Evidence from positron emission tomography. *Neuron, 17*, 267–274.

Schacter, D. L., Reiman, E., Uecker, A., Polster, M. R., Yun, L. S., & Cooper, L. A. (1995). Brain regions associated with retrieval of structurally coherent visual information. *Nature, 376*, 587–590.

Schacter, D. L., Savage, C. R., Alpert, N. M., Rauch, S. L., & Albert, M. S. (1996). The role of hippocampus and frontal cortex in age-related memory changes: A PET study. *NeuroReport, 7*, 1165–1169.

Schacter, D. L., Verfaellie, M., & Anes, M. D. (1997). Illusory memories in amnesic patients: Conceptual and perceptual false recognition. *Neuropsychology, 11*, 331–342.

Schacter, D. L., Verfaellie, M., & Pradere, D. (1996). The neuropsychology of memory illusions: False recall and recognition in amnesic patients. *Journal of Memory and Language, 35*, 319–334.

Shallice, T., Fletcher, P., Frith, C. D., Grasby, P., Frackowiak, R. S. J., & Dolan, R. J. (1994). Brain regions associated with acquisition and retrieval of verbal episodic memory. *Nature, 368*, 633–635.

Squire, L. R. (1987). *Memory and brain.* New York: Oxford University Press.

Squire, L. R. (1992). Memory and the hippocampus: A synthesis from findings with rats, monkeys, and humans. *Psychological Review, 99*, 195–231.

Squire, L. R., Ojemann, J. G., Miezin, F. M., Petersen, S. E., Videen, T. O., & Raichle, M. E. (1992). Activation of the hippocampus in normal humans: A functional anatomical study of memory. *Proceedings of the National Academy of Sciences, 89*, 1837–1841.

Tulving, E. (1983). *Elements of episodic memory.* Oxford, UK: Clarendon.

Tulving, E. (1985). Memory and consciousness. *Canadian Psychologist, 26*, 1–12.

Tulving, E., Kapur, S., Markowitsch, H. J., Craik, F. I. M., Habib, R., & Houle, S. (1994). Neuroanatomical correlates of retrieval in episodic memory: Auditory sentence recognition. *Proceedings of the National Academy of Sciences, 91*, 2012–2015.

Tulving, E., & Schacter, D. L. (1990). Priming and human memory systems. *Science, 247*, 301–306.

Underwood, B. J. (1965). False recognition produced by implicit verbal responses. *Journal of Experimental Psychology, 70*, 122–129.

Ungerleider, L. G. (1995). Functional brain imaging studies of cortical mechanisms for memory. *Science, 270*, 760–775.

7

The Impact of Metacognitive Reflection On Cognitive Control

Cesare Cornoldi
University of Padova, Italy

This chapter examines the impact of metacognitive reflection (i.e., people's beliefs and interpretations about their cognitive activity) on cognitive behavior. I present evidence in favor of the hypothesis that this impact is important. From one point of view this hypothesis can appear obvious. In fact, how could it be possible that what we think about our actions does not influence what we are doing? However, some skepticism about this hypothesis does exist.

To examine this issue I first introduce some terms and definitions. I will distinguish between pre-existing metacognitive knowledge and the metacognitive conceptualization that is activated when a person is faced with a cognitive task. I then argue that metacognitive knowledge cannot be reduced to a corpus of declarative knowledge. I also focus on two different ways metacognitive knowledge can influence cognitive behavior, one due to the individual's attitude toward cognitive tasks (here called *metacognitive attitude*) and the other related to the subject's specific metacognitive knowledge. I end by examining a particular type of metacognitive influence that occurs when metacognitive conceptualization has a disruptive effect on cognitive activity.

To clarify the main distinctions and definitions introduced in these first paragraphs, Table 7.1 offers an overview of the main distinctions and definitions introduced in these paragraphs.

TABLE 7.1

Components of Metacognitive Reflection

Metacognitive reflection: People's beliefs and interpretation of cognitive activity. It can be distinguished in two aspects: (a) metacognitive knowledge, and (b) metacognitive conceptualization of a task.

Metacognitive knowledge: People's beliefs concerning all possible aspects of cognitive activity (nature, functioning, self-evaluation, etc.), preexisting before actual cognitive tasks must be carried out. It may be general or specific, more or less conscious, verbalizable, and so forth.

Metacognitive conceptualization of a task: Metacognitive reflection present at the moment of starting a task and during its execution.

Metacognitive attitude: Overall level of metacognitive knowledge, with cognitive, emotional-motivational, and behavioral implications (see also this section).

Specific metacognitive knowledge: Knowledge concerning specific aspects of cognitive functioning.

METACOGNITIVE REFLECTION

Introspective evidence shows that doing cognitive tasks is typically accompanied by a metacognitive reflection concerning the task. Suppose we have to memorize a poem.

Our first reaction will probably be to estimate how much effort and trouble will be produced by this task. We can estimate this, roughly, even without reading the verses, by basing our estimation on our knowledge of similar experiences. For our estimation we will then consider a conspicuous series of variables, like the nature of the material, the nature of the task, of the test, the expected retention interval, the desired level of acquisition, and so forth. When we begin to examine the verses, we might use additional information to make metacognitive judgments about the task; for example, we could decide that the task is easier than expected because we could use particular strategies and, for example, take advantage of rhymes, similarities in sounds, redundancy, and so on.

All these metacognitive considerations belong to a broad area of metacognitive reflection, concerning ideas a person has about the characteristics of a cognitive task. It is evident that metacognitive reflection has different components. In particular we can distinguish between the type of reflection the individual had in advance (I have called this preexisting reflection metacognitive knowledge; Cornoldi & Vianello, 1992) and the type of reflection the person develops when faced with the cognitive task (I have called it metacognitive conceptualization). This last aspect is not a simple application of metacognitive knowledge to the specific case, but it is subjected to modifications and articulations due to the particular context of the moment.

THE CHARACTERISTICS OF METACOGNITIVE KNOWLEDGE

A few different lines of research have tried to describe characteristics of metacognitive knowledge; these studies include Flavell's (1981) explorations of children's ideas about different aspects of cognitive functioning; the researchers involved in the study of folk psychology, or people's naive comprehension of their own mental states (Goldman, 1993; Stich, 1983); and researchers whose work was more specifically focused on the development of a theory of mind (i.e., the ability to recognize that other people's mental states are different from our own; e.g., Wimmer & Perner, 1983).

I have argued elsewhere that metacognitive knowledge can be considered similar to any other form of knowledge, or examined in a similar way. This could seem not inappropriate, as metacognitive knowledge can appear different from other forms of declarative knowledge that are more explicit and well organized. For example knowledge about mammals (that they can move, have four legs, skin, hair, etc.) appears well defined, organized, and easy to verbalize. The same cannot be said of many points of metacognitive knowledge. If we consider again the to-be-memorized verses of a poem, we can also develop emotional feelings related to the verses per se and to the task, aspects that may be partially unconscious and difficult to verbalize, but that could nonetheless interact with other more explicit aspects of metacognitive knowledge. In this respect, metacognitive knowledge is different from other forms of knowledge.

However, the same point can be raised about the apparently well organized domains of knowledge. If we come back to the example about mammals, we observe that our knowledge also includes ill-structured information such as that cats are pleasant animals and we could probably estimate how much we would like all other mammals in the same way (connotative knowledge); we know how to milk cows (procedural knowledge); we have a personal memory of a horse we saw one day casting sheep's eyes at us (autobiographical memory for a single event); and so on.

Therefore, if the knowledge about a well-organized knowledge domain, like mammals, presents such a variety of stored information, we cannot be surprised by the fact that the same also applies to metacognitive knowledge.

When we examine the relation between metacognitive knowledge and cognitive behaviors some aspects of metacognitive knowledge appear particularly important. In this perspective I started by distinguishing two aspects of metacognitive knowledge that could be differently related to behavior, to show how metacognitive reflection can influence cognitive activity. The first aspect is a general component of metacognitive knowledge I first called strategic attitude (Cornoldi, 1987) and then metacognitive attitude (Cornoldi & Caponi, 1991). The second aspect is represented by specific metacognitive knowledge. This distinction overlaps with other specifications present in the literature. For example, the idea of a general metacognitive attitude partially overlaps with the concept of sensitivity proposed by Flavell (1976, 1981) and the concept of general metacognitive knowledge proposed by Borkowski and co-authors (e.g. Borkowski, Weyhing, & Carr, 1988). The more general definition of Cornoldi and Caponi (1991) focused on a core subdomain of the domain of metacognitive knowledge, an intersection of general ideas, emotional evaluations, and inclination to use metacognitive knowledge; hence the use of the term attitude, typically associated in social psycology with the joint intervention of cognitive, emotiona,l and behavioral aspects.

Furthermore, as suggested by Cornoldi and Vianello (1992), metacognitive knowledge can be characterized with reference to a series of aspects such as its level of specificity, its range of application, the ease of access, whether it can be verbalized or not, the modality of acquisition, the level of awareness, its applicability, the number of connections with other knowledge domains, its level of coherence, and many aspects. Given these premises, examining one person's metacognitive knowledge can be a difficult task that requires, as I mentioned in previous work (e.g. Cornoldi, 1995), consideration of an additional series of issues (problems) listed in Table 7.2.

THE RELATION BETWEEN METACOGNITIVE KNOWLEDGE AND COGNITIVE BEHAVIOR: THE SKEPTICAL VIEWS

It is intuitive that, if we have some ideas concerning a particular cognitive activity, these ideas should influence that activity. In the history of philosophy I first found this intuition in the small treaty on memory of Aristotle (see Aristotle, 1965, p. 62) In the passage, Aristotle discussed different ways of remembering and described an active way of remembering (which can be translated into recollection) that is influenced by the ideas a person has about memory, and in particular by the idea inspiring human memory retrieval. The

TABLE 7.2

Sources of Errors (or Variability) in the Examination of Metacognitive Knowledge

1. Variables affecting the interaction during the examination.

2. Linguistic competence.

3. Decontextualized questions.

4. Prolonged examination.

5. No independence with respect to cognitive behavior.

6. Inability to individuate proneness to application.

7. Low psychometric properties.

8. Absence of validations.

9. Confusion between knowledge of the mental event and its external referents.

10. No possibility of distinguishing between a metacognitive level and the levels in other intellectual abilities.

11. Biases in the interview.

12. Absence of other convergent measures.

idea is that, if an information entered into the mind, in principle it should still be there. Therefore a retrieval failure does not mean a memory loss. It is on the basis of this idea that a person decides to work harder in order to find the missing information. In other words, Aristotle assumed that an idea can influence the amount of effort spent in a cognitive task and modify the quality of the memory processes.

A naive way of establishing the relation between metacognitive knowledge and behavior is to assume that this relation is perfect.

This position is based on unrealistic assumptions concerning the perfect efficiency, rationality, and power (influence) of the human mind to activate, at a certain moment, all the relevant ideas it has about the task.

In the absence of such a perfect correspondence, psychologists are tempted to disregard the relation between metacognitive knowledge and cognitive behavior. This skepticism has found unexpected support in positions favoring the assumption of nonpenetrability of cognitive processes. Some theories (e.g., Fodor, 1983) were focused on simple, hard-wired units of cognitive processing, corresponding to well-defined units of neural functioning, which can be primed and developed without the individual's control and then, a fortiori, without the influence of a specific metacognitive conceptualization. This position was also appealing for complex cognitive processes the penetrability of which was under discussion.

Skeptical conceptions about the influence of metacognitive knowledge on cognitive behaviour can assume two different forms: independent coexistence and epiphenomenal experience. From an independent coexistence point of view, metacognitive knowledge has independent development but does not have any real influence on cognitive behavior. From an epiphenomenal experience point of view, metacognitive knowledge is a simple epiphenomenon, a by-product of cognitive behavior, having only the role of making such behavior aware, but without exerting any influence on it. The epiphenomenal position is obviously completely critical to the hypothesis guiding this chapter (i.e., that metacognitive knowledge affects behavior in substantial way), and offers a different interpretation of the correlational data showing rather strong significant correlations between metacognitive knowledge and cognitive behavior. For example, Schneider and Pressley (1989) reported mean correlations of 0.47 for 10 to–11-years-old children between knowledge about organizational strategies and their use (as inferred from clustering scores) and, considering a variety of different studies, the mean correlation between metacognition and cognitive behavior was 0.41 (Schneider & Pressley, 1989). According to the epiphenomenal experience view, a more adequate metacognitive knowledge is the consequence of a more adequate cognitive behavior, and not vice versa.

METACOGNITIVE ATTITUDE
AND ITS INFLUENCE ON BEHAVIOR

The metacognitive attitude (Cornoldi & Caponi, 1991) concerns the general tendency of a person to develop reflection about the nature of his or her own cognitive activity and to think about the possibility of extending and using this reflection. A metacognitive attitude may help people when they do not have specific metacognitive knowledge about the cognitive task they must undergo. The ability to transfer known strategies to new tasks and the amount of time and effort spent in trying to accomplish the task are both related to metacognitive attitude.

This definition has two implications concerning the relation between metacognitive knowledge and cognitive behavior. First, we expect people who have better metacognitive attitude to be more inclined to use their metacognitive knowledge. In turn, this should lead people with high metacognitive attitude to have a high correlation between metacognitive knowledge and cognitive behavior. Second, high metacognitive attitude individuals should develop more resources, information, and strategies, and therefore perform better on cognitive tasks.

The first implication is (modestly) confirmed by the fact that typically the correlations between specific metacognitive knowledge and cognitive behavior increase with age (Schneider & Pressley, 1989). Older children, who typically have higher metacognitive attitude, also often present higher correlations between metacognitive knowledge and cognitive behavior.

With reference to the second implication, there is some evidence confirming the predicted relation, specifically the fact that effort (one of the main aspects of metacognitive attitude) has a positive effect on performance. The consideration of this aspect was largely influenced by the attribution theory when applied to explain the results of our actions (Weiner, 1985). Usually, self-attributions are examined by asking participants to explain the reason for their successes or failures (e.g., a good performance at an examination, a failure in solving a problem, etc.). Participants are invited to choose among factors like effort, luck, received help, ability, and so forth. It has been observed that self-effort explanations (i.e., successes explained on the basis of the devoted effort and failures explained on the basis of a lack of effort) correspond to better performance in a variety of cognitive tasks. For example, Cornoldi and De Beni (1996, Experiment 2) divided elderly people into two effort attribution groups according to the number of times (out of eight) effort attributions was chosen as the cause of their success or failure in a cognitive task. Approximately 50% of the participants had more than three effort attributions (high self-effort), and these participants also had significantly better performance in a series of memory tests in which they were required to use specific strategies. This performance was about 20% better than the performance of low-self-effort attribution participants. Similar results were obtained by other researchers with developmental populations (Borkowski, Carr, Rellinger, & Pressley, 1990). The pattern of relation between self-effort attribution and quality of cognitive performance is further specified by the repeated observation that poor learners also give a lower number of self-effort attributions, especially when they have to explain their failures (e.g., Pearl, Bryan, & Donahue, 1980). Data obtained with poor learners, however, raise the problem of the direction of the relation:Is effort attribution that produces an improvement in performance, or it is good performance that creates the opportunity to attribute successes and failures to effort? In fact, when the role of self-attribution is considered in individuals of different levels of ability, it is plausible to expect that high-ability individuals have a better performance and the possibility to experience the positive effect of greater effort more than low-ability participants.

With developmental populations, a widely used procedure for examining the relation between general aspects of metacognitive knowledge and cognitive behavior employed psychometric estimation of the individual's general level of metacognitive knowledge. Typically the estimation was based on the answers given by a child to a sample of questions about metacognitive knowledge (e.g., Kreutzer, Leonard, & Flavell, 1975). It can be assumed that people who have, in general, better metacognitive knowledge also have a better metacognitive attitude. Using this procedure, we (Caponi & Cornoldi, 1989) found in 6 to 8-year-old children a highly significant positive correlation between metacognitive knowledge and free recall (.70). The score in metacognitive knowledge highly also correlated with a strategy use score (given by two judges who observed the child's behavior on a videotape) despite the fact that none of the observed strategies was considered in the questionnaire used to measure metacognitive knowledge.

In our research, we have often measured metacognitive knowledge by using a procedure that is more sensitive to the core aspects of metacognitive knowledge and that can overcome some of the measure problems shown in Table 7.2. In our procedure, we tell the child a story that deals with central aspects of metacognitive knowledge. In our most frequently used story, a prince forgets, after a long trip, the instructions he received in order to free a princess who was imprisoned in a castle. We ask the child to anticipate the forgetting event, to explain it, to help the prince to remember and then to memorize again the critical instructions (Cornoldi, Gobbo, & Mazzoni, 1991). In this case the number of different types of knowledge that we tested is not high, but it is nevertheless representative of the most important ideas concerning memory. Scores obtained with this procedure were always significantly correlated with memory behavior (Cornoldi, 1995).

With reference to reading, the influence of metacognitive attitude on cognitive behavior has been confirmed in a number of studies (e.g., Pazzaglia, Cornoldi, & De Beni, 1995) showing that poor readers not only have poorer metacognitive knowledge about reading than good readers, but also have less metacognitive knowledge related to other areas of cognitive functioning like memory (e.g., Papetti, Cornoldi, Pettavino, Mazzoni, & Borkowski, 1992), or mathematics (Lucangeli, Cornoldi, & Tessari, 1991). This result suggests that a metacognitive knowledge deficit can be general and can affect different cognitive areas. The strongest evidence in favor of the role of a metacognitive attitude comes from the fact that, by changing only metacognitive knowledge without affecting other variables, we can obtain positive effects on cognitive behavior. Such positive effects can also be observed when cognitive behavior involves the use of strategies and processes on which participants were not directly trained.

In principle, research on the effect of programs aimed at improving metacognitive knowledge that do not include parallel training in the use of control cognitive processes can offer the most compelling evidence concerning the causal role of metacognitive knowledge and metacognitive attitude in modifying cognitive behavior. Consider two perfectly matched groups, each having a different training program, where only one group is subjected to training in metacognitive knowledge. If, after training, the two groups show significant differences, these differences could be attributed to a causal role of metacognitive knowledge.

Lucangeli, Galderisi and Cornoldi (1994) did two training experiments in which they created situations that developed participant's metacognitive knowledge about memory and increased their level of metacognitive attitude. In the first experiment fifthgraders, at the end of the training, not only had better knowledge about memory, but also better performed in a free recall task. In the second experiment, third- to fifth-graders trained in metamemory were better not only in memory tasks, but also in reading comprehension and problem solving.

A further result in this research appears important. Lucangeli et al. (1994, Experiment 1) found that participants trained in metacognitive knowledge were better at transferring a learned strategy to a new context. Both control and experimental groups were trained in the use of an alphabetical strategy (consisting of scanning the whole alphabet) to retrieve series of letters, and after the training they obtained similar results on the specific task. When the task was partially changed, however, the members of the metacognitive group were significantly better than control participants at transferring the learned strategy to the new task. This result allows the development of a specific prediction related to the concept of metacognitive attitude, (i. e., that individuals with higher metacognitive attitude are better at transferring learned strategies to new contexts; see also Borkowski, Ryan, Kurtz, & Reid, 1983; Cavanaugh & Borkowski, 1980).

THE EFFECT OF SPECIFIC METACOGNITIVE KNOWLEDGE
ON COGNITIVE BEHAVIOR

A particularly evident case of the relation between specific metacognitive knowledge and cognitive behavior concerns specific strategy knowledge. A crude way of considering this issue could be the following. If you can successfully undergo a cognitive task by using Strategy A, will specific knowledge of that strategy increase the probability of using it (and the probability of success in the task)?

A positive answer to this question is apparently rather obvious. However, at a theoretical level, knowledge and use appear distinguishable, as confirmed by the possibility of talking about strategies without using them. Strategy knowledge also includes a general element of metacognitive knowledge; that is, that a strategic effort may enhance performance and that it can be more effective under some circumstances than others, but knowing why a strategy is effective is different from knowing how to use the strategy (Kramer & Engle, 1981), and different from knowing how a strategy works (Paris, Newman, & McVey, 1982).

A problem in studying cognitive strategies is related to the difficulty in defining what a strategy is (e.g., Kirby, 1984; Simon, 1978). For example the strategy of rehearsing the material to be memorized , or the strategy of thinking of all the possible alternative steps during problem solving are very general and content-independent. On the contrary, there are strategies that are strictly related to the memory content, (e.g., categorical organization in memorization), or that even indicate the specific operations required for succeeding in a task, (e.g., thinking about the possibility that a segment occupies space outside the square when trying to solve the Mayer's square problem of joining nine dots arranged in a square with four straight lines). It is evident that specific metacognitive knowledge can have different influences on cognitive behavior, depending on which specific strategy is involved.

The complexity of the relation between specific strategy knowledge and strategy use can be nicely illustrated by the strategy of categorical organization during encoding and retrieval. For example, children who have recognized the advantage of having to memorize categorizable material compared to material that could not be grouped into categories do not apply this knowledge during their memory tasks (see Sodian, Schneider, & Perlmutter, 1986). The opposite was also found: Children were found to use the strategy efficiently, but without being able to demonstrate that they were aware of the advantages of the strategy. Others (e.g., Bjorklund & Green, 1992) observed a strategy utilization deficit in children who started to use a strategy but were not able to draw complete benefit from its use. In an unpublished study we found that poor metacognitive knowledge could be the cause of this strategy utilization deficit, as children who used the categorical organization strategy without benefit were also less aware of its nature and its use than children who benefited from its use.

Other examples of the complexity of the relation between specific metacognitive knowledge and cognitive behaviors (such as strategy use) concern people who attended memory courses but did not use mnemonics because they had the (false) impression that mnemonics require much more effort than traditional memorization methods (Higbee, 1988). Even memory scholars, despite their sophisticated knowledge about memory, do not use sophisticated methods to remember. There is no difference between them, other nonpsychological academics, and university students in their use of strategies. In addition, they neither use nor recommend the use of mnemonics.

The case of mnemonics is interesting because it offers an example of how knowledge of a strategy can conflict with other metacognitive beliefs. In my follow-up interviews with people who had attended memory courses some months earlier, these people generally appeared convinced about the positive benefits of the use of mnemonics, but they did not use them. They explained the fact they had not used the mnemonics on the basis of two main principles that I call memory overestimation and initiating costs overestimation. In the first case, participants had generally the idea that the task was too simple to require the use of mnemonics; more traditional strategies would have been equally effective. In the second case, individuals believed that mnemonics require great effort, and they are not worth it.

Here I describe how the two principles can contribute to the behavioral decision. People have beliefs related to the use of mnemonics: They think that the advantages of their use are high only with complex tasks for whch the risk of failure is high. They also incorrectly estimate that the cost in cognitive resources implied by the use of mnemonics is high. Furthermore, faced with a cognitive task, people tend to underestimate its difficulty, with the consequence that they consider the use of mnemonics inappropriate.

A PARTICULAR CASE OF THE DEBATE ON THE RELATION BETWEEN KNOWLEDGE ABOUT A COGNITIVE PHENOMENON AND COGNITIVE BEHAVIOR: MENTAL IMAGERY

In the preceding paragraphs we considered the case of specific metacognitive knowledge concerning strategies and their actual use. Here we consider a different case of interconnection between specific metacognitive knowledge and cognitive activity: knowledge of the phenomenon. One example of knowledge of the phenomenon can be found in the studies on imagery, where the evaluation of the impact of the individual's knowledge about the phenomenon has become critical for the consideration of the phenomenon itself. People are assumed to consider visual imagery similar to visual perception. Therefore they may use their tacit knowledge about cognitive functioning in a perceptual task, and they behave, in the imagery tasks, as they think they behave in a perceptual condition (Pylyshyn, 1981). The argument can be incorporated in a radical anti-imaginistic position, proposing that the individual only tries to replicate the result expected in a perceptual condition and therefore that the outcome of an imagery task is a simple artifact. However the argument is coherent with our theory of mental imagery, which suggests that mental images, in contrast to visual perceptions, are more directly under the person's control and can be influenced by the person's knowledge about the world and about mental imagery (Cornoldi, 1995; Cornoldi, De Beni, Giusberti, & Massironi, 1998; see also Intons-Peterson, 1983). Research on ideas people have about imagery phenomena becomes consequently important. Denis and Carfantan (1985, 1990) obtained a variety of important results, and proposed that sometimes people have ideas about the possible outcomes of imagery experiments that are different from the actual outcomes. We have replicated their studies and found that people express different ideas according to the question format (Cornoldi, De Beni, & Giusberti, 1996). In this research, we presented participants with a metacognitive questionnaire on mental imagery that focused on how people behave in a classical and largely discussed mental imagery experiment (i.e., the mental scanning of a pathway). Kosslyn, Bal, and Reiser (1978) asked their participants to imagine an already memorized map of an island and to imagine a spot moving from one point to another point of the island. They found that the time required for doing this was proportional to the distance between the two points, suggesting that the imagined movement is isomorphic to real eye movement scanning between the two points on the map.

As we mentioned before, in our study we observed that people have different hypotheses about the outcome of this experiment, and that when participants based their answer on a concrete example, their predictions about the outcome were closer to their actual outcome. For example, when presented with a concrete example, only 21% of the participants still maintained that mental scanning is not related to distance, whereas 61% of the same participants held this opinion before the concrete example was presented.

The tendency to relate time for mental scanning to distance becomes general when individuals are placed in front of the task, as shown in another experiment held in two phases. In Phase 1, participants filled out a metacognitive questionnaire on which they were asked to estimate whether the time required to mentally scan between two towns on a map is proportional to the distance between the two towns. In phase 2, 3 months later, they were interviewed in a completely different context, during the preparation for the scanning task. In this case participants were invited to give an estimate of the possible time required to scan the pathway between pairs of European towns on a map that had been briefly shown earlier. In Phase 1, 26 participants out of 39 stated that the scanning time is proportional to the distance. In the concrete question proposed before the experiment, these individuals estimated that the scanning time between the two closest towns in Europe would require 1,251 ms less than the scanning time between the two farthest towns. The 13 participants who in Phase 1 stated that time is not proportional to distance, in Phase 2 estimated that scanning between the two towns would require, 1070 ms, a value not significantly different from the value (1,251) of the other group. Faced with a concrete task participants tended to estimate that time is proportional to distance, independently of their initial belief. In fact, we did not find any significant relation between the belief expressed in Phase 1 and the belief expressed in Phase 2.

Only for approximately one third of the participants the Pearson's correlation between predicted time —in phase 2— and real distance was greater than .89. For these participants also the imagery scanning time was also very close to actual distance between the two towns on the map; scanning time for individuals with a lower relation between predicted time and distance was not as close to actual distance as for the previous group of participants. It could be argued that the experimental task is artificial, and the person cannot base the response on preexisting experiences. However, participants did not seem to have difficulty on this task, and seemed to use processes similar to these in describing environments. DeBeni and Giusberti (1990) found that people are able to imagine both moving regularly along the pathway from one point to another and quickly changing position. As the human mind seems able to execute both imaginal processes, using one of them rather than the other can depend on a variety of factors, including the momentarily metacognitive conceptualization. In fact, there is no need to use an anti-imagistic argument to explain why an imagery task can be influenced by the individual's metacognitive conceptualization.

A correspondence between metacognitive conceptualization and cognitive activity is not enough evidence to assume that the first is causally related to the second. In such a task, participants could have anticipated or known in advance how to perform the task. However, the results of additional experiments (Cornoldi et al., 1996) have offered further evidence for the causal role of metacognitive conceptualization on cognitive activities. This aspect is developed in the next section.

FURTHER EVIDENCE CONCERNING THE CAUSAL ROLE OF METACOGNITIVE KNOWLEDGE

Converging evidence on the role of metacognitive knowledge in cognitive activity comes from research showing that metacognitive knowledge is not simply an experiential by-product of cognitive activity. Developmental research shows that sometimes children develop knowledge about a strategy (e.g., mental rehearsal, organization) before using it. Consider the specific metacognitive knowledge that the repetition of the material to be memorized can enhance the ability to memorize it. We have found that this can be an early intuition and it is typically present in 5-year-old children (Cornoldi & Vianello, 1992), whereas some of the literature reports that rehearsal clearly appears only at age 6 (Kail, 1979). This belief appears earlier than the behavior, suggesting that the belief can have an influence on the behavior.

Similar evidence comes from research showing lack of correspondence between metacognitive knowledge and cognitive activity. In a study on how children solve arithmetical problems, we (Lucangeli, Caccio', Cornoldi, & Salerni, 1997) had a group of children with a strong belief that large numbers produce difficulty in problem solving and a group who did not hold this belief. We reasoned that, if the belief is the consequence of an actual experience, children with a "large numbers" belief should have more difficulty with large numbers. If, on the contrary, beliefs modulate behavior, children with a large numbers belief should focus their attention on computations with large numbers. Our finding was that children with a large numbers belief made fewer computational errors (e.g., when adding or subtracting) than the other children, but made more procedural errors (e.g., chose the wrong operation). We argued that procedural errors could be due to an excessive preoccupation with the large numbers. Other evidence comes from research on monitoring and allocation of resources. Nelson and Leonesio (1988) suggested that the allocation of resources in processing different pieces of information is guided by the metacognitive estimation of the specific difficulty of each piece. Typically, people allocate more time to the most difficult items and less time to the easiest ones.

However, there is evidence that the allocation of resources does not necessarily follow the rule "more difficult–more elaboration" (Mazzoni, Cornoldi, & Marchitelli, 1990). Furthermore, task expectation (e.g., recall vs. recognition), rather than simple item difficulty, can affect study time allocation strategies (Mazzoni & Cornoldi, 1993). It was observed that individuals devote less time to studing the same items for a recognition test than for a recall test, also when the recognition test is manipulated in a way that makes it more difficult than a recall test. These data are consistent with the observation that, faced with a shopping list, people devote more effort to infrequent items because they incorrectly think that these items will be more difficult to remember (Mazzoni, Cornoldi, Tomat, & Vecchi, 1997).

THE DISRUPTIVE ROLE OF INSTRUCTIONS WHEN THEY COMPETE WITH METACOGNITIVE KNOWLEDGE OR TYPICAL TASK OUTCOME

An unpublished experiment carried out during my course by the student Edoardo Muffolini can help us to understand the role of instructions competing with both metacognitive knowledge and typical outcome. We presented 12 triplets of words to 36 students of a technical school. Six triplets were formed by concrete words and the other six were formed by abstract words. Half of the participants received instructions that stressed that remembering more concrete words than abstract words is an index of intelligence. For the other half of the participants instructions stressed that remembering more abstract words was an index of intelligence. A preceding examination of a similar group of participants showed that people typically know that concrete words are easier to remember than abstract words (i.e., they correctly think that concrete words are easier to remember). Therefore, instructions for the abstract group were conflicting with both the typical outcome and with the general expectations about the outcome.

Triplets were presented at a rate of 8 s (5 s for reading the words and 3 s for intertriplet interval). After a short retention interval in which participants were informed that instructions concerning intelligence were a joke, they were invited to recall the words using a response sheet on which the first word of each triplet was presented. In the scoring, we considered a response correct only when it was associated with the appropriate triplet. Table 7.3 presents the mean scores obtained by the two groups.

A comparison with a few control participants suggested that both the concrete and abstract group had a performance lower than the performance that could be obtained without any suggestion. If we limit the analysis to the two groups, we can see that instructions affected performance. There was a significant effect of the material and a significant interaction, suggesting that in this case the instructions directed the memorization effort as required.

From my point of view, the most interesting result is represented by the group effect that was nearly significant. This result shows that the abstract group had a lower performance than the concrete group and suggests that instructions contrasting preexisting metacognitive knowledge may have a disruptive effect on performance.

A MEMORY SITUATION IN WHICH METACOGNITIVE KNOWLEDGE CAN CONFLICT WITH COGNITIVE BEHAVIOR: THE MISSING "BIZARRENESS EFFECT"

There are sometimes discrepancies that offer the opportunity to better understand the relation between metacognition and cognitive behavior. In

TABLE 7.3

Mean Number of Correct Recall Responses for Concrete and Abstract Words in Two Conditions: with Instructions Stressing That Remembering More Concrete Words Is an Index of Intelligence (Concrete) and with Instructions Stressing That Remembering Abstract Words Is an Index of Intelligence (Abstract).

Groups	Concrete		Abstract	
	M	SD	M	SD
Concrete	4.44	1.98	1.83	2.12
Abstract	2.35	1.82	2.09	1.78

the field of memory and imagery, we observe a typical overestimation of the memorability of bizarre items. In standard interviews, 90% of people think they will be able to remember more bizarre than concrete sentences (Cornoldi, 1995). This incorrect belief is also maintained in contexts where there is no advantage for the bizarre items and even in contrast to evidence. Cavedon, Cornoldi, De Beni, and Pra Baldi (1986) found that, after an experiment that had failed to show a bizarreness effect, 20 out of 23 participants still thought they had remembered more bizarre than concrete items.

Kroll, Schepeler, and Angin (1986) observed that we are left, then, with an anomaly. People, including mnemonists, experimental psychologists, and experimental participants, believe that bizarre imagery helps their memories, but, once the degree of interaction is controlled, it does not; or, at very least, its effect on memory is much smaller than the effect of interaction. It seems that the interesting phenomenon that needs to be studied is not the effect of bizarre imagery on memory, but rather its effect on metamemory. Why do we believe that bizareness improves our memory? What is the influence of such belief on the cognitive behavior in memory tasks with common and bizarre words?

In the context of the relation between metacognitive knowledge and cognitive behavior the case of bizarre items seems to represent a situation in which our expectations contrast with the actual outcome. However, it also has some peculiar characteristics. For example, people overestimate recall of bizarre items only when a generic, estimation is requested; overestimation is no more present when estimation is done on an item-by-item basis. In a pilot study I asked eight undergraduates to predict if they were better at remembering sentences describing bizarre or common situations after they had received examples of each category. I found that people overestimated the memorability of bizarre items when they had to give an overall prediction, but the overestimation disappeared when they had to give separate judgments of learning on a 5-point scale ranging from (*poor expected performance*) to 5 (*high*) for each of 12 sentences (six common and six bizarre).

Despite the fact that, in this particular case, bizarre items produced better recall than common items (4.13 vs 3.29 sentences), judgments of learning were lower for bizarre (M = 2.98) than for common sentences (M = 3.5). This observation suggests that initial overestimation of bizarre material interacts with actual task difficulty. Experience can change beliefs that, in turn, can affect cognitive behaviors.

A better controlled series of experiments examined the effects of changing the participant's metacognitive conceptualization in the memorization of bizarre items (Cornoldi & De Beni, in preparation). We addressed the question I raised earlier in this chapter: Does the experimental manipulation of the ideas individuals have at the time of performing a task affect their way of performing it?

Recall of common and bizarre material was studied in an experimental situation in which in a baseline condition, common material was recalled at the same extent as bizarre material. We found that overestimation of bizarre material was more likely to occur when participants did not expect to actually perform the task. It was also observed that when predictions preceded recall, our participants did not expect to remember more bizarre than common items. However, the important point here is that in these conditions, bizarre items were indeed better remembered than common items. When predictions preceded the memory task, participants were more often looking for bizarre connections to retrieve the item than when predictions followed the task. Although a third experiment showed that the better recall of bizarre material was not due to the instructions shifting the participant's attention during recall toward bizarre items, a fourth experiment demonstrated that the effect was due to the fact that people were trying harder to recall bizarre than common items.

These results confirmed the hypothesis that people's initial beliefs (metacognitive conceptualization) have a strong impact on cognitive behavior, and in the case of bizarre items, direct retrieval effort.

CONCLUSIONS

Cognitive psychology has for a long time focused on the processes carried out in doing cognitive tasks, but only more recently has interest been directed toward participants' intentional and aware control and strategic choice.

This chapter suggests that one important aspect of the cognitive activity is an individual's metacognitive reflection, which precedes and influences the execution of cognitive tasks. Metacognitive reflection is not identified with voluntary control and strategy choice but is related to them.

It is a truism to declare that, in order to voluntarily initiate a cognitive activity, an individual must have some metacognitive conceptualization of the task. For example, comprehension of instructions in an experiment requires the experimental participants to develop a metacognitive conceptualization of what to do. It is also a truism to state that comprehension of instructions and the metacognitive conceptualization of the task are affected by preexisting knowledge, including knowledge about the way our mind works, the cognitive tasks, and so forth.

In this chapter, however, I have tried to show that considering these aspects of metacognition is not simply a subtle sophistication about irrelevant subjective experiences. In fact I have described some convergent evidence showing that metacognitive reflection can influence cognitive activity. On one hand, metacognitive reflection is not only represented by its most evident, aware, verbalizable portion; it also includes a part not so easy to verbalize that refers to intuitions, sensations, emotions, autobiographical memories, and self-evaluations. A consequence of this is that verbalizable metacognitive knowledge is not necessarily the aspect of metacognition that most critically affect cognitive activity. In addition, we found that sometimes explicit attempts to modify the verbalizable aspect of metacognitive knowledge can have disruptive effects on cognitive performance, probably due to a change in the balance of various components of metacognitive knowledge.

In particular, I have shown that cognition is affected by the metacognitive conceptualization preceding and metacognitive knowledge triggered by the specific task. I have also argued that a metacognitive conceptualization is the result of the integration of preexisting metacognitive knowledge and of specific metacognitive knowledge activated during the task. Preexisting metacognitive knowledge includes more general aspects (metacognitive attitude) and more specific knowledge. A general metacognitive attitude may produce a greater tendency to develop metacognitive reflection, to spend effort in the task, to transfer a learned strategy to a new context, and so on. Specific metacognitive knowledge may induce use of specific strategies when required.

REFERENCES

Aristoteles. (1965) Petits traités d' histoire naturelle [Essays of natural history] Paris: Presse Universitaire de France.

Bjorklund, D. F., & Green, B. L. (1992), The adaptive nature of cognitive immaturity. *American Psychologist, 47*, 46–54.

Borkowski, J., Carr, M., Rellinger, E., & Pressley, M. (1990). Self-regulated cognition: Interdependence of metacognition, attributions, and self-esteem. In B. F.Jones & L. Idol (Eds.). *Dimensions of thinking and cognitive instruction*, (pp. 53–92.). Hillsdale, NJ: Lawrence Erlbaum Associates.

Borkowski, J. G., Ryan, E. B., Kurtz, B. E., & Reid, M. K. (1983). Metamemory and metalinguistic development: Correlates of children's intelligence and achievement. *Bulletin of the Psychonomic Society, 21*, 393–396.

158   CORNOLDI

Borkowski, J. G., Weyhing, R. S., & Carr, M. (1988). Effects of attributional retraining on strategy-based reading comprehension in learning-disabled students. *Journal of Educational Psychology, 80*, 46–53.
Caponi, B., & Cornoldi, C. (1989). Metamemoria, strategicita' & ricordo in bambini della scuola elementare. (Metamemory, strategies and recall in 6-10 year old children). *Eta' Evolutiva, 34*, 5–15.
Cavanaugh, J. C., & Borkowski, J. G. (1980). Searching for metamemory-memory connections: A developmental study. *Developmental Psychology, 16*, 441–453.
Cavedon, A., Cornoldi, C., De Beni, R., & Pra Baldi, A. (1986). Recall of common, unusual and bizarre sentences under imagery instructions. In D. G. Russell, D. F. Marks, & J. T. E. Richardson (Eds.), *Imagery 2*, (pp. 17–21). Dunedeen, New Zealand: Human Performance Associates.
Cornoldi, C. (1987). Origins of intentional strategic memory in the child. In B. Inhelder, D. De Caprona, & A. Cornu-Wells (Eds.), *Piaget today* (pp. 183–201). Hillsdale, NJ: Lawrence Erlbaum Associates.
Cornoldi, C. (1995). *Metacognizione e apprendimento* (Metacognition and Learning). Bologna, Italy: Il Mulino.
Cornoldi, C., & Caponi, B. (1991). *Memoria e metacognizione* (Memory and Metacognition). Trento, Italy: Erickson.
Cornoldi, C., & De Beni, R. (1996). Mnemonics and metacognition. In D. Herrmann, K. McEvoy, C. Hertzog, P. Hertel, & M. Johnson (Eds., *Basic and applied memory research: Practical applications.* (pp. 237–253. Mahwah, NJ: Lawrence Erlbaum Associates.
Cornoldi, C., & De Beni, R. (in preparation). *How bizarre is bizarreness effect.*
Cornoldi, C., De Beni, R., & Giusberti, F. (1996). Meta-imagery: conceptualization of mental imagery and its relationship with cognitive behavior. *Psychologische Beitrage, 38*, 484–499.
Cornoldi, C., Gobbo, C., & Mazzoni, G. (1991). Metamemory and strategy transfer. *International Journal of Behavioral Development, 14*, 101–121.
Cornoldi, C. F., & Vianello, R. (1992). Metacognitive knowledge, learning disorders and mental retardation. In T. E. Scruggs & M. Mastropieri (Eds.), *Advances in learning and behavioral disabilities* (Vol. 7, (pp. 87–134). Greenwich, CT: JAI.
Cornoldi, C., De Beni, R., Giusberti, F., & Massironi, M. (1998). Memory and imagery: A visual trace is not a visual image. In S. Gathercole, M. Conway, & C. Cornoldi (Eds.), *Theories of memory*, (pp. 87–110). Hove, UK: Psychology Press.
De Beni, R., & Giusberti, F. (1990). Conoscenze esplicite & tacite sulle immagini mentali. Uno studio metacognitivo (Explicit and tacit knowledge about mental images: A metacognitive study). *Ricerche di Psicologia, 58–72.*
Denis, M. & Carfantan, M. Y. (1985). People's knowledge about images. *Cognition, 20*, 49–60.
Denis, M. & Carfantan, M. Y. (1990). Enhancing people's knowledge about images. In P. J. Hampson, D. F. Marks & J. T. E. Richardson (Eds.), *Imagery: Current Developments.* (pp. 197–222). London: Routledge.
Flavell, J. H. (1976). Metacognitive aspects of problem solving. In L. B. Resnick (Ed.), *The nature of intelligence*, Hillsdale, NJ: Lawrence Erlbaum Associates.
Flavell, J. H. (1981). Cognitive monitoring. In W. P. Dickson (Ed.), *Children's oral communication skills*, (pp. 35–60). New York: Academic Press.
Fodor, J. A. (1983). *The modularity of mind.* Cambridge, MA: MIT Press.
Goldman, A. I. (1993). The psychology of folk psychology. *Behavioral and Brain Sciences, 16*, 15–29.
Higbee, K. (1988). Some motivational aspects of visual imagery mnemonics. In (Cornoldi (Ed.) *Imagery and cognition: Pre-proceedings of the Second Workshop on Imagery and Cognition*, (pp. 173–184). Padova, Italy.
Intons-Peterson, M. J. (1983). Imagery paradigms: How vulnerable are they to experimenters' expectations. *Journal of Experimental Psychology: Human Perception and Performance, 9*, 394–412.
Kail, R. (1979). *The development of memory in children.* San Francisco: Freeman.
Kirby, J. (Ed.). (1984). *Cognitive strategies and educational performance.* Orlando, FL: Academic Press.
Kosslyn, S. M., Bal, T. M., & Reiser, B. J. (1978). Visual images preserve metric spatial information: Evidence from studies of imagery scanning. *Journal of Experimental Psychology: Human Perception and Performance, 4*, 47–60.
Kramer, J. J., & Engle, R. (1981). Teaching awareness of strategic behavior in combination with strategy training: Effects on children's memory. *Journal of Experimental Child Psychology, 32*, 513–530.
Kreutzer, M. A., Leonard, C., & Flavell, J. H. (1975). An interview study of children's knowledge about memory. *Monographs of the Society for Research in Child Development, 40*(1, Serial 159).

Kroll, N., Schepeler, E., Angin, K. (1986). Bizarre imagery: The misremembered mnemonic. *Journal of Experimental Psychology: Learning Memory, and cognition, 16*, 466–470.

Lucangeli, D., Cornoldi, C., & Tessari, S. (1991). Bambini con disturbi di apprendimento in lettura & matematica: Aspetti comuni & specificita' nei deficit cognitivi & di conoscenza metacognitiva (Reading and Mathematical learning disabilities: common and specific deficits, in cognitive processes and metacognitive knowledge). *Psichiatria dell'infanzia & dell'adolescenza, 58*, 629–642.

Lucangeli, D., Galderisi, D., & Cornoldi, C. (1994). Transfer effects after metacognitive training. *Learning Disabilities. Research and Practice, 10*, 11–21.

Lucangeli, D., Caccio', L., Cornoldi, C., & Salerni, C. (1997). Conoscenze metacognitive e successo in problem solving aritmetico (Metacognitive knowledge and success in arithmetical problem solving). *Studi di Psicologia dell'Educazione, 15*, 37–60.

Mazzoni, G., & Cornoldi, C. (1993). Strategies in study time allocation: Why is study time sometimes not effective? *Journal of Experimental Psychology: General, 122*, 47–60.

Mazzoni, G., Cornoldi, C., & Marchitelli, G. (1990). Do memorability ratings affect study-time allocation? *Memory & Cognition, 18*, 196–204.

Mazzoni, G., Cornoldi, C., Tomat, L., & Vecchi, T. (1997). Remembering the grocery shopping list: A study in metacognitive biases. *Journal of Applied Cognitive Psychology, 11*, 253–267.

Nelson, T. O., & Leonesio, R. J. (1988). Allocation of self-paced study-time and the "labor-in-vain effect." *Journal of Experimental Psychology: Learning, Memory and Cognition, 14*, 676–686.

Papetti, O., Cornoldi, C., Pettavino, A., Mazzoni, G., & Borkowski, J. (1992). Memory judgements and allocation of study times in good and poor comprehenders. In T. E. Scruggs & M. A. Mastropieri (Eds.), *Advances in learning and behavioral disabilities, 7*, (pp. 3–33). Greenwich, CT: JAI.

Paris, S. G., Newman, R. S., & McVey, K. A. (1982). Learning the functional significance of mnemonic actions: A microgenetic study of strategy acquisition. *Journal of Experimental Child Psychology, 6*, 25–56.

Pazzaglia, F., Cornoldi, C., & De Beni, R. (1995). Metacognitive knowledge about reading and self esteem in poor readers. *Advances in Learning and Behavioral Disabilities, 9*, (pp. 91–117).

Pearl, R.. Bryan, T., & Donahue, M. (1980). Learning disabled children's attributions for cognitive behaviors and failure. *Learning Disability Quarterly, 3*, 3–9.

Pylyshyn, Z. W. (1981). The imagery debate: Analogue media versus tacit knowledge. *Psychological Review, 87*, 16–45.

Schneider, W., & Pressley, M. (1989). *Memory development between 2 and 20*. New York: Springer-Verlag.

Simon, H. A. (1978). What the knower knows: Alternative strategies for problem-solving tasks. In F. Klix (Ed.), *Human and artificial intelligence*. Berlin.

Sodian, B., Schneider, W., & Perlmutter, M. (1986). Recall, clustering, and metamemory in young children. *Journal of Experimental Child Psychology, 41*, 395–410.

Stich, S. (1983). *From folk psychology to cognitive science*. Cambridge, MA: MIT Press.

Weiner, B. (1985). An attributional theory of achievement motivation and emotion. *Psychological Review, 92*, 548–573.

Wimmer, H., & Perner, J. (1983). Beliefs about beliefs: Representation and constraining function of wrong beliefs in young children's understanding of deception. *Cognition, 13*, 103–128.

8

Effect of Acute Alcohol Intoxication on Recall and on Judgments of Learning During the Acquisition of New Information

Thomas O. Nelson
University of Maryland
Aurora Graf
University of Washington
John Dunlosky
University of North Carolina at Greensboro
Alan Marlatt
Denise Walker
Kristine Luce
University of Washington

A variety of scientific approaches has been frequently used to investigate metamemory, including cognitive, developmental, and neurophysiological. In this research, we investigate metamemory using a psychopharmacological approach, which has already proven valuable in developing various theories of memory (for a review, see Polster, 1993). For instance, drug effects have produced dissociations that provide clues to the underlying representation of memory. Alcohol intoxication does not affect retrieval on tests of recently learned items (Birnbaum, Parker, Hartley, & Noble, 1978) but impairs retrieval on tests of general information learned prior to the experiment

(Nelson, McSpadden, Fromme, & Marlatt, 1986). An important point to keep in mind is that this approach should be viewed not as a replacement of other approaches but as a useful addition to other research on human cognition and metamemory.

Although the effects of drugs on metamemory have not been widely investigated, Nelson et al. (1986) examined how alcohol affects people's feeling-of-knowing (FOK) judgments and their retrospective confidence judgments. Participants were given either alcohol or a placebo, and then they answered general information questions (e.g., "What is the name of the navigation instrument used at sea to plot position by the stars?"). For each answer attempted during recall, a given participant made a retrospective confidence judgment about the likelihood that his or her answer was correct. After 12 questions had been incorrectly answered, the participant made an FOK judgment for each missed question, which is the person's prediction about the likelihood of later recognizing the correct answer. Finally, the participant received a 7-alternative forced-choice recognition test on each of the 12 questions.

Several findings from this experiment are relevant to the present research, which also focuses on alcohol intoxication and metamemory. First, recall was worse for the alcohol group than the recall group. Retrospective confidence judgments made during recall did not differ for the two groups, although this finding may be partially attributable to ceiling effects (i.e., median confidence was 96% for both groups). Second, alcohol intoxication did not affect the accuracy of people's FOK judgments at predicting subsequent recognition performance, which suggests alcohol has a minimal effect on how a person monitors his or her own memory. Third, the mean FOK judgments did not significantly differ for the two groups, which "implies that intoxicated subjects do not exhibit extra overconfidence (beyond that of unintoxicated subjects) while assessing their likelihood of retrieving verbal information from long-term memory" (Nelson et al. 1986, p. 251).

A primary goal of this research was to examine the effects of alcohol intoxication on judgments of learning (JOLs). A JOL is made during acquisition and is a person's prediction of the likelihood of correctly recalling a recently studied item on an upcoming test of memory. A person can make a JOL for an item either immediately after studying the item (called *immediate* JOL) or can wait until after a delay before making the JOL (called *delayed* JOL; Nelson & Dunlosky, 1991). When JOLs are cued by the stimulus alone (i.e., "dog – spoon" is studied, and the cue for the JOL is "dog – ?"), the sensitivity of JOLs to various manipulations are greater for delayed than immediate JOLs. For instance, Dunlosky and Nelson (1994) showed that delayed JOLs were more sensitive to the effects of interactive imagery (vs. rote repetition) and to the distributed presentations of items (vs. massed presentations). Accordingly, both kinds of JOL were investigated to evaluate the possibility that intoxicated people are not overconfident in memory-related situations.

JOLs can be contrasted with the FOK judgments used by Nelson et al. (1986). JOLs are made during the acquisition of new items and occur for all studied items, whereas FOK judgments are made on previously learned items and occur for only a subset of items (i.e., those not correctly recalled). Furthermore, Leonesio and Nelson (1990) examined the relation between FOK judgments and delayed JOLs cued by the stimulus–response cue, which have nominal similarities both to the immediate and delayed JOLs already described (Dunlosky & Nelson, 1997). The correlation between FOK judgments and JOLs was relatively low, indicating that the two metamemory judgments are based on different aspects of whatever underlies memory (Leonesio & Nelson, 1990). Given these differences, a negligible effect of alcohol intoxication on JOLs would provide converging evidence for the generalizability of the findings from Nelson et al. (1986).

MONITORING-RETRIEVAL HYPOTHESES OF JOLS

Other predictions concerning how alcohol intoxication will affect people's JOLs can be derived from current theories of how people make JOLs. One class of hypotheses, called the *monitoring-retrieval hypotheses*, provide a relatively straightforward explanation for how people make JOLs (for detailed discussion of instances of these hypotheses see Dunlosky & Nelson, 1994, 1997). When a person is prompted to make a JOL, he or she first attempts to retrieve the to-be-judged item from memory (cf. accessibility hypothesis, Koriat, 1993; products-of-retrieval hypothesis, Schwartz, 1994). For instance, consider a person who had studied "dog – spoon" and was later shown "dog – ?" as a cue for the JOL. The person presumably attempts to retrieve information about that item, such as an internal representation of the response, how the item had been studied, and so forth. The JOL is then based on the outcome of that retrieval attempt. The idea here is that people do not monitor the underlying object-level memory system per se, but instead monitor the output from this system (ala monitoring the output of a neurological system, as discussed by Moscovitch, 1992).

Delaying the JOL of an item results in a retrieval attempt of the response for the to-be-judged item, which in turn affects the JOLs. For instance, when a delayed JOL is cued by the stimulus alone, people presumably monitor the outcome of at least whether the response had been retrieved (Nelson & Dunlosky, 1991, 1992; Spellman & Bjork, 1992), with higher JOLs being given when responses are retrieved than when they are not. Based on this rationale and the effect of alcohol intoxication on memory, a prediction can be derived about the effect of alcohol intoxication on people's delayed JOLs. Namely, a well-documented conclusion is that alcohol intoxication disrupts encoding during the acquisition of new materials (for reviews see Birnbaum & Parker, 1977; Hull & Reilly, 1986; Loke & Lai, 1993), which will result in lower delayed memory performance for intoxicated people than for sober people. Thus, covert retrieval at the time delayed JOLs are made will be impaired by alcohol, and in turn this will lower delayed JOLs for intoxicated people.

For immediate JOLs cued by the stimulus alone, however, a covert retrieval attempt of the response will be less salient for making JOLs, because most—if not all—of the responses will be retrieved. The notion here is that retrieval of the response at the time of immediate JOLs is relatively uninformative concerning which items will later be retrieved, because retrieval occurs when the representation of the item is still in short-term memory (a la the monitoring-dual-memories hypothesis in Nelson & Dunlosky, 1991). Thus, people will base immediate JOLs on other factors that which presumably are relevant to the processing of the item during study (for possible bases of immediate JOLs see Begg, Duft, Lalonde, Melnick, & Sanvito, 1989; Dunlosky & Nelson, 1994).

Concerning the present research, alcohol intoxication may disrupt retrieval of items from short-term memory. Rundell and Williams (1977) examined the effect of alcohol intoxication on free recall. Alcohol intoxication impaired performance across the entire serial-position curve, with recall of the last two items presented during study being about .65 for the alcohol group but .80 for the placebo group (from Rundell & Williams, 1977, Fig. 2; but see Jones & Jones, 1977, for lack of an effect on the last serial position). Although Ryback's (1971) review of the literature on memory span indicated a negligible effect of alcohol intoxication on immediate memory, others have noted that some earlier research may have been inconclusive due to low statistical power. In sum, Rosen and Lee (1976) concluded that "the possibility of impairment in registration of incoming information into short-term store in intoxicated subjects must be consid-

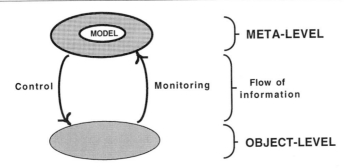

FIG. 8.1. A two-level model showing the relations between a metalevel system and object-level system (adapted from Nelson & Narens, 1994). The model shown in the metalevel system is a subjective representation (e.g., derived from metacognitive knowledge, which may be inaccurate) of the underlying object-level system.

ered, [but] the level of impairment is probably not high" (p. 316). Assuming alcohol has at least a marginal effect on retrieval performance from short-term memory, a prediction from the monitoring-retrieval hypothesis is that immediate JOLs will be lower for intoxicated than for sober people. Although this effect may be relatively weak, the rationale highlights the possible trade-off between basing JOLs on the on-line monitoring of (decreased) object-level performance versus basing JOLs on any general increase in subjective confidence that results from alcohol intoxication.

Besides evaluating the aforementioned predictions about the level of JOLs per se, a more exploratory aspect of this research involved examining the effect of alcohol on the accuracy of people's JOLs at predicting the recall of one item versus another; that is, will alcohol intoxication affect JOL accuracy? To help develop an intuition about possible outcomes, consider the relation between a metalevel system versus an object-level system, illustrated in Fig. 8.1. The metalevel system receives information (via monitoring) from the object-level system, which in case is the underlying memory system. In terms of the monitoring-retrieval hypothesis, the metalevel system receives information concerning the retrieval of information about the to-be-judged item from memory (i.e., it receives output from the object-level system).

The aforementioned predictions can be derived from this two-level model, along with the assumption that alcohol impairs the information output from the object-level system. But what if alcohol also impairs the metalevel system or some aspect of information transfer from the object-level system to the metalevel system? For instance, perhaps alcohol disrupts the flow of information about the object-level memory of an item to the metalevel system, which would reduce the likelihood that the person's perception of the item would match the underlying state of the item in long-term memory. Such an impairment involving the metalevel system would reduce the accuracy of people's JOLs at predicting recall. At one extreme, if alcohol minimizes functioning of the metalevel system, a person's JOLs may be greatly affected by alcohol, as if the person were unable to assess the output from the object-level memory system. Considering that alcohol has a negligible effect on FOK accuracy (Nelson et al., 1986), we did not expect that alcohol would minimize JOL accuracy. However, given the differences between these two kinds of judgments, perhaps the accuracy of JOLs will be sensitive to the effects of alcohol intoxication. Exploring this possibility was a secondary goal of this research.

OVERVIEW

We evaluated the aforementioned predictions by having participants study paired-associate items and make both immediate and delayed JOLs for a subsequent test of paired-associate recall. Half of the participants drank alcohol prior to the study test trial (alcohol group) and the other half drank a nonalcoholic beverage (placebo group). Furthermore, to link better with Nelson et al.'s (1986) investigation of alcohol intoxication and metamemory, participants also made retrospective confidence judgments for attempted answers during a second test trial. Thus, a variety of issues is addressed by examining the effects of alcohol intoxication on recall performance, JOLs, JOL accuracy at predicting subsequent recall, retrospective confidence judgments, and on the relations between JOLs and the confidence judgments.

METHOD

Participants

The participants were 42 male social drinkers between the ages of 21 and 35. They received either course credit or $25 for their participation. Those receiving credit were University of Washington undergraduates taking psychology courses, and the paid participants were either students or members of the local community. All participants were screened over the telephone to ensure that they drank alcohol regularly (a few times a week) but not excessively. Information regarding existing medical conditions and medications was also obtained to ensure that drinking alcohol would not have adverse side effects. Anywhere from one to three participants were run in a given session.

Design

The between-subjects variable in this experiment was alcohol (participants were either in the placebo or the alcohol group). The within-subject variable was kind of JOL (half of the JOLs were immediate, and the remainder were delayed). Participants were either in an alcohol or a placebo group, but all participants were led to believe they would receive alcohol. They were also informed that they might be misled.

Preparation

Prior to each session, an experimenter prepared the bottles from which the drinks were mixed. For each session, participants were run in either the alcohol or placebo group (i.e., all participants within a given session were run in the same condition). For each session, one vodka bottle and three tonic bottles were prepared. If the session involved alcohol, all four bottles contained a vodka-and-tonic solution that was one part vodka and four parts tonic. If the session involved the tonic placebo, all four bottles contained tonic water. On arrival, participants were given consent forms and asked to complete a personal history questionnaire.

Alcohol Administration

The participants were escorted to a lab room designed to look like a bar. In this 'barlab", participants' baseline blood alcohol levels (BALs) were measured to ensure that they had not been drinking prior to the experiment. They were also weighed (alcohol dosage was determined by weight; the dose was 1.82 mls of 100-proof vodka per kilogram body weight). The drink mixer consulted a chart that listed the appropriate ratios of vodka and tonic by weight. The ratio of tonic to vodka was always 1:4. For each participant, the drink mixer poured the appropriate amount of "vodka" (which was either pure tonic or the vodka-and-tonic mixture) into a small beaker, the appropriate amount of "tonic" (which was either pure tonic or the vodka-and-tonic mixture) into a large beaker, and mixed the contents of both beakers in the large beaker. The drink mixer poured the mixed solution into two (or three, depending on the participant's weight) glasses with ice and squirted lime into each glass. Before drinking, participants were asked to rinse with mouthwash (this was to dull the tastebuds). They were given 21 minutes for drinking and were told to try to keep their drinking rate constant throughout the 21 minutes. Everyone finished their drinks, and almost all finished them within 21 minutes. Following consumption, participants rode an elevator to the computer lab. Each participant was run individually in a separate room, and a different experimenter ran each participant. The experimenters were blind to the condition the participants were in. In each room, a given participant and the experimenter sat side by side in front of an LC II Macintosh computer, and the experimenter typed all of the participant's responses.

Absorption Period

After entering the computer room, each participant played a computer game, Reversi, for 30 minutes. This was to allow them time to absorb the alcohol (BAL peaks at 30 minutes following consumption). Following the absorption period, BAL was measured. The drink mixer knocked on the door of the computer room, the experimenter exited, and the drink mixer measured the BAL. Following this, the experimenter came back into the computer room and began the experimental task.

Experimental Task

All instructions pertaining to the experiment appeared on the computer screen. Participants were instructed to read the instructions silently as the experimenter read them aloud. All of the participant's responses were made verbally, and the experimenter typed the responses into the computer. The task included the following stages: (a) familiarization, (b) study with JOLs, (c) an aggregate JOL, (d) first recall trial, (e) second recall trial with retrospective confidence judgments, and (f) an aggregate retrospective confidence judgment. Because the aggregate judgments are not central to the major aims of this chapter they are not discussed further. However, analyses involving these aggregate judgments can be obtained from the third author.

Items

Items were 66 noun–noun paired associates (e.g., "dog – spoon") used in Nelson and Dunlosky (1991). The first six items presented for study comprised a set of practice items that were not tested during recall.

Familiarization

A familiarization trial was included to avoid floor effects on recall perform-ance. During this trial, the order of items was randomized, and then each item was presented for study at an 8-second rate. Participants were in-structed to study the items so that they could recall the second word of an item when shown the first.

Study and JOLs

This phase of the experiment was based on the procedure developed by Nelson and Dunlosky (1991). For study, the order of items was randomized anew and each was again presented for 8 seconds. The prompt for each JOL was the first word of the item. For example, if "dog – spoon" had been presented during study, the JOL prompt was "dog –" followed by the query, "How confident are you that in about 10 minutes from now you will be able to recall the second word of the item when prompted with the first (0 = definitely won't recall, 20 = 20% sure, 40 ..., 60 ..., 80 ..., 100 = definitely will recall)?" JOLs were self-paced.

The 60 critical items were randomly slated to two blocks of 30 items per block. Half of the items (15) in each block were randomly slated to receive immediate JOLs; the remaining 15 items in each block were slated to receive delayed JOLs. The only restriction on assignment was that no more than three consecutive items would receive the same kind of JOL. For items slated to receive immediate JOLs in a given block, the JOL prompt immediately followed the offset of the study presentation of the item. For items slated to receive delayed JOLs in a given block, the corresponding JOL prompts appeared immediately after the study and immediate JOLs had been com-pleted for a given block. The prompts for delayed JOLs were randomized as in Nelson and Dunlosky (1991), which ensured that the delayed JOLs for Block 1 followed all of the immediate JOLs for Block 1, but occurred before any of the immediate JOLs for Block 2.

Warmup Test Trial.   Immediately prior to the warmup test trial, a prompt on the computer screen warned the experimenter to take another BAL reading. The experimenter went across the hall where the drink mixer was waiting, and the drink mixer went to measure the BAL. When the reading was taken, the drink mixer retrieved the experimenter who went back to finish the experiment.

The order of presentation was randomized anew from study trials to test trials. For each item, the first word from the pair seen at study was presented, and the participant was instructed to complete the pair with the second word. Recall trials were self-paced. Guessing was encouraged, but omissions were allowed. Participants were instructed to say "next" if they wanted to omit an item. This was done to discourage them from omitting items to get through the task more quickly.

Critical Test Trial With Retrospective Confidence Judgments.   I t e m s were again presented in a new random order. This trial was the same as the other test trial, except that the participant was asked to make (after every attempt at recall) a retrospective confidence judgment. Confidence judgments were not made for omissions. If the participant provided a response other than "next," the following prompt appeared: "How confident are you that the response you just made is correct? (0 = *definitely is not correct*, 20 = 20% *sure*, 40 ..., 60 ..., 80 ..., and 100 = *definitely is correct*)." After the experimenter entered the participant's judgment, the computer proceeded to the next item.

Debriefing

Following the experiment, the participant remained in the laboratory under the supervision of an experimenter until his BAL fell below .03. The participant was debriefed and informed whether or not he had received alcohol. If the participant received alcohol, he was warned not to operate heavy machinery for at least 3 hours, and then was either driven home or allowed to walk home.

RESULTS AND DISCUSSION

Blood Alcohol Levels

Both for the first reading and for the second reading, mean BALs for participants in the alcohol group were .075 (SEM = .003) . Mean BALs for those in the placebo group were 0. These levels were similar to those reported by Nelson et al. (1986).

Effects of Alcohol on Recall

Recall Performance.   For each participant, the mean proportion of correct recall performance was calculated separately for the warmup trial and for the trial involving retrospective confidence judgments. The mean across individual participants' proportions on the warmup trial was .46 (SEM = .05) for the alcohol group and .59 (SEM = .04) for the placebo group. The mean proportion correct on the second test trial that included retrospective confidence judgments was .47 (SEM = .05) for the alcohol group and .61 (SEM = .04) for the placebo group. The levels of recall were substantially different, both on the warmup trial, $t(40) = 1.99$, $p = .053$, and on the second trial, $t(40) = 2.03$, $p < .05$. Given the slightly larger effect of alcohol on the second trial and the fact that retrospective confidence judgments were made only during the second trial, subsequent analyses focus on performance from the second trial. The finding that the alcohol dose was sufficient to impair recall performance confirms an assumption (alcohol impairs delayed retrieval) underlying this evaluation of the monitoring-retrieval hypothesis in relation to delayed JOLs.

Proportion of Commissions Given a Recall Failure. Given that people did not correctly retrieve a response, the likelihood that they would produce an incorrect response (commission error) was .28 (SEM = .05) in the alcohol group and .26 (SEM = .04) in the placebo group, $t(40) = .36$, $p = .72$. Thus, although alcohol intoxication affected overall levels of recall, it did not affect the likelihood people would output an incorrect response when retrieval of the correct response failed. This finding is consistent with those of Nelson et al. (1986) who found that alcohol intoxication did not affect the likelihood of responding with a commission error when failing to answer general information questions. By contrast, other drugs such as marijuana (Darley, Tinklenberg, Roth, Vernon, & Kopelt, 1977) and lithium (Weingartner, Rudorfer, & Linnoila, 1985) produce an increase in the rate of commission errors, suggesting that those drugs make people less conservative in withholding potential answers during retrieval.

Effect of Alcohol on JOLs

Magnitude of the JOLs. The mean across each individual's median item-by-item judgments was calculated separately for immediate JOLs and for delayed JOLs. These values are shown in the first two rows of Table 8.1.

Alcohol intoxication had a relatively substantial effect on delayed JOLs. As predicted from the monitoring-retrieval hypothesis, the magnitude of delayed JOLs was lower for the alcohol group than the placebo group. By contrast, alcohol intoxication had little, if any, effect on people's immediate JOLs, although the trend of the effect (with lower immediate JOLs for

TABLE 8.1

Magnitude of Item-by-Item Metamemory Judgments

Kind of Judgment	Drug Group	
	Alcohol	Placebo
Judgments of learning		
Immediate	50	54
Delayed	46	54
Retrospective confidence	46	62

Note. Entries are mean of every individual's median judgments. Standard error of the mean ≤ 5.4 for all entries.

intoxicated than sober people) was in the predicted direction. Furthermore, note that the magnitudes of delayed JOLs are relatively well-matched with the corresponding levels of recall performance for the two groups. These values are inconsistent with the hypothesis that alcohol intoxication generally increases people's confidence (cf. Nelson et al., 1986).

Distributions of the JOLs. A finer-grained analysis of how people made JOLs is provided by examining how the JOL ratings were distributed across items. For each participant, the proportion of items that received each JOL rating was calculated for immediate JOLs versus delayed JOLs (as in Dunlosky & Nelson, 1994). The mean across the individual participants' proportions is shown for each JOL rating in Fig. 8.2.

Alcohol intoxication did not change the general shape of the curves. Regardless of drug group, curves for delayed JOLs showed the characteristic U shape, whereas curves for immediate JOLs showed the characteristic inverted-U shape (cf. Dunlosky & Nelson, 1997). However, as expected from differences in the magnitude of JOLs, the curves appear to diverge at several places across the JOL ratings. First consider the curves for delayed JOLs, which are shown in the upper panel of Fig. 8.2. A crossover interaction occurs in which the higher JOLs (across ratings of 60, 80, and 100) were made less frequently by the alcohol group than by the placebo group, whereas the lower JOLs (0, 20, and 40) were made more frequently by the alcohol group than by the placebo group.

The same trend is also evident for immediate JOLs: The higher JOLs (across ratings of 60, 80, and 100) were made somewhat less frequently by the alcohol group than by the placebo group, whereas the opposite occurred for the lower JOLs. This pattern of findings, although weaker in relation to

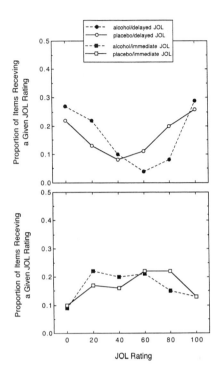

FIG. 8.2. The mean (across participants) of the proportion of items that had received a given JOL rating for delayed JOLs (upper panel) and for of JOLs, it has a quantitative effect on the degree with which specific JOL ratings are used. immediate JOLs (lower panel). These curves indicate that although alcohol intoxication does not have a qualitative effect on the distribution

immediate JOLs than to delayed JOLs, is consistent with the predictions from the monitoring-retrieval hypothesis.

Accuracy of the Relative Aspects of the Jols. Relative accuracy of people's JOLs at predicting recall performance was assessed using the Goodman–Kruskal gamma correlation (for reasons, see Gonzalez & Nelson, 1996; Nelson, 1984). Gamma correlations were computed for each participant, and the means of those correlations are reported in Fig. 8.3 as a function of the drug group and the delay between study and JOL (immediate vs. delayed).

As evident from inspection of Fig. 8.3, accuracy was greater for delayed JOLs than for immediate JOLs, with this delayed-JOL effect occurring for both drug groups. Furthermore, although alcohol intoxication had a negligible effect on the accuracy of people's delayed JOLs, $t(39) = 1.17$, the

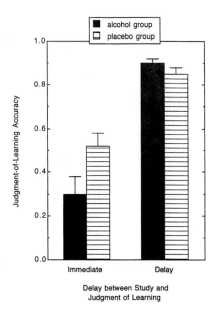

FIG, 8.3. The mean (across participants) of the gamma correlation between an individual's JOLs and subsequent recall on the second test trial. Standard errors of the mean are shown as bars.

accuracy of immediate JOLs was significantly lower for the alcohol group than for the placebo group, $t(40) = 2.09, p < .05$.[1] Possible explanations for this effect are considered in the General Discussion section.

Effect of Alcohol on Retrospective Confidence Judgments

The mean across each individual's median retrospective judgments was calculated across all items, with omission responses treated as if they had been given a confidence rating of 0. These values are reported in the third row of Table 8.1. Retrospective confidence judgments were lower for the alcohol group than for the placebo group. Also consider the relation between retrospective confidence and recall performance. The values for mean retrospective confidence almost perfectly match the corresponding values for mean recall, which demonstrates the high level of accuracy that has been typically shown by retrospective confidence judgments for recently learned

---

[1]The corresponding values for the relative accuracy of JOLs at predicting performance on the warmup trial showed the same trend, with the (statistically nonsignificant) difference in mean gammas for immediate JOLs being +.14 less for the alcohol group than for the placebo group.

Relations Between JOLs and Retrospective Confidence Judgments

As shown in Table 8.1, the effect of alcohol appears relatively similar for retrospective confidence judgments and for the delayed JOLs, whereas the effect of alcohol on immediate JOLs is relatively diminished. We further explored the relations between these metamemory judgments by calculating a gamma correlation between each participant's JOLs and retrospective confidence judgments.

The mean gamma across individual participants' correlations between JOLs and retrospective confidence judgments is shown in Fig. 8.4 for each condition. The mean gammas between delayed JOLs and retrospective confidence were +.84 for the alcohol group and +.81 for the placebo group, $SEMs = .03$, $t(39) = .68$, $p = .50$. For immediate JOLs and retrospective confidence judgments, the means were +.30 for the alcohol group and +.45 for the placebo group, $SEMs \_ .06$, $t(40) = 1.51$, $p = .14$. Several aspects of these values are worth noting. First, the strong relations between delayed JOLs and retrospective confidence judgments replicate findings reported by

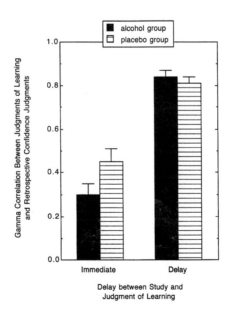

FIG, 8.4. The mean (across participants) of the gamma correlation between an individual's JOLs and retrospective confidence judgments. Standard errors of the mean are shown as bars.

Thiede and Dunlosky (1994). This outcome suggests that both of those kinds of judgments are based on a similar underlying construct, presumably retrieval of the response for the to-be-judged item. Further, alcohol intoxication had little, if any, effect on this relation.

Second, the relation between delayed JOLs and retrospective confidence was much greater than the relation between immediate JOLs and retrospective confidence. The relatively low relation between immediate JOLs and retrospective confidence judgments suggest that these two kinds of judgments are based on at least one different psychological dimension or the two kinds of judgment are based on a different weighting of the same dimensions (or both). For instance, the retrieval of responses that presumably drive retrospective confidence judgments may have relatively little weight when people make immediate JOLs. The same conclusion is suggested by rationalistic argument: Given that retrieval of responses is near perfect when immediate JOLs are made, such retrieval is a less useful indicator of which items will later be remembered and therefore people use some other bases (e.g., ease of learning or inference about future recall) for making immediate JOLs. Note, however, the gamma here was reliably different than 0, indicating that even immediate JOLs appear to share at least some common aspects with retrospective confidence judgments (cf. Leonesio & Nelson, 1990).

GENERAL DISCUSSION

Effect of Alcohol on People's Metamemory Judgments

A major goal of this research was to examine the effect of alcohol intoxication on people's JOLs to answer the question, "Does alcohol intoxication increase people's confidence in this memory-related situation?" In summary, alcohol intoxication significantly reduced the magnitude of two metamemory judgments (delayed JOLs and retrospective confidence judgments). These results extend those of Nelson et al. (1986) in showing that alcohol does not generally produce overconfidence in memory.

The effect of alcohol on these metamemory judgments also confirms the monitoring-retrieval hypotheses, which emphasizes the important role that covert retrieval plays in making JOLs. These results also provide a mystery concerning the basis of FOK judgments. A leading hypothesis concerning the basis of FOK judgments is that "the cues for FOK reside in the products of the retrieval process itself" (Koriat, 1995, p. 312; cf. Schwartz, 1994). That is, as in the monitoring-retrieval hypotheses for JOLs, this *accessibility hypothesis* states that FOK judgments are based on the covert retrieval of information about the item to be judged. If JOLs and FOK judgments are both based on covert retrieval of information about an item, alcohol intoxication should have similar effects on the magnitude of JOLs and FOK judgments. However, we found that the magnitude of JOLs is reduced by alcohol intoxication, but earlier research showed that the magnitude of FOK judgments is not affected by alcohol intoxication (Nelson et al., 1986). Perhaps the different kinds of items used in the two experiments were the cause of the different outcomes for JOLs versus FOK judgments, or perhaps the different outcomes are due more to different mechanisms for the two kinds of judgments (cf. Leonesio & Nelson, 1990).

Effect of Alcohol on JOL Accuracy

An unexpected finding was that alcohol impaired the accuracy of people's immediate JOLs. One relatively uninteresting explanation here is that the effect of alcohol diminished from the JOL trial to the test trials. If so, this finding may reflect a kind of state-dependent effect in which monitoring during encoding is not impaired by alcohol intoxication, but instead the memory itself fluctuates more across time for the alcohol group than for the placebo group. For instance, the cues produced by alcohol intoxication during encoding may be a basis for people's immediate JOLs, but if the alcohol intoxication wanes throughout the experimental session, the alcohol-induced cues will be less likely sampled during the later test trials. This explanation seems unlikely for two reasons. First, the BAL levels did not change from early in the experimental session to later in the session, suggesting that the effect of alcohol was relatively constant throughout the study–test trials. Second, this explanation also predicts that alcohol intoxication would affect the accuracy of both immediate JOLs and delayed JOLs, because both were made at the same time in the experimental session. However, alcohol intoxication had little effect on the accuracy of delayed JOLs—if anything, the mean level of delayed JOL accuracy tends to be higher for the alcohol group than for the placebo group.

To the best of our knowledge, the findings illustrated in Fig. 8.3 provide the first demonstration of a drug effect on the accuracy of any kind of metamemory judgment. Although we currently do not know why alcohol intoxication affects immediate JOL accuracy, we provide some speculation that may help guide future research. Alcohol intoxication may decrease the stability of people's judgments across time, which would reduce the relation between JOLs and subsequent recall (or any other measure). A testable prediction here is that alcohol intoxication will affect the accuracy of all metamemory judgments. However, intoxicated people have a high level of delayed JOL accuracy (Fig. 8.3), and they show normal levels of FOK accuracy (as reported by Nelson et al., 1986). Nelson et al. (1986) also found that intoxicated people's FOK judgments were highly reliable (.91) and the likelihood of intransitivities in their FOK judgments was relatively low (.08, which was somewhat higher than that of the sober group). Unless alcohol selectively affects the stability of immediate JOLs and not other kinds of metamemory judgments, this evidence suggests that the effect of alcohol on immediate JOL accuracy is not entirely an artifact of the instability of people's immediate JOLs.

Alcohol intoxication may impair neurological systems that underlie the metalevel processes involved in making metamemory judgments. For instance, perhaps alcohol intoxication affects portions of the frontal lobe, which in turn may affect the accuracy of metamemory judgments. Consistent with this link between frontal lobe functioning and the predictive accuracy of metamemory judgments, Janowsky, Shimamura, and Squire (1989) found that patients with frontal lobe lesions had impaired levels of FOK accuracy. Although plausible, the possibility that alcohol intoxication affects metamemory accuracy via impairing frontal-lobe functioning will have limited scope, because Nelson et al. (1986) found that alcohol intoxication did not affect FOK accuracy. Assuming alcohol affects frontal functioning, perhaps the differential effect of alcohol on immediate JOLs versus on FOK judgments indicates that these judgments rely on frontal-lobe functioning to differing degrees. Critical experiments about this topic will involve examining the effects of various drugs on each of these metamemory judgments within a single experiment.

ACKNOWLEDGEMENTS

This research was supported by grant R01-MH32205 and a career development award (K05-MH1075) from the National Institute of Mental Health to Thomas O. Nelson.

REFERENCES

Begg, I., Duft, S., Lalonde, P., Melnick, R., & Sanvito, J. (1989). Memory predictions are based on ease of processing. *Journal of Memory and Language1, 28*, 610–632.

Birnbaum, I. M., & Parker, E. S. (1977). *Alcohol and human memory*. Hillsdale, NJ: Lawrence Erlbaum Associates.

Birnbaum, I. M., Parker, E. S., Hartley, J. T., & Noble, E. P. (1978). Alcohol and memory: retrieval processes. *Journal of Verbal Learning and Verbal Behavior, 17,* 325–335.

Darley, C. F., Tinklenberg, J. R., Roth, W. T., Vernon, S., & Kopelt, B. S. (1977). Marijuana effects on long-term memory assessment and retrieval. *Psychopharmacology, 52,* 239–241.

Dunlosky, J., & Nelson, T. O. (1992). Importance of the kind of cue for judgments of learning (JOLs) and the delayed-JOL effect. *Memory & Cognition, 20,* 373–380.

Dunlosky, J., & Nelson, T. O. (1994). Does the sensitivity of judgments of learning (JOLs) to the effects of various study activities depend on when the JOLs occur? *Journal of Memory and Language, 33,* 545–565.

Dunlosky, J., & Nelson, T. O. (1997). Similarity between the cue for judgments of learning (JOL) and the cue for test is not the primary determinant of JOL accuracy. *Journal of Memory and Language, 36,* 34–49.

Gonzalez, R. & Nelson, T. O. (1996). Measuring ordinal association in situations that contain tied scores. *Psychological Bulletin, 119,* 159–165.

Hull, J. G., & Reilly, N. P. (1986). An information processing approach to alcohol use and its consequences. In R. E. Ingram (Ed.), *Information processing approaches to clinical psychology* (pp. 151–167). New York: Academic Press.

Janowsky, J., Shimamura, A., & Squire, L. (1989). Memory and metamemory: Comparison between patients with frontal-lobe lesions and amnesic patients. *Psychobiology, 17,* 3–11.

Jones, B. M., & Jones, M. K. (1977). Alcohol and memory impairment in male and female social drinkers. In I. M. Birnbaum & E. S. Parker (Eds.), *Alcohol and human memory* (pp. 127–138). Hillsdale NJ: Lawrence Erlbaum Associates.

Koriat, A. (1993). How do we know that we know? The accessibility model of the feeling of knowing. *Psychological Review, 100,* 609–639.

Koriat, A. (1995). Dissociating knowing from feeling of knowing: Further evidence for the accessibility model. *Journal of Experimental Psychology: General, 124,* 311–333.

Leonesio, R. J., & Nelson, T. O. (1990). Do different measures of metamemory tap the same underlying aspects of memory? *Journal of Experimental Psychology: Learning, Memory, & Cognition, 16,* 464–470.

Loke, W. H., & Lai, M. L. (1993). Methodological considerations in the study of alcohol and memory. *Psychologia, 36,* 39–46.

Moscovitch, M. (1992). A neuropsychological model of memory and consciousness. In L. R. Squire & N. Butters (Eds.), *Neuropsychology of memory* (pp. 5–22). New York: Guilford.

Nelson, T. O. (1984). A comparison of current measures of feeling-of-knowing accuracy. *Psychological Bulletin, 95,* 109–133.

Nelson, T. O., & Dunlosky, J. (1991). When people's judgments of learning (JOLs) are extremely accurate at predicting subsequent recall: The "delayed-JOL effect." *Psychological Science, 2,* 267–270.

Nelson, T. O., & Dunlosky, J. (1992). How shall we explain the delayed-judgment-of-learning effect? *Psychological Science, 3,* 317–318.

Nelson, T. O., McSpadden, M., Fromme, K., & Marlatt, G. A. (1986). Effects of alcohol intoxication on metamemory and retrieval from long term memory. *Journal of Experimental Psychology: General, 15,* 247–254.

Nelson, T. O., & Narens, L. (1994). Why investigate metacognition? In J. Metcalfe & A. P. Shimamura (Eds.), *Metacognition: Knowing about knowing* (pp. 1–25). Cambridge, MA: MIT Press.

Polster, M. R. (1993). Drug-induced amnesia: Implications for cognitive neuropsychological investigations of memory. *Psychological Bulletin, 114,* 477–493.

Rosen, L. J., & Lee, C. L. (1976). Acute and chronic effects of alcohol use on organization processes in memory. *Journal of Abnormal Psychology, 3,* 309–317.

Rundell, O. H., Jr., & Williams, H. L. (1977). Effects of alcohol on organizational aspects of human memory. In F. A. Seixas (Ed.), *Currents in alcoholism: Psychiatric, psychological, social, and epidemiological studies* (Vol. 2, pp. 175–186). New York: Grune & Stratton.

Ryback, R. S. (1971). The continuum and specificity of the effects of alcohol on memory: A review. *Journal of Studies on Alcohol, 32,* 995–1016.

Schwartz, B. L. (1994). Sources of information in metamemory: Judgments of learning and feelings of knowing. *Psychonomic Bulletin and Review, 1,* 357–375.

Spellman, B. A., & Bjork, R. A. (1992). People's judgments of learning are extremely accurate at predicting subsequent recall when retrieval practice mediates both tasks. *Psychological Science, 3*, 315–316.

Weingartner, H., Rudorfer, M. V., & Linnoila, M. (1985). Cognitive effects of lithium treatment in normal volunteers. *Psychopharmacology, 86*, 472–474.

9

Insight and Metacognition

Janet Metcalfe
Columbia University

In this chapter the possibility that cognitive representations may change very rapidly, or that a process commonly called *insight* may be psychologically and biologically plausible, is discussed. Some researchers have argued that all problem-solving processes, including those called *insight problem solving*, proceed via gradual, incremental steps. These researchers claim that the idea that representations may change suddenly is untenable and indeed mystical. In contrast, I argue that many common physical and biological processes have the quality of spontaneous change—the construct itself is scientifically reputable, and the validity of the construct of spontaneous psychological processes in problem solving cannot be ruled out on a priori grounds. Whether such processes actually occur in specific cases of human problem solving, is, therefore, an empirical question open to normal scientific investigation.

Researchers who argue that the construct of insight is not viable propose, instead, a memory explanation of this kind of problem solving. Thus, in addition to addressing the question of whether insight is possible in principle, three areas of investigation relevant to the alternative proposal—that all problem solving rests solely on remembering—are reviewed. First, the metacognitive data are reviewed. Feeling-of-knowing data comparing people's predictions during memory retrieval and insight problem solving, and the dynamics of people's knowledge about their own proximity to solution are outlined. Second, the literature on the capabilities of amnesic patients is reviewed. Amnesiacs show severe memory dysfunctions. If insight problem solving depends critically on memory, amnesiacs should also be severely impaired on these problems. Third, it is shown that the memory-retrieval-

181

only view of insight problem solving runs headlong into Menon's paradox, including the infinite regress it implies. *Menon's paradox* refers to an ancient conundrum outlined originally by Plato, who purported to demonstrate that the slave boy, Menon, was able to *remember*, with the help of clever questioning by Socrates, the proof of Pythagoras' theorem. Thus, Plato was the first to argue that even very complex and difficult problem solving might be attributable to memory retrieval alone.

Finally, I conclude that to accept the recommendation (Weisberg, 1991) to abandon the concept of insight problem solving on the grounds that it is unscientific entails a high risk of throwing out the pearl with the oyster. If we fail to investigate the possibility that spontaneous restructuring may exist we may inappropriately preclude understanding some of the most interesting and important human cognitive capabilities. Instead, it is suggested here, that more detailed study of the concept itself, as well as additional empirical research to test for the characteristics, concomitants, representations, and biological underpinnings, is needed.

SCIENTIFIC BASIS OF NONINCREMENTAL CHANGE

Weisberg (1986, Weisberg & Alba,1981, 1982) has challenged the existence of insight or structural change in human thought, that all problem solving involves slow incremental processing and depends critically on normal memory processes. The insight proposal, rather than merely being given as an alternative to this accumulative view, has, instead, been dubbed as mystical and unscientific, in spite of the cautions of a number of scientists who have taken issue with this characterization (Dominowski, 1981; El-len,1982; Lung & Dominowski, 1985; Montgomery, 1988; Ohlsson, 1984; Sternberg & Davidson, 1982; and see also Holyoak, 1990, and Maitlin, 1989). Weisberg's disaffection for the insight construct is most obvious in his 1986 book entitled *Creativity, Genius, and Other Myths*. There, he argued specifically that the concept of insight is tantamount to a 'messenger of God' view. He stated that his aim was to debunk the idea:

> The messenger of God view assumes that creative products come about through leaps. The creative person suddenly begins to produce something complete without knowing where it is coming from. This view has come down to us at least from the Greeks, who believed that the gods or the Muses breathed creative ideas into the artist.... Studies of famous scientists and artists often emphasize their spontaneous "aha!" aspect of creativity.... If creative achievements do indeed come about through great leaps of insight, brought about by extraordinary thought processes, in individuals who possess

some unanalyzable quality called genius, then little more can be said. Creative thinking must remain mysterious and unknowable. ... The creative capacity that the ancient Greeks assigned to the mythical gods has in our era been assigned to the unconscious and other exotic processes. (Weisberg, 1986, pp. 1–3).

Weisberg (1986) claimed that "the modern view is no less a myth" (p. 3). The alternative that he proposed is a gradualist view based on cued retrieval from memory: "No great leaps of conscious or unconscious insight necessarily occur. Rather creative action is slow and incremental, the familiar way of dealing with a problem gradually evolving into something new" (p. 12).

One issue raised by Weisberg, if irrefutable, provides a genuine cause for concern: Perhaps the construct of fast-changing mental processes, restructuring, or insight is unscientific. Postulation of such processes may be akin to a belief in supernatural forces, if Weisberg is correct. In the next few paragraphs, I argue that fast-changing mental processes are not a priori unscientific, and may indeed provoke interesting new hypotheses about the nature of problem solving. If the existence of fast structural changes were unknown in the physical and biological world, then this absence would suggest that their purported presence only in the world of mental phenomena is questionable. Insofar as such phenomena are commonplace physical phenomena, however, there seems to be no reason to evoke supernatural causes for their possible advent in mental processes, or to rule out the fast-structural-change hypothesis as either mysterious or unknowable.

Restructuring in Nonliving Systems

There are many cases of spontaneous restructuring in the physical sciences, that, a number of researchers have taken to explaining by using complex nonlinear models and advanced mathematical techniques. These nonlinear changes continue to generate particular curiosity and intense interest, and often provide key understandings in the fields in which they are found. To give a very simple illustration (sometimes given in mathematical textbooks), consider a strip of thin metal held at the two ends by pins that allow it to flex either up or down. Press the thin metal strip together (still held in place by the pins) until it forms a tense arch. Now, one by one, place small bricks at the peak of the arch. As more bricks are added apparently nothing happens. The metal arch holds its shape. However at some point a catastrophic change in structure occurs. The metal springs and stabilizes in a U pointing down rather than an arch pointing up. The transition is sudden, and the result is a different structure. Real bridges breaking show a similar dynamic. Earthquakes show a similar dynamic.

Phase changes between a liquid state and a solid state provide another physical example of relatively fast structural change. The atoms of water in a liquid state float in a random motion. When the temperature is lowered to a certain point, a new structure—in this case a lattice—is formed and the characteristics of the H_2O we observe are qualitatively altered. This process may hold particular interest for psychologists because it parallels the kind of reports given of creative discoveries. For example, Poincare (1913) said, "ideas rose in crowds; I felt them collide until pairs interlocked, so to speak, making a stable combination" (p.81). Kekule, according to Shepard and Cooper's (1982) account, had idle reveries of atoms joining and rejoining to form chainlike molecules whirling in a giddy dance, prior to discovering the structure of benzene. The visualized structure became stable only when it crystallized into a closed ring. This occurred in an 'aha' experience that happened in a dream that awoke him immediately.[1]

Changes in structure, far from being unknowable, have received extensive mathematical analysis in the physical sciences. Thom (1975) and Zeeman (1976) formulated a mathematical theory called *catastrophe theory* to account for some such changes (see Saunders, 1980). Catastrophe theory is not the only (or even perhaps the best accepted) conceptualization being explored for these changes (see Abraham & Shaw, 1982). The dynamics of phase changes are of special interest in dissipative systems; that is, in open systems that consume energy. Such self-organizing energy-eating systems seem akin to the human cognitive system insofar as they become more organized at the expense of the surrounding environment, and they need energy for their sustenance. Prigogine and Stengers (1984, and see Prigogine, 1980) provided many examples of such self-organizing biological systems, as well as the mathematical theories that detail their workings. In a similar vein, Haken (1977), within the synergetics framework, and Yates (1986) delineated some interesting examples of self-organizing energy-consuming systems including, for example, the laser. Some of the constructs of most interest in dynamics and self-organizing systems, such as phase

---

[1]Not all structural changes in a representation result in the phenomenology of insight, however. For example, Watson (1968) manipulated the elements of DNA both mentally and by using cardboard models in many random-appearing ways until the stable double-helix structure with the bases running in complement appeared. In contrast to Kekule, Watson did not report an 'aha' experience accompanying this structural change, perhaps because the manipulation of the symbols was physical rather than mental.

changes, attractor states, entrainment, and bifurcations, have become familiar to psychologists via the study of the behavior of neural networks, and, indeed, most neural network models of learning are nonlinear, and, as such, allow for dramatic changes in state.

Physical phase change may provide an apt metaphor for insight because it gives a grounding for the concept of a change in structure. Physically, *phase change* is defined in terms of a change from state or Structure A to a different stable state or Structure B that occurs without *coherent* (or stable) intermediate forms. This definition does not say there are no intermediate forms, but only that they are unstable, and cannot persist independently under the circumstances of the dynamic situation. In the example of the metal bridge given earlier, the metal, of course, must pass through the positions between the arch and the U. However, none of the intervening positions is stable. The instability of the intermediate states given in nonlinear dynamics bears some resemblance to the unstable decallage state noted by Piaget (1968) between the stable developmental stages he posited.

The lack of stability rather than the speed of occurrence of the state change is the most important definitional characteristic, although these changes frequently occur quickly, and relative rapidity is also a characteristic demarcating a phase change. With supersaturated solutions, for example, the change in structure from a liquid to a solid occurs very rapidly—close to the speed of sound. In contrast to Weisberg's arguments suggesting that spontaneous change implies divine intervention, this near spontaneity in crystallization does not, of course, mean that (a) the phase change does not really occur or that (b) it is attributable to extraphysical causes.

Restructuring in Living Systems

Structural changes are common in living as well as nonliving systems. Evolutionary examples of radical change or punctuated equilibrium, where the essential meaning or function of a structure is suddenly altered, have been provided by Gould (1977). For example, with evolution, the functions of certain bone configurations have taken on radically different functions. According to Gould:

> The first fishes did not have jaws. How could such an intricate device, consisting of several interlocking bones, ever evolve from scratch? "From scratch" turns out to be a red herring. The bones were present in ancestors, but they were doing something else—they were supporting a gill arch located behind the mouth. They were well designed for their respiratory role; they had been selected for this alone and "knew" nothing of any future function. In hindsight, the bones were admirably preadapted to

become jaws. The intricate device was already assembled, but it was being used for breathing, not eating. (p. 108).

Although both functions are well coordinated, there is no coherent intermediary that is half-breathing and half-eating. Therefore, this abrupt change in function qualifies as a phase or state change. These same bones later took on a third function, becoming the ossicles of the middle ear:

> The bone that suspended an ancestral fish's upper jaw to its cranium became the bone that transmits sound to the ears of reptiles. Two bones that articulated the jaws of that reptile then became the other two sound-transmitting bones of the mammalian middle ear. When we see how beautifully our hammer, anvil, and stirrup function in hearing, who would imagine that one bone once suspended jaw to cranium, while two others articulated the jaws. (Gould, 1983, p.63).

Examples of structural changes in organization of motor behavior (as opposed to thought) in humans and other animals come from studies of movements done by Turvey and his colleagues (e.g., Kugler & Turvey, 1987) Thelan, Kelso, and Fogel (1987) provided examples and analyses of motor movements changing structure in infants. The flavor of some of this work can be seen in studies by Kelso and Schoner (1988), who investigated state changes in coordinated hand movements. If one swings both hands so that the fingers are pointed to the left, then to the right, then left, and so on, and gradually increases the speed, one will find that at some point the 'out of phase' left then right organization will be impossible to maintain and the phase relation will switch to (and stabilize in) an in-phase mode in which the hands will converge and then separate, then converge and separate, and so on. Between the in-phase organization and the out-of-phase organization there is an intermediate positioning of the hands—but it is not coherent, coordinated, or stable. A similar change in organization of the movement (or structure of the movement) occurs when a horse changes gait from a walk to a trot, to a canter, or, indeed, when a person changes from a walk to a run.

Restructuring in Cognitive Systems

But motor movements are not themselves thought processes, arguments about their likely influence on cognition notwithstanding. Demonstrations of catastrophic changes in organization at a purely mental level are, therefore, critical. A number of such examples are well known. Within the area of perception, for example, there are a number of examples of spontaneous mental changes in representation—the Necker cube, the wife/mother-in-law figure, the Janov duck-rabbit, a number of Dali paintings, and many other bistable figures. The idea that a person must gradually and slowly retrieve memorial information from explicit memory to see the alternate interpretation does not seem to apply in these cases. Within the domain of human learning, Rumelhart and Norman (1978) considered three modes of learning: accretion, tuning, and restructuring. Although not downplaying the importance of accretion or tuning, they noted that "often the point of the learning is the formation of the new structures, not the accumulation of knowledge. Once the appropriate structures exist, the learner can be said to understand the material, and that is often a satisfactory endpoint of the learning process" (p. 39). In summary, then, the idea that fast changes in structure need be linked to unscientific thinking, to exotic causes, or to special blessings by mysterious muses is specious.

CONSCIOUSNESS, RESTRUCTURING, AND INCREMENTAL CHANGE

In addition to fast restructuring there also are incremental processes involved in phase change: The temperature of the water *decreases* when water changes to ice; the wrist movements *accelerate* in Kelso's example, producing the phase change. There are a number of possibilities concerning the role of the incremental factors that may underlie changes in structure. One is the conjecture that the change from one representation to another occurs at a certain threshold value in the incremental factor. In Sieglar's (1978) balance task, before restructuring, children understand each dimension—weight and distance from the fulcrum—separately. Afterward, they integrate and coordinate both dimensions and can deal with a new construct—torque. Presumably, there is one or more incremental factor that changes to allow this new structure to emerge—perhaps brain maturation, background experience, or some combination of the two. Similarly, in a conservation task, before being able to conserve, children are able to use only one dimension (e.g., the height of the juice in the glass), but after the restructuring they are able to take into account trade-offs among dimensions (e.g., that the width also has an effect). Given that older children are able and younger children are not able to solve this problem, it seems likely that an age-related incremental factor comes into play. An understanding of both the incremental factor and the structural change are necessary for the analysis of the thought process.

Like these well-studied cases, insight problems frequently force the person to consider a dimension that is not immediately available to them. To solve the Gardener's problem (How can you plant four special trees such that they are all equally distant from one another?), the person must restructure his or her thinking from considering only a planar surface to taking into account a three-dimensional space. The reason the relevant dimension is unavailable to the person may not be because they do not, developmentally, have the capacity to consider the relevant dimension, however. Furthermore, the consideration of the needed dimension may or may not result from some incremental pressure. The possible existence of incremental factors in insight problem solving, although worthy of study, does not obviate the reality of the structural changes.

Of course, not all problem solving requires restructuring. The temperature of water can be changed 10° in such a way that no restructuring occurs. Similarly in problem solving, some goals may be attained without the restructuring of any thought processes or modifications of mental representations. There is a sense in which such problems, though, are not problems at all, if, along with Wertheimer, we think of problems as being problematic only when there is some obstruction to reaching the goal. Thus a simple incremental unobstructed approach to a goal might not be considered problem solving at all—the person knows what the goal is and he or she knows how to get there, so what, exactly, is the problem? Although acknowledging this argument, here it is considered that unobstructed approach is a different kind of problem solving from insight problem solving—but it is still considered to be problem solving.

Some problems can be solved by remembering previous solutions, either to the exact problem given or to ones that are highly similar to it. If the problem is similar rather than exactly the same as one that one previously solved or was taught the solution, the only 'leap' needed may be in grasping the structural similarity. Much research has been conducted on the topic of metaphor (see, Gentner, 1983; Holyoak & Spellman, 1993)—addressing the issue of how it is that people are able to make this sometimes difficult to attain connection.

Metacognitive data, reviewed in more detail shortly, suggest that there may be a near-spontaneous change in representations in insight problem solving that contrasts to the incremental changes that underlie routine problem solving. Individuals who report their nearness to solution to insight problems most of the time do not know that they are approaching the solution. They arrive at it suddenly—seemingly, from "out of a blue sky," to use Hebb's (1949) language for insight. Note that Hebb did not deny the existence or the importance of "out-of-a-blue-sky" cognitive or brain processes, but used the Nova Scotian terminology descriptively.

The output of the processing—the representational structure—does not appear to be slowly changing in the studies that are reviewed here. The phase change metaphor also may be useful in helping to delineate the role of consciousness in insight problem solving. In keeping with Nisbett and Wilson's (1977) argument, it seems likely that most mental processes themselves are unavailable to conscious inspection. However, the output, representations, content, or information that results from the operations may be available. It is as if people are able to monitor the water molecules and say whether they are drifting around randomly or have formed into a lattice (or, alternatively, to say whether the substance is a liquid or a solid) but they do not have conscious access to the refrigerating unit (or, indeed, to a thermometer that measures the temperature) that is causing the temperature drop that produces the change in structure.

THE ROLE OF MEMORY
IN INSIGHT PROBLEM SOLVING

This section addresses three issues concerning the relation between memory and insight. First, is insight problem solving the same as memory retrieval? Several experiments investigating people's metacognitions before and during insight problem solving investigate some similarities and differences of these processes. Second, is explicit memory retrieval necessary and sufficient for insight problem solving? If it is needed, then it follows that people who are profoundly deficient in memory retrieval—amnesic patients—should be incapable of insight. And third, there is an ancient paradox about the memory retrieval view of problem solving—Menon's paradox. The view that insight problem solving involves nothing more than memory retrieval, championed first by Plato. runs headlong into the problem of having to propose an infinite regress. I take up each of these three issues in turn.

Insight Problem Solving and Metacognition

Metcalfe and Wiebe (1987), and Metcalfe (1986a) tested the idea that if insight problem solving and memory retrieval were essentially similar processes then they should produce a similar pattern of results on a variety of tasks. If the patterns of results were different, then it would indicate that there might be important differences between the two domains. The most obvious of these tasks—and the one they investigated—was a feeling-of-knowing task. In the feeling-of-knowing paradigm the participants were asked to predict the likelihood with which they would be able either to remember the answer to memory questions to which they could not immediately provide the answers or to produce the solutions to problems that they could not immediately solve. Typically, there is a positive correlation between feeling-of-knowing judgments and later memory performance on a criterion task. One explanation of this positive correlation is that memory retrieval involves the gradual accrual of partial information, and that the judgments are based on this partial information (see Koriat, 1993, cf. Metcalfe, 1993, 1996; Schwartz & Metcalfe, 1992). If insight problems were solved, in a similar way, by accruing partial information, then the feeling-of-knowing judgments on the unsolved insight problems should also be based on this partial information (retrieved from memory) and should show a positive correlation with their later solution. However, if insight problem solving is a nonincremental process, then one would expect no reliable feeling-of-knowing correlation. More than simply providing a general comparison between memory and problem solving, then, this particular task provided the opportunity to investigate a focal dimension on which insight problem solving and memory retrieval might be thought to either be similar or different—the conjectured incrementality of the insight process.

The results of the experiment showed that people who were given general information memory questions were able to rank order reliably the unrecalled items in terms of how likely they would be to recognize each of the correct answers later (in keeping with much past research; e.g., Blake, 1973; Freedman & Landauer, 1966; Krinsky & Nelson, 1985; Nelson, 1988; Reder, 1988; Schacter, 1983; Shimamura & Squire, 1986). However, the gamma correlations relating the rankings of the insight questions to their later solution were not different from zero. This straightforward test of whether people had accessible partial information in insight problem solving yielded negative results.

In a second test, Metcalfe (1986b) compared the dynamical metacognitions during insight problem solving to those in routine problem solving. Participants were asked to indicate how near they were to solution, or how "warm" they felt, at 5 or 10 second intervals during the course of solving these two kinds of problems. The dynamical patterns showed that participants had little foreknowledge of the impending solution to the insight problems, as compared to routine problems, and they were able to reliably indicate nearness to solution with the routine problems. There was a very small increment in warmth with the insight problems. Because participants, in these experiments were told to anchor their starting judgments at zero, which was the endpoint of the scale that indicated "far from solution," rather than at some intermediate position, it is possible that the small trend toward increasing "warmth" in the insight problem protocols was a regression effect rather than a true increment in perceived nearness to solution. Even so, the increment was very slight, and it was much smaller for the insight problems than for the routine problems. Anagram-solving tasks (Metcalfe, 1986b) also showed an insightlike metacognitive dynamic.

Metcalfe (1996) discussed two possible explanations for these data. First, the processes underlying insight may undergo a sudden shift—reflected in the metacognitive judgments. Second, the processes may be incremental but unavailable to conscious inspection. At the present time, it is unknown which account is the correct one.

Insight Problem Solving and Amnesia

In an experiment that I conducted with Eaton (Metcalfe & Eaton, unpublished manuscript), we found that unprimed word fragment completion and unprimed picture fragment completion tasks also produce an insightlike metacognitive dynamic; that is, people report almost no increment in their perceived nearness to solving these problems prior to their actual solution. As was shown in Metcalfe (1986b), anagram solving also shows an insightlike dynamic. These three tasks relate to implicit memory tasks, which amnesic patients can accomplish as readily as can normal individuals (see Schacter, 1991, for a review). In addition, in a manner that is unlike the situation for explicit recognition or recall, amnesics show normal priming on word fragment or anagram solving tasks. If insight and insightlike tasks necessarily involve explicit retrieval from memory, and if amnesics have severe deficiencies in this kind of memory, then they should not show this priming. The data are consistent with the idea that insightlike tasks rely on mechanisms or representations that are distinct from explicit memory retrieval mechanisms.

McAndrews, Glisky, and Schacter (1987) provided amnesic patients and normals with puzzles that are perhaps even more self-evidently insightlike, entailing resolving of word definition problems devised by Auble and Franks (1978). As noted by McAndrews et al. (1987), and also by Auble and Franks

(1978, 1979), these problems, which were puzzle sentences such as : "The haystack was important because the cloth ripped—parachute," or " The person was unhappy because the hole closed — earrings," seem to involve an "aha" reaction. Amnesics showed near-normal performance, even at a week's delay, on this task. This result contradicts the hypothesis that insight relies exclusively on recollection.

The interesting possibility exists that the tasks that have been labeled implicit memory tasks may correspond to those showing an insightlike dynamic. Classically, insight has been considered a process of comprehension. When the new stable structure emerges, one may be said to then have reached an understanding. Such a process may be quite common in human cognition. When we perceive objects, not just in picture fragment tasks but also in our day-to-day perception of the world, presumably there is some perceptual binding whereby the diverse parts are seen to all comprise the same object and to have a particular structure. The problematic nature of perceptual binding becomes more apparent when fragments of pictures or words or noisy versions of pictures or words are given to individuals and the usually immediate comprehension of the whole is impaired. Under these conditions, temporal retardation of a normally quick and apparently effortless process may occur. An insightlike dynamic, as seen in the unprimed fragment completion task, may typify comprehension tasks and relate to processes involved in implicit memory tasks—processes that may stand in contrast to the incremental processes seen in explicit memory tasks. Anagrams, picture fragments, word fragments, and insight problems all seem to have the characteristic that the parts need to configure in a particular way for a coherent and comprehensible whole to emerge, suggesting the possibility that insight-like tasks and implicit memory tasks are one and the same. If so, then the critical processes entailed in these tasks may involve coherence extraction, which is a catastrophic process, rather than retrieval from explicit memory, which is an incremental process.

Menon's Paradox

In this final section, I review an age-old discussion of problem solving, and particularly of the view that recollective memory is critically involved. A paradox lurks in this memory-only position.

Plato illustrated the memory-only view in his tale of Menon's remembering the Pythagorian theorem. This so-called memory feat is demonstrated when Socrates asks the slave boy leading questions that allow these "memories" to be recovered. Plato suggested that all knowledge—the solution to all problems—was there already just waiting to be uncovered or remembered.

The problem that Plato (and any strict memory-only theorist) encounters is that the person may not have had the relevant experience needed to solve the problem. Menon's paradox, then, refers to the conundrum encountered if it is assumed, as did Plato, that a person solves a problem at Time t, by remembering the solution from Time $t - x$. At some point in the past there must have been a time (it might have been at Time $t - x$, but it is possible that at that $t - x$ the person remembered the solution from some earlier time, $t - x - y$, etc.) when that person (or, perhaps the person who directly taught the person the solution, or the person who taught the person who taught the person, etc.) actually solved the problem. Remembering alone does not allow the problem to be solved the first time. Plato tried to finesse this problem by allowing remembrances from past lives—a proposition that is likely to prove untenable, not only because of its lack of plausibility, but also because even allowing it, one has still to postulate an infinite regress. How did one get the exact memory needed for precisely this problem-solving situation in one's past life? Presumably at some point, in some past life, someone (maybe not the current problem solver—who may have been just a witness) has to have actually *solved* the problem. Otherwise there is no solving event for the current problem solver to remember, and if there is no solving event then one cannot be simply remembering such an event. The memory-only view crumbles on logical grounds.

Of course, this is not to deny that , indisputably, the problem solver needs some knowledge base. And sometimes people may remember a solution to a problem they have already solved or seen someone else solve, but it is not clear that these remembered solutions are correctly classified as problem *solving*. It is similar to hearing a joke for the second time: The experience of remembering the punch line is different from "getting it." We have tried to remove these cases of remembering the solution from our empirical studies by allowing participants to tell us the solutions they know immediately and eliminating those from further consideration on the assumption that such immediate responses may be based on remembering the problem rather than solving it. Skills, experience, and expertise are indisputably important in insight problem solving, although the contributions of these variables is not yet fully understood—the processes and control processes involved in insight problem solving require further empirical research.

In summary, then, if what Weisberg means by the cued-memory view of problem solving is that explicit recollections of past experiences, without restructuring, yield up the solutions to the problems, then (a) our data weigh against it, (b) the capabilities of amnesics weigh against it, and (c) the view runs headlong into Menon's paradox. Alternatively, it seems reasonable to postulate that there exists some process by which events, structures or solutions that are *new* emerge.

DEFINING INSIGHT

To further study of the processes that underlie restructuring it is important to be able to say whether a particular change involves restructuring or not. Three possibilities have been suggested. The first—highlighted in the organization-of-movement literature—is based on the speed of the change. If the change in movement organizational structure occurs suddenly, then it is considered to be a gait change. If it occurs gradually, then it is not. Thus, the change from walking to trotting is a gait change, as is the change from trotting to cantering. But the canter and the gallop are considered to be the same gait. The latter is faster than the former but it is accomplished gradually.

Second, Wiebe and I (Metcalfe & Wiebe, 1987) proposed that if participants' metacognitions showed a sudden solution, then we should call those problems insight problems, and if they do not then we should not. In so arguing we assumed that the ontological issue was already resolved positively and we were now facing a classification problem. One difficulty with this proposal is that an insight process might be a critical, but not the only process needed to solve a given problem. The metacognitions might, then, appear incremental because of the involvement of other, noninsight processes. The nine-dot problem, for example, probably involves a restructuring, but it also likely includes other processes as well. If one wanted to isolate the insight process, the nine-dot problem would be a bad choice. M. Levine (personal communication, 1988) suggested using a four-dot problem that involves the same restructuring as the nine-dot problem but with little else to cloud the metacognitive results.

The third definition is the one adopted in physics. Phase change is defined by the lack of stable intermediate forms. Even with this definition, however, the relative speed of the process is still considered important. Stability itself is a relative concept, and the concept nests an idea of rate of change. We do not yet know how this definition concerned with the lack of stability of intermediate forms might apply in the study of mental processes and representations.

The difficulty in defining insight is an old one. Hebb (1949), in contrasting the behaviorist view to the configurationist view, noted that only some problems are candidates for provoking insight—those that are extremely difficult, but not impossible:

> With a problem of such borderline difficulty, the solution may appear out of a blue sky. There is a period first of fruitless effort in one direction, or perhaps a period of attempted solutions. Then suddenly there is a complete change in the direction of effort, and a clean-cut solution of the task. This then is the first criterion for the occurrence of *insight*. The behavior cannot be described as a gradual accretion of learning; it is evident that something has happened in the animal at the moment of solution. *(What* happens is another matter). (p. 160)

With recent advances in complex nonlinear dynamics and the spontaneous emergence of structure, we may now, 50 years later, be at a bifurcation point, with one route leading to the demise of research on insight, but the other leading to real progress on this question of "what."

ACKNOWLEDGMENTS

I appreciate the comments of Carol Fowler, Walter Mischel, and Bennett Schwartz. The preparation of this paper was fostered by a CSEP grant from the James S. McDonnell Foundation.

REFERENCES

Abraham, R. H., & Shaw, C. D. (1982). *Dynamics: The geometry of behavior, Parts 1, 2, and 3.* Santa Cruz, CA: Ariel Press.

Auble, P. M., & Franks, J. J. (1978). The effects of efforts towards comprehension on recall. *Memory & Cognition, 6,* 20–25.

Auble, P. M., & Franks, J. J. (1979). Effort toward comprehension: Elaboration or "aha"? *Memory & Cognition, 7,* 426–434.

Blake, M. (1973). Prediction of recognition when recall fails: Exploring the feeling-of-knowing phenomenon. *Journal of Verbal Learning and Verbal Behavior, 12,* 311–319.

Dominowski, R. L. (1981). Comment on "An examination of the alleged role of 'fixation' in the solution of 'insight' problems." *Journal of Experimental Psychology: General, 110,* 199–203.

Ellen, P. (1982). Direction, past experience, and hints in creative problem solving: Reply to Weisberg and Alba. *Journal of Experimental Psychology: General, 111,* 316–325.

Freedman, J. L., & Landauer, T. K. (1966). Retrieval of long-term memory: "Tip of the tongue" phenomenon. *Psychonomic Science, 4,* 309–310.

Gentner, D. (1983). Structure mapping: A theoretical framework for analogy. *Cognitive Science, 7,* 155–170.

Gould, S. J. (1977). *Ever since Darwin: Reflections in natural history.* New York: Norton.

Gould, S. J. (1983). *Hen's teeth and horse's toes: Further reflections in natural history.* New York: Norton.

Haken, H. (1977). *Synergetics.* Heidelberg, Germany: Springer-Verlag.

Hebb, D. O. (1949). *The organization of behavior.* New York: Wiley.

Holyoak, K. J. (1990). Problem solving. In D. N. Osherson & E. E. Smith (Eds.), *An invitation to cognitive science: Vol. 3, Thinking,* (pp. xxxx). Cambridge, MA: MIT Press.

Holyoak, K. J., & Spellman, R. A. (1993). *Thinking Annual Review of Psychology, 44,* 263–315.

Kelso, J. A. S., & Schoner, G. (1988). Self-organization of coordinative movement patterns. *Human Movement Science, 7,* 27–46.

Koriat, A. (1993). How do we know? The accessability model of feeling of knowing. *Psychological Review, 100,* 609–639.

Krinsky, R., & Nelson, T. O. (1985). The feeling of knowing for different types of retrieval failure. *Acta Psychologica, 58,* 141–158.

Kugler, P. N., & Turvey, M. T. (1987). Information, natural law, and the self-assembly of rhythmic movement. Hillsdale, NJ: Lawrence Erlbaum Associates.

Lung, C.-T., & Dominowski, R. L. (1985). Effects of strategy, instructions, and practice on nine-dot problem solving. *Journal of Experimental Psychology: Learning, Memory, and Cognition, 11,* 804–811.

Maitlin, M. (1989). *Cognition (2nd ed.).* New York: Holt, Rinehart, & Winston.

McAndrews, M. D., Glisky, E. L. & Schacter, D. L. (1987). When priming persists: Long-lasting implicit memory for a single episode in amnesic patients. *Neuropsychologia, 25,* 497–506.

Metcalfe, J. (1986a). Feeling of knowing in memory and problem solving. *Journal of Experimental Psychology: Learning, Memory, and Cognition, 12,* 288–294.

Metcalfe, J. (1986b). Premonitions of insight predict impending error. *Journal of Experimental Psychology: Learning, Memory, and Cognition, 12,* 623–634.

Metcalfe, J. (1993). Novelty monitoring, metacognition, and control in a composite holographic associative recall model: Implications for Korsakoff amnesia. *Psychological Review, 100,* 3–22.

Metcalfe, J. (1996). Metacognitive processes. In E. L. Bjork & R. A. Bjork (Eds.). *The Handbook of Perception and Cognition Vol. 10., Memory.* Academic Press: San Diego, pp. 383–411.

Metcalfe, J., & Eaton, G. J. (Unpublished manuscript). Dynamical metacognition in two redintegrative tasks: Picture and word fragment completion.

Metcalfe, J., & Wiebe, D. (1987). Intuition in insight and non-insight problem solving. *Memory & Cognition, 15,* 238–246.

Montgomery, H. (1988). Mental models and problem solving: Three challenges to a theory of restructuring and insight. *Scandinavian Journal of Psychology, 29,* 85–94.

Nelson, T. O. (1988). Predictive accuracy of the feeling of knowing across different criterion tasks and across different subject populations and individuals. In M. M. Gruneberg, P. E. Morris, & R. N. Sykes (Eds.), *Practical aspects of memory: Current research and issues* (Vol. 1, pp. 190–196). New York: Wiley.

Nisbett, R. E., & Wilson, T. D. (1977). Telling more than we can know: Verbal reports on mental processes. *Psychological Review, 84,* 107–123.

Ohlsson, S. (1984). Restructuring revisited: II. An information processing theory of restructuring and insight. *Scandinavian Journal of Psychology, 25,* 117–129.

Piaget, J. (1968). *Structuralism.* New York: Harper & Row.

Poincaré, H. (1913). Mathematical creation. In *The Foundations of Science.* (G. H. Halstead, Trans.) New York: Science Press.

Prigogine, I. (1980). *From being to becoming: Time and complexity in the physical sciences.* San Francisco: Freeman.

Prigogine, I., & Stengers, I. (1984). *Order out of chaos.* Boulder, CO: New Science Library, Random House.

Reder, L. (1988). Strategic control of retrieval strategies. *The Psychology of Learning and Motivation, 22,* 227–259.

Rumelhart, D. E., & Norman, D. A. (1978). Accretion, tuning and restructuring: Three modes of learning. In J. W. Cotton & R. L. Klatsky (Eds.), *Semantic factors in cognition* (pp. 37–53). Hillsdale, NJ: Lawrence Erlbaum Associates.

Saunders, P. T. (1980). *Introduction to catastrophe theory.* London: Cambridge University Press.

Schacter, D. (1983). Feeling of knowing in episodic memory. *Journal of Experimental Psychology: Learning, Memory, and Cognition, 9,* 39–54.

Schacter, D. (1991). Implicit memory: History and current status. *Journal of Experimental Psychology: Learning, Memory, and Cognition, 13,* 501-518.

Schwartz, B. L., & Metcalfe, J. (1992). Cue familiarity but not target retrievability enhances feeling-of-knowing judgments. *Journal of Experimental Psychology: Learning, Memory, and Cognition, 18,* 1074–1083.

Shepard, R. N., & Cooper, L. A. (1982). *Mental images and their transformations.* Cambridge, MA: MIT Press.

Shimamura, A. P., & Squire, L. R. (1986). Memory and metamemory: A study of the feeling of knowing in amnesic patients. *Journal of Experimental Psychology: Learning, Memory, and Cognition, 12*, 452–460.

Sieglar, R. S. (1978). The origins of scientific reasoning. In R. S. Sieglar (Ed.) *Children's thinking: What develops? Hillsdale, NJ: Lawrence Erlbaum Associates.*

Sternberg, R. J., & Davidson, J. E. (1982, June). The mind of a puzzler. *Psychology Today*, 37–44.

Thelan, E., Kelso, J. A. S., & Fogel, A. (1987). Self-organizing systems in infant motor development. *Developmental Review, 7*, 39–65.

Thom, R. (1975). *Structural stability and morphogenesis.* Reading, MA: Benjamin.

Watson, J. D. (1968). *The double helix,* New York: Atheneum.

Weisberg, R. W. (1986). *Creativity, genius and other myths.* New York: Freeman.

Weisberg, R. W. (1991). Metacognition and insight during problem solving. *Journal of Experimental Psychology: Learning, Memory, and Cognition, 17*, 169–192.

Weisberg, R. W., & Alba, J. W. (1981). An examination of the alleged role of 'fixation' in the solution of "insight" problems. *Journal of Experimental Psychology: General, 110*, 169–192.

Weisberg, R. W., & Alba, J. W. (1982). Problem solving is not like perception: More on gestalt theory. *Journal of Experimental Psychology: General, 111*, 326–330.

Yates, F. E. (1986). *Self-organizing systems: The emergence of order.* New York: Plenum.

Zeeman, E. C. (1976). Catastrophe theory. *Scientific American, 234*, 65–83.

Author Index

Subject Index

A

Accuracy-recall relations, 14–15
Acquisition, *see also under* Knowledge; Learning
  vs. retention, 24
Action disorganization syndrome (ADS), 76
Action schemas, 47
Alcohol intoxication, 161, 170–178
  JOL accuracy and, 177
  metamemory judgments and, 176–177
  short-term retrieval and, 164–165
Alzheimer's disease (AD), 84
Amnesics
  false recognition, 129–132, 135
  insight problem solving, 191–192
Anagram solving, 191
Aristotle, 142
Attention
  allocation, 11–13, 15
  dissociation between monitoring and, 109–110
  selective, 11, 47–48
    inhibitory component of, 39
Autism, 83

B

Behavior, *see* Cognitive behavior
Bizarre items, 155–156
"Bizarreness effect," 154–156
Brain imaging, 64
Broca's area, 59
Brodmann's areas, 59, 60

C

Calibration, 112
Capacity sharing model, 43–45
Categorical organization strategy, 148–149
Causal modeling procedure, 18
Central executive, 78

experimental measurement of, 84–85
Change
  incremental, 187–189
  nonincremental, scientific basis of, 182–187
  speed of, 194
Closed-head-injuries (CHIs), 41–50
Cognitive behavior
  conflict with metacognitive knowledge, 154–156
  effect of metacognitive knowledge on, 148–149
  metacognitive conceptualization and, 156
  relation to metacognitive attitude skeptical views on, 142–144
Cognitive change, *see* Change
Cognitive control, *see* Control
Cognitive functioning
  metalevels *vs.* object levels of, 3
Cognitive models
  localization arguments from, 86
Cognitive monitoring, *see* Monitoring Cognitive processes
Competitive filter, 38
Computerized tomography (CT) scans, 64
Confabulation, 125
Confidence, under- *vs.* over-, 112, *see also under* Judgments of learning
Consciousness, role in insight problem solving, 189
Contention scheduling, 73
Control, 37–39, *see also* Control processes
  metacognitive reflection and voluntary, 156
Control functions, 39–41
  frontal lobe functioning and, 40
Control processes, 39, 50, 107–108, *see also* Contention scheduling; Supervisory attentional system
  dependence on specific brain structures, 50
  memory performance and, 98, 100, 110–111